Volkswagen
Transporter
the first **60** *years*

Volkswagen
Transporter
the first 60 years

Richard Copping
with Brian Screaton

Haynes Publishing

◀ Two magical letters and
three perfect examples
of the first generation
Transporter – Volkswagen's
publicity shot proclaims
success on both counts. *(BS)*

First published in April 2009

A catalogue record for this book is available from the British Library

ISBN 978 1 84425 579 5

Library of Congress catalog control no. 2008943623

Published by Haynes Publishing, Sparkford, Yeovil, Somerset BA22 7JJ, UK
Tel: +44 (0)1963 442030 Fax: +44 (0)1963 440001
Email: sales@haynes.co.uk
Website: www.haynes.co.uk

Haynes North America Inc., 861 Lawrence Drive, Newbury Park, California 91320, USA

Picture copyright and sources
Pages 1–329: all pictures copyright Volkswagen Alktiengesellschaft apart from:
Porsche Werksfoto 16/17
Richard Copping 42 bottom (both), 43, 168/169, 289, 324, 327
Brian Screaton 207, 249
Devon Motor Caravans 268
Pon's Automobielhandel BV 195 top
D'leteren archive 231 top, 232-233

Pages 330–400: all pictures copyright respective camper conversion companies apart from:
Volkswagen Alktiengesellschaft: 330-340, 342-356, 365 bottom, 392, 393 bottom, 394/395
Richard Copping 393 top (both)
Brian Screaton 341 top (both)

All pictures sourced from Volkswagen Alktiengesellschaft unless otherwise stated.
Abbreviations used:
(BS) Brian Screaton collection,
plus pages 106–110, 153
(RC) Richard Copping collection.

Designed and typeset by James Robertson
Printed and bound in the UK

A note regarding *Pferdestärken* (PS)
In the company's early days Volkswagen expressed performance in terms of metric horsepower, or *Pferdestärken* (PS). PS measurements have consequently been adopted throughout this book. As a by-product this also avoids the confusion that frequently arises when referring to brake horsepower, and the difference between British and American bhp. To convert PS figures into British horsepower, multiply by 0.986.

Contents

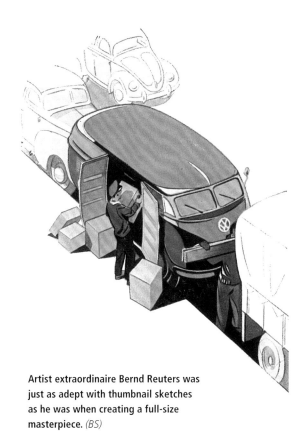

Artist extraordinaire Bernd Reuters was just as adept with thumbnail sketches as he was when creating a full-size masterpiece. *(BS)*

Introduction

The growth of interest in Volkswagen's legendary Transporter over the last 15 years or so has been nothing short of meteoric. Once it was little more than a workhorse, a people carrier, or a useful camper; a vehicle to be used and sold on in exchange for a newer model, until after a succession of owners the time finally came when, exhausted and terminally blighted with rust, only the scrap-yard beckoned.

The owner of a current generation model, known as the T5, or conceivably a late example of its predecessor, the T4, corporate or individual, might well visit the local Volkswagen Van Centre to upgrade to the latest shiny offering to emerge from Hanover, just as drivers of Ford, Vauxhall, Renault and the myriad of other makes do as a matter of course. Such owners might recognise the Volkswagen Transporter, or people carrier, as a quality product without being drawn into the cult surrounding its five generations of production. However, when it comes to older Volkswagens the story is undoubtedly very different. Enthusiasm abounds and materialises in a definite demand to acquire and cherish some T4s, a large percentage of T3s (or T25s), and just about every second- and first-generation model that still exists.

It is to the older Transporters that this book is primarily devoted – the generations whose value today far outstrips not only the vehicles' original selling prices, but also those of many a newer model. But why a celebratory volume now, for that is undoubtedly what this is? The answer is in the date of publication: a diamond occasion!

Some would argue that the first generation Transporter was born when, in 1947, an extravert Dutchman named Ben Pon drew his now legendary sketch of a light commercial, a drawing that bore a remarkable resemblance to the vehicle today known affectionately as the Splitty, or in Germany as the Bulli. If that is so (and some at Volkswagen are certainly of such an opinion), then the proverbial boat has more or less been missed. Others, however, dismiss this embryonic doodle as largely irrelevant, and favour either February or March 1950 – when the first production models started to roll off the Wolfsburg assembly line – as the Transporter's actual date of birth. If such claims are decreed definitive, then this book is premature. However, the fact that 1949 saw the first prototypes emerge, and witnessed Volkswagen Director General Heinz Nordhoff's announcement to the world that a second vehicle bearing the VW badge was joining the Beetle, would seem to confirm that its diamond jubilee is being acknowledged at exactly the right point.

What is certain is that this book is a commemorative history, and that a primary aim has been to collate as much interesting information relating to the Transporter as was feasible in the 100,000 words allocated to the task. No key element of its 60-year story has been excluded, while the unusual or largely unknown has been included wherever possible.

From delving deeply into the original planned line-up of variations on the Delivery or Panel Van theme, to the rapid escalation of *sonderausführungren* or special models – the options that made the Transporter more versatile than even Nordhoff could have imagined – the first-generation model is assigned a generous slice of the story. A bonus arrives in the form of the Transporters despatched from Wolfsburg, and later Hanover, with little more than a coat of primer to protect them, to become wonderful mobile advertising machines thanks to their clever liveries. Of even greater interest is a section devoted to the dynamic ground-breaking advertising campaigns of the American Doyle

▼ 1949–67

Dane Bernbach agency, without question the catalyst to burgeoning sales.

Gliding from the first generation, or Splitty, to the second, or Bay-window, the key revamp that occurred in 1955 was echoed when the new model of 1967 (for the '68 model year) vintage was itself given an overhaul in the summer of 1972. The comprehensive availability of all variants of this model from day one makes its own headline, while the rapid succession of engine upgrades from single to twin port 1600, followed by the addition of a 1700, its replacement by an 1800, and finally a 2.0-litre block, is equally noteworthy. Of only marginally less interest has to be the survival of the Bay design for some 29 years through production in Mexico and Brazil, the latter country showing no signs of abandoning the ancient design. The Bay's elegant looks might be partially disfigured by a radiator up front, while a water-cooled unit might propel it these days, but, Beetle-like, it has survived.

The third generation Transporter, launched in the summer of 1979 and known officially as the T3 on the Continent and as the T25 in Britain, but to all Americans simply as the Vanagon, illustrates perfectly the quirky aspects of a 60-year progression. Conceived in the mid-1970s, when the transition from air-cooled power to water-cooled precision was sufficiently advanced as to make the Beetle little more than an also-ran, the fact that the wedge-shaped vehicle should retain both air-cooling and a rear-wheel-drive configuration is truly amazing. That it should have been conceived by the man who led Volkswagen towards water-cooled supremacy, Rudolf Leiding, is startling in its revelation and no doubt beyond the credibility of many. Commonly nicknamed the Wedge, this is the vehicle that not only changed direction part way through its production run, with the arrival of a diesel unit (which of near necessity demanded a radiator and water), only to be followed by an invasion of boxer design liquid-cooled engines, but also saw simple and traditional trim terminology evaporate in favour of Caravelles and, at least for a time, Carats.

The fourth generation, a product of the 1990s, heralded the arrival of modern-day conventionality with a vengeance. For here was a vehicle with front-wheel drive and its engine in a location where most manufacturers have deemed a power unit should be. Instantly the age-old problem for Volkswagen, of customers struggling to manoeuvre loads over a space-consuming rear-mounted engine, could be dismissed, while the notion of a 'stand-alone' versatile ladder chassis became an instantaneous reality. Despite a slightly reduced load or passenger carrying quarter, due to the lack of space-saving constraints afforded by an extensive area of windscreen glass and an intrusive engine block in the vicinity of traditional cab space,

Volkswagen successfully pulled off another miracle of seamless transition from one design to another. Yet despite this earth-shattering event in the Transporter's story, just as the Golf 6 is a very different car to the Golf 5 while retaining the same basic look, so too the T4 and its predecessor preserved a visual similarity.

Turning to the fifth generation Transporter, known – at least colloquially – as the T5, the latest descendant in a direct line dating back to 1949, history, analysis and in most instances nostalgia make way for a combination of product description and test-drive style review. Without any doubt comparative luxury is evident even with the simplest workhorse, just as it is when it comes to what would once have been described as straightforward family transport models. However, the single key factor behind the fifth generation

▲ **1967–79** *(BS)*

▼ **1979–92**

▲ 1990–2003

▼ 2003–

Transporter has to be the production of Volkswagen's own California Camper; a move necessitated by long-time partner in this field Westfalia's takeover by the Daimler, Chrysler, Mercedes-Benz conglomerate's around the time the T5 was launched.

Even the briefest mention of the words Camper and Volkswagen in connection with each other requires that we celebrate the intrinsically linked boost to sales provided by Kombis and Micro Buses, and even Panel Vans, in years gone by. While it might not be feasible for a number of reasons to celebrate the finer points of each and every conversion, it is entirely practical to make more than passing reference to many of the names, both past and present, involved in the Camper

conversion business. Westfalia cannot be overlooked, nor can the brands and designs endorsed at one time or another by Volkswagen, whether they are based on a Splitty or a T4.

A final textual element must be mentioned in this introductory synopsis. Images of Volkswagen's renowned first Director General Heinz Nordhoff speaking to the world and his workforce as yet another production barrier was broken are reasonably well known, but what he was saying to them is not. Thanks to the auspices of the *Historische Kommunikation* department at Wolfsburg this is no longer the case. All the key figures in the birth of the Transporter are duly profiled, and the story is enhanced by extracts from their speeches and contemporary press releases.

Directly linked to the availability of written material, the book contains a wide selection of previously unpublished or rarely seen images, many of which emanate from records preserved through the medium of sales brochures and photographs commissioned by Volkswagen either for its own use or that of the world's press. To emphasise this aspect, even the images used to present the T5 are from the collection produced by Volkswagen to promote the vehicles through motoring publications and newspapers. Hanover in its infancy is depicted, and the occasions of great celebrations at the factory have been unearthed, to highlight just two fascinating examples.

This unique combination of the rare and the well-known provides the backbone to the celebratory nature of this book. Sixty diamond years; a remarkable achievement of which Volkswagen are justifiably proud, and particularly so as the models produced by other marques less than half as long ago are already long since forgotten.

Acknowledgements

I suspect that you will join me in thinking that this book is special, and if you do, I can reveal a threefold reason for this.

Much as I would like to claim that the idea to write a book celebrating the diamond jubilee of Transporter production was mine, it wasn't. The proposal was generated by the fertile brains of Mark Hughes and Derek Smith of Haynes Publishing, while the end result has only been achieved through their assistance and guidance throughout.

Without the permission of Volkswagen AG to visit the archive in Wolfsburg and to delve into its wealth of preserved documents, some of the key elements of the Transporter's history wouldn't have emerged, or might have been portrayed incorrectly. My particular thanks go to Dr Ulrike Gutzmann of the Corporate History Department, who went to great lengths to ensure that what was desired was made available, both in terms of words and imagery.

Last, but not least, my task was made so much easier thanks to the auspices of Brian Screaton that it seemed only fair to elevate him to the rank of co-author. Many of the images in the book were sourced from his extensive archive, including photographs and drawings that I certainly hadn't seen before. Brian accompanied me to Germany, where he led the research and directed me towards additional material. Since returning, he has trawled far and wide to obtain further material I have requested, while also researching and penning one of the most interesting sections of the book.

In addition to the three already mentioned, one other person deserves a special word of thanks. I have worked with Ken Cservenka on a variety of projects over the course of the last decade and more, but this book, which wasn't intrinsically technical and didn't rely on modern photography of older vehicles, wasn't one where Ken's particular talents were essential; or were they? Before the manuscript was submitted Ken kindly checked through each chapter, line by line, word by word and, as is his wont, unearthed a number of 'gremlins', some of which might easily have made it all the way to publication.

Richard A. Copping
January 2009

▶ Professor Dr Heinz Nordhoff, Chairman of the Board of Management, *Volkswagenwerk* AG 1948–68. Without Nordhoff it is unlikely that VW would have rapidly matured into the phenomenal success story it became, while the Transporter might well have remained nothing more than a scribbled sketch in what would, as a result, have become a long-forgotten notebook. Fans of the Transporter in all its guises owe an enormous debt of gratitude to Nordhoff. *(BS)*

Prelude to the first 20 years

▼ On the occasion of the two-millionth Transporter's completion, the vehicle's mentor, Heinz Nordhoff, delivered an unusually short speech to gathered dignitaries, journalists and workers at Hanover. The vehicle by his side was a Titian Red Clipper L with a Cloud White roof.

One cold, bleak winter's day in early February 1968 a seemingly frail and undoubtedly elderly man, physically transformed by recent illness and hence barely recognisable to those who had known and worked with or for him for the last 20 years, addressed assembled journalists, dignitaries and factory employees. Standing on a specially erected podium, behind a flower-bedecked pedestal and close to a lusciously garlanded second generation Micro Bus De Luxe finished in Titian Red with a Cloud White roof panel, his speech was uncharacteristically short. This was the man who previously would have relished the opportunity to regale his audience with a dialogue relayed from up to 30 pages of closely typed notes, each carefully annotated with alterations, additions and amendments.

Despite the forebodings of those closest to Heinrich Nordhoff, Volkswagen's omnipotent Director General, the occasion was genuinely celebratory, for those gathered at VW's Hanover factory were present to mark the emergence from the assembly line of the two-millionth Transporter, an unequalled milestone at the time for a vehicle of this type, and further testament, if it were needed, to the King of Wolfsburg's outstanding ability to mould success from humble origins.

The 69-year-old Director General of the multi-

faceted Volkswagen empire had successfully controlled the Transporter's progress for the best part of two decades. From its starting point as a design concept, Nordhoff had guided it through the early months, when daily production amounted to little more than ten vehicles on a leisurely single assembly line boxed away in a corner of the vastness of Wolfsburg, to the days of a myriad of variations on the basic Panel Van theme. He'd decreed that there would be a purpose-built factory in Hanover, some 25 miles from Wolfsburg, specifically for its production. Nordhoff had insisted upon countless modifications, varying from a fundamental redesign of parts to accommodate demands for more satisfactory cab air circulation, to straightforward increases in engine size. Finally, he'd spearheaded the introduction of a completely new Transporter a little over six months previously.

The speech Nordhoff made on that day was destined to be one of his last, and certainly his finale as far as the Transporter was concerned, for within little more than a month he had been stricken once more and following a short period in Wolfsburg's hospital died on Good Friday, 12 April 1968. As his epitaph on matters pertaining to the Transporter, the following extracts from Nordhoff's speech, which in themselves account for some 90 to 95 per cent of the total wordage delivered, reflect all the key issues of the first two decades of the vehicle's history which help to set this anniversary volume apart from what has been written to date.

'It's in the nature of things that records mean the least to the people who set them,' he said, 'but of course they have their relevance in the expression of a special achievement and an unusual success.'

By longstanding tradition the father of the Transporter is said to have been either the British officer in charge at Wolfsburg in the immediate post-war period, or the man (perhaps best described as the first true Volkswagen enthusiast) who, inspired by the rudimentary Beetle-based platform-wagon, sketched what is deemed – by legend if nothing else – to be the seed that bore fruit a couple of years later as the first generation Delivery Van. Both the eager but inevitably inexperienced Major Ivan Hirst and, particularly, the exuberant, highly vocal, entrepreneurial Dutchman Ben Pon might have raised an eyebrow in surprise when, in late 1949, they heard that another would claim the Transporter as his own, as many will do now, 60 years later. When he spoke of 'the people', the modest Nordhoff of February 1968 was undoubtedly referring to the *Vorstand* or management body, his inner sanctum of courtiers who were only too aware that Nordhoff's word was law. What Nordhoff elected to skim over was his self-declared message, first uttered even before production of the Transporter began, that he was the true father of this new and revolutionary load-lugging or people-carrying Transporter.

'When we started building the VW Transporter in Wolfsburg the numbers were small but as early as 1956 the decision had been taken to build in additional capacity by transferring production to a purpose-built factory in Hanover. The fact that we bought a million square metres then was met by some with incredulity; today we would be happier if we had taken two million square metres. Our reason is that the VW Transporter made a unique journey to success. In 1962 our achievement was the millionth, taking twelve-and-a-half years to do this, while today the two-millionth VW Transporter is with us, five-and-a-half years after the first. Now that daily production has been increased to 900 Transporters, one can work out pretty well when the third-millionth one will be due, especially if you add in the production of our factories abroad.'

Without doubt, the 1950s was a time of incredible growth for Volkswagen. The stories of ever-increasing Beetle production still lagging far behind ever-increasing demand for the product are well known, a situation which lasted at least to the end of the decade. However, despite such a major issue Nordhoff pressed ahead with a meteoric expansion programme, intending to mould Volkswagen into a worldwide sales organisation. Part of the Beetle's success story has to be attributed to Nordhoff's policy of continual improvement, rather than a change of model for change's sake. The Director General's outlook determined the Transporter's future too.

Surprisingly, considering the successes noted in Nordhoff's speech of 1968, initial sales of the commercial vehicle and passenger-carrying Transporters could not be taken for granted. While some countries readily accepted the Transporter for the revolutionary vehicle it was and took it to their hearts immediately, others, including the all-important American market, appeared singularly unimpressed. Volkswagen of America's dilemma in this respect might have eventually been solved by the most original and dynamic advertising campaign the automobile world had yet to encounter, but this does not explain why Nordhoff should countenance the building of a factory dedicated to Transporter production in the mid-'50s. It is the contention here that Hanover was built for the Beetle, to safeguard maximum car production at Wolfsburg at a time when the factory was threatened by even a single assembly line being devoted to anything that wasn't pointed in the direction of increased daily saloon car production. The area surrounding Wolfsburg was by this point devoid of further men, or for that matter women, that the factory could call upon easily – but the potential workforce of the city of Hanover was underutilised. That the Hanover factory did exist ensured that when the boom times came – guaranteed by year-on-year improvements, after-sales service and growth in the legend of air-cooled infallibility across Europe and beyond, and thanks primarily to distinctive advertising in the United States – capacity to meet demand was available.

If Nordhoff's pivotal role in the birth of the Transporter could prove controversial, the narrative surrounding its development and growth should not; this was the final major issue of Nordhoff's swansong Micro Bus and Delivery Van speech:

'Since the introduction of the current VW Transporter we can only satisfy demand by working additional shifts. This vehicle has created a new class which unites about two-thirds of all Transporters up to 1.25-tonne payload in the German Republic, and has not been influenced by economic fluctuations.'

Almost immediately after the death of Heinrich Nordhoff, Volkswagen's new hierarchy rushed into the arms of the small but increasingly vociferous group who had called for the Beetle to be replaced. Soon it was a common assumption that Nordhoff had been incapable of casting any member of his small family aside; that he had become besotted with his policy of continual improvement to the detriment of all other options. That Nordhoff had been able to say that additional shifts were necessary because a new model of Transporter had been launched, while posterity recorded him standing by its side, should have swept such mutterings right out of the door. However, it didn't, and curiously much of the initial marketing of the new Nordhoff-approved second-generation Transporter only served to add credence to the myths surrounding his inability to acknowledge change. It is perhaps not so amazing, then, that even in the current millennium the myth of Nordhoff's intransigence is perpetuated in certain circles, where, to be frank, the well-researched author should know better.

Nordhoff was grateful, on that momentous day in 1968, to all those who accepted the invitation to be Volkswagen's guests at the festivities to mark the appearance of the two-millionth Transporter, a vehicle generously donated to the Charitable Foundation for Children with the heartfelt wish that it would 'bring some happiness to these under-privileged children'. Perhaps he would have been equally happy to know that some 40+ years hence his story in the birth and development of the first- and second-generation Transporters was to be retold, not in some vaguely nostalgic way to rekindle interest in long defunct and forgotten vehicles, but as a crucial part in an anniversary volume celebrating 60 years of Transporter production and sales, currently, in just about all its five guises, the single most popular Volkswagen of them all.

▶ The garland-bedecked two-millionth Transporter portrayed with its siblings.
Left: single cab Pick-up, double cab Pick-up, Micro Bus and Micro Bus De Luxe.
Right: Ambulance, single cab Pick-up with extended platform, Kombi, Delivery Van.

1948–50

PART I

Fast track to production

▶ In his desire to bring the Transporter into production, Nordhoff put considerable pressure on the design team. This prototype has still a little way to go in terms of refinements.

No participation from Porsche and the Nazis

Ferdinand Porsche, the renowned creator of the Beetle, played no part in the conception of the Transporter. At the time the humble Delivery Van was conceived Porsche, no longer a young man, was languishing in a French jail, having fled from his wartime role at the Strength-Through-Joy factory we know today as Wolfsburg, to his native Austria as the defeat of the Third Reich became increasingly inevitable.

Before and during the war tentative attempts were made to produce load-carrying versions of the Beetle, but such vehicles were little more than cut-down adaptations of the saloon. Take as an example the Type 68, listed as delivery van Model A. This was a vehicle with a normal Beetle body hacked away behind the doors to make space for a long flat bed to which could be fitted a canvas canopy. The initial two-seater conversion was developed out of the final car in the Beetle prototype VW38 production series. Later, another delivery van emerged, this time designated as the Type 88 and labelled as the Model B. Again little more than a saloon with most of the rear removed, on this occasion the rear end was redesigned, while the platform was shorter than previously. Both variations on the theme can best be summarised as pick-ups rather than delivery vans, the latter designation being best reserved for a further development.

The Type 81, of which only one example was built, first saw the light of day in 1940, and once more looked like a saloon when viewed from the front. However, on this occasion a normal van shape, complete with a totally flat hinged door, emerged behind the B-pillars. A transverse beam below the rear door made access to the engine somewhat difficult, while the enclosed nature of the flat-four, with its air inlets high up on the side panels, brought into question the efficiency of its cooling.

Probably the most often seen Beetle-based van relates to a later version of the Pick-up model. This was a vehicle listed and actually produced after Porsche had taken flight. Rudolph Brörmann, the plant manager at Wolfsburg in the early post-war days when the British were in control, drew up a chart of all the possible Beetle options as early as September 1945, each of which was based on models designed by Porsche previously. Brörmann's Type 83, complete with the description 'Delivery van (closed body) *Reichpost* type', might best be described as a Beetle saloon with the usual areas chopped away to be replaced by little more than a metal-panelled garden shed unceremoniously dumped on what was left of the car.

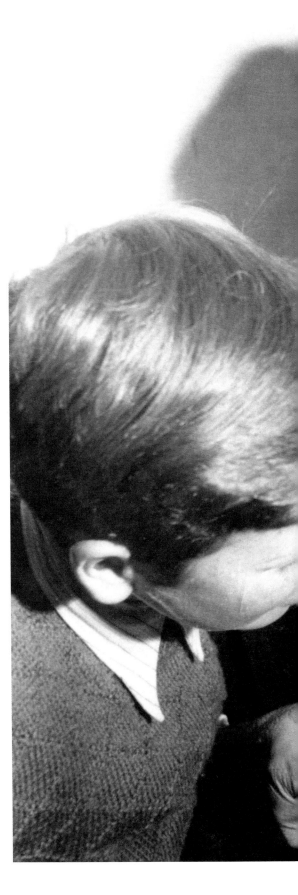

▶ Although Ferdinand Porsche played no part in the design and production of the Transporter, it was powered by his flat-four engine. This picture, taken when Porsche was approaching the end of his life, is of particular interest in that it features Ferdinand Piech (right), the man in charge at Volkswagen during much of the lifetime of the fourth generation Transporter, and still an influential figure today.

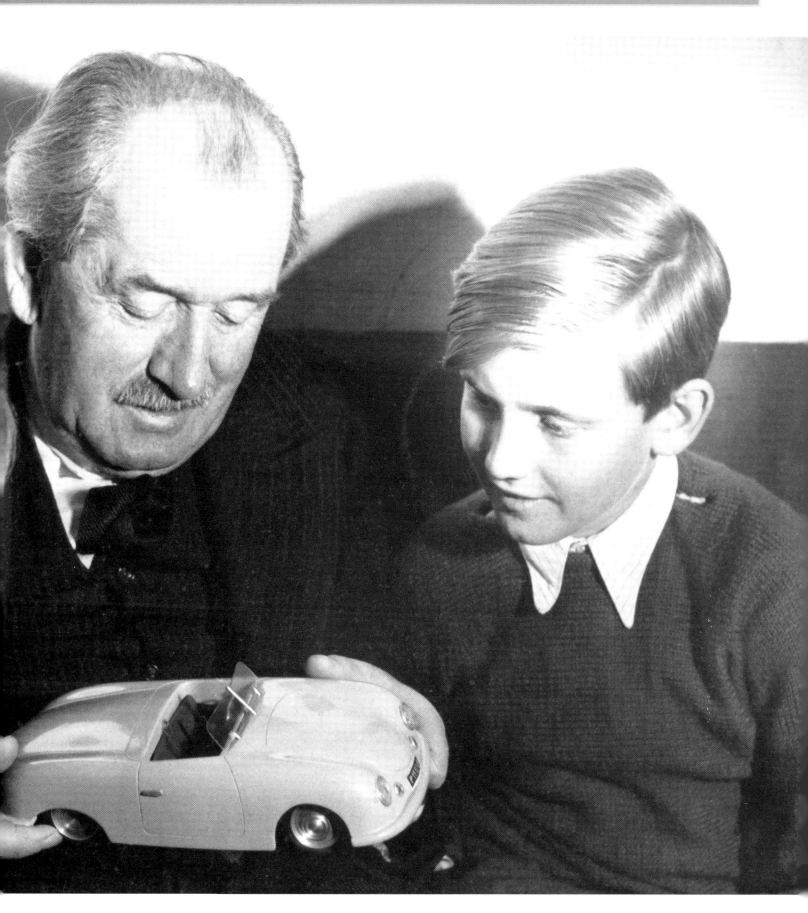

A factory and a product without purpose?

By definition, if Porsche wasn't involved with the Transporter neither were the Nazis. However, this is also where it must be said that without either, in all probability there wouldn't have been a Transporter as we know it. That the Nazi party was forced into the situation of owning a car-manufacturing plant, purpose-built for production of the Beetle, is reasonably well-known. Hitler wished to motorise the German population. Porsche had the genius at his fingertips to create a revolutionary design while almost complying with Hitler's demands in terms of affordability. To create a *volkswagen*, a people's car, was something Porsche had strived long and hard for, his previous attempts always having been thwarted at some stage on the long, twisty road to manufacture. The German motor manufacturing industry's reluctance to assist with the creation of a vehicle that would form competition to its own products, and in reality the RDA's (*Reichsverband der deutschen Automobilindustrie*, or German Motor Car Industry Association) belief that procrastination would lead to any such programme's long-term cancellation, led directly to Hitler demanding that his party should benefit by taking on the responsibility of building a grandiose factory specifically for Beetle production.

Created out of near open countryside, requisitioned from the estates of the von Schulenburg family amongst others, the mile-long factory had no purpose in peacetime but to build *KdF-Wagens*, Strength-Through-Joy cars, during the Nazi era and Beetles after the war. Following the collapse of the Third Reich and the ruling that made the Nazi Party an illegal organisation, the factory became ownerless. Demolition was one option, but there was a community living around its walls dependent on its existence for their future, however unsure. Another option was reparations, but as is well known, although interest was shown, nobody entertained either the building, or its sole product, seriously.

In many ways it was the desperate need in post-war Germany for transport for the occupying forces that saved Wolfsburg. This demand was far from overlooked by the senior resident British officer at the factory. Indeed, Major Ivan Hirst went out of his way to secure a future for the workers and residents of Wolfsburg. With sizeable orders cleverly secured, manufacture began, admittedly in a rather haphazard manner that resulted largely from the lack of supplies and the plant being badly affected by bomb damage.

However grossly oversimplified, the foundations for the creation of the Transporter were now in place. Not only did a large factory exist in which such a vehicle could be built, thanks to the Nazis, but also an economical air-cooled engine employed in a vehicle with a separate chassis, the norm for the times anyway, courtesy of Ferdinand Porsche, awaited utilisation. All that had to happen was for someone to think of the idea of building a wholly new type of small commercial vehicle.

The idea

By tradition, at least in the higher echelons of the current day Volkswagen hierarchy amongst many others, two men were responsible for the concept of the Transporter. The ingenuity of one inspired the other to sketch the rudimentary elements of what is undoubtedly recognisable as the first generation Transporter. The names of both are well known. Major Ivan Hirst's solution to a problem triggered the fertile mind of car dealer and businessman Ben Pon into action, and the idea behind the Transporter was duly conceived on 23 April 1947. For it was on this day that little more than a scribbled drawing was produced by Pon. The essence of his sketch was a box-shaped vehicle of 750kg, with an apparently contoured front, its driver and any passengers sitting over the front wheels. The engine was depicted as being mounted above the rear axle and accessible for routine maintenance and servicing via an upward-opening lid.

Over 50 years later, Ivan Hirst delighted in recalling that momentous day. Sat with the author in a homely little café in the neighbouring hamlet to his native Yorkshire village of Marsden, Ivan produced a pencil stub from a convenient pocket, plucked a white serviette from a glass and proceeded to reproduce what Pon had sketched 52 years earlier. This was his superbly timed prelude to a cleverly acted account of his creation of a vehicle known as the *Plattenwagen*; an ingenious contraption devised to overcome yet another problem which had occurred as the British tried to kick-start Wolfsburg back into life.

Ivan Hirst

In later life Ivan Hirst was a consummate actor and a great showman. There is a distinct sense that this was a lifelong trait, as evidenced by the now legendary tale of Heinz Nordhoff's appointment to the position of Director General at Wolfsburg. The year was 1947, and the decision had been made that the German administrator at Wolfsburg, the lawyer Hermann Munch, was in desperate need of someone with a thorough understanding of the car industry to assist him in the long-term running of Wolfsburg, a factory of which the British always deemed themselves to be caretakers. Nordhoff's name was plucked from the capacious pot of dispossessed managers and he was duly interviewed by Hirst. After an intense two-day period the Major announced in solemn tone that he was unable to recommend Nordhoff as the ideal candidate for the job. A dispirited Nordhoff started to pack his briefcase in readiness to leave. Hirst said nothing and maintained a stony expression. Mentally he was counting the seconds of a two-minute silence. At the crucial moment and to maximum effect, he added that he was going to advise his superiors that Nordhoff should be given the top job!

Ivan Hirst always carried a pipe with him and a box of matches. Whether he actually smoked much of the dreaded weed is open to question, for when recalling events of years gone by the pipe and particularly the matches played a crucial role in the vital pause before the punch-line of any story was delivered. A brilliant raconteur, a wit and a genuine English gentleman, Ivan Hirst captured the hearts of many a Wolfsburg manager and enthusiast alike many years after his period at Volkswagen. However, during his time at the factory it wasn't his car-manufacturing skills that set him apart from others, for they were non-existent: it was his ability to improvise in the face of adversity.

Born in 1916, Ivan's early childhood at least was one of privilege. The Great War had been good to Hirst's father and grandfather, their wholesale watch business spiralling upwards as they turned their attentions to making much-demanded precision instruments. With Germany defeated and the Kaiser in exile, the Hirsts turned their attention to watchmaking. Such was the scale of the enterprise that a new and impressively modern factory was built. While customs duties on German luxury goods were retained at the rate of 33.3 per cent times were good for the Hirst enterprise. Throughout this period of prosperity the young Ivan was encouraged to visit and spend time at the factory. This led him to comment later that he knew what an automatic lathe was before he had even the slightest understanding of either Latin or Greek.

Sadly for the entrepreneurial Hirsts, custom duties were removed as the 1920s gathered pace, a move which made competitiveness far harder in the face of cheap foreign imports. Such was the downturn in their fortunes that during the course of 1927 there was no other option left to them but to sell the factory. For Ivan, fortunately, the effects were not really far-reaching, as within just a few short years university beckoned. His chosen course directed him towards a career as an optician, while academia also opened the door to happy times spent at military training camps. By the outbreak of war Hirst held

▼ This well-known photograph of Ivan Hirst was taken at Wolfsburg in the period when he was the Senior Resident Officer.

▲ In case we forget – this picture, taken in front of the damaged office suites of the factory, features Ivan Hirst on the right. Wolfsburg, named so by the British, remained under the control of the military for several years after the defeat of the Nazis and the end of Hitler's Reich.

the rank of captain, although by this time his day job for a number of years had been running a workshop for the repair of optical instruments. Sadly, his almost immediate call-up on the outbreak of war curtailed his business interests, his absence forcing the permanent closure of the premises.

Following active service in France and a period as an engineer in a tank workshop, his strengths as both an optician and someone with knowledge of fine mechanics had been duly recognised. In the autumn of 1942 Hirst proved an ideal candidate to join the newly established Corps of Royal Electrical and Mechanical Engineers, known as the REME, a body set up to support the machinery behind the technical modernisation of the armed forces. Following Germany's defeat the REME's role inevitably changed, but was still of high importance. Repair and maintenance work relating to the equipment and vehicles owned by the British army continued, but additionally the REME was charged with supervising production at all the most important industrial sites, ensuring in the process that the demands of the Allies were met. Hirst had been allocated to No 4 General Troops Workshops in Brussels when the call came for officers to apply for assignments in Germany. The

military government – the Control Commission for Germany, or CCG – was finding it difficult to recruit suitable candidates, many of those best qualified having been despatched to fight in the continuing war in Asia. When a by now somewhat dispirited Hirst applied he was considered ideal, his family's business relations with pre-war Germany being considered an added advantage.

Hirst's own account of his arrival at Wolfsburg in August 1945 as the senior resident officer is well chronicled. That he had 'no specific orders other than to take control' serves to indicate that it was largely due to his ingenuity, quick thinking and ability to improvise that what appeared to consist of little more than a REME workshop which was not his direct responsibility, and a vast series of derelict buildings with only a few disheartened men working in them, was quickly developed into a production unit capable of providing much-needed transport for the Allied forces.

The story of how Hirst tackled a whole series of issues associated with, and obstacles to production of the Beetle in those early days is not one to be told in this volume, save to mention his ingenious solution to one difficulty that was to prove the inspiration behind Pon's legendary sketch of a Delivery Van.

The *Plattenwagen*

Hirst frequently recalled the story behind the *Plattenwagen* (literally 'flat car'), his words being recorded for posterity on one occasion at least. When asked to elaborate on the trials and tribulations of manoeuvring material from one part of the factory to another in a place that was so vast, the Major spoke of the decided lack of electro-cars, or battery vehicles. His initial well thought-out solution to the problem was to beg the use of some of the army's forklift trucks. Unfortunately, the time soon came when they were needed lock, stock and barrel for more pressing work elsewhere. Aghast, the German plant manager at the time, Rudolph Brörmann, was convinced that this act of near treachery would be the prelude to the end of Beetle manufacture. Hirst recalled saying something to the effect of not being so stupid: 'We're a car factory, surely we can do something… We'll take a *Kübelwagen* or a *Käfer* chassis, put a flat board at one end, [and] put a driver's seat over the engine [at the other].' This was the simplicity of the *Plattenwagen*; little more than a trussed tubular steel frame that supported a flat platform, yet so successful in its composition that examples were still in service in the 1970s. Hirst's ingenuity lay in his decision to place the driver's seat above the engine, as this freed up the entire front, while the simple expediency of an extended steering link guaranteed manoeuvrability and resulted in a tight turning circle deemed to be just the ticket for work on the factory floor. Although

it was an immediate success Hirst confirmed to his interviewer that no steps were taken to expand its usage, as just enough were built to satisfy the requirements of the factory.

▼ Three images of the *Plattenwagen*, each taken during the early days of the vehicle's lengthy semi-official production run.

Ben Pon

Ebullient, extravert and flamboyant are just three of the most frequently used words to describe Ben Pon, from Amersfoot in Holland, a key figure not only in the emerging story of the Transporter, but also with regard to the Beetle. While Pon's brother Wijn appeared happy to simply accept what life threw at him, Ben always demonstrated a determination to carve a name for himself and generate a fortune for the family.

Ben Pon's interest in Volkswagen stemmed back to the earliest days of Porsche's Volksauto project. To put it simply, the Pon family had experienced a heavy body blow when, as Opel dealers, they were forced to relinquish their franchise following the acquisition of one of Germany's premier vehicle manufacturing firms by the American giant General Motors. According to the custom of GM, Opel's apparently haphazard arrangements had allowed too many agencies to develop per country, had failed in its attempts to build a system of interchangeable parts, and had sanctioned by default the making of components by a series of dealer machine shops. General Motors quickly decreed that their own practices from now on would be employed, a system which gave no leeway for independence of thought or action. The Pons, feeling unable to comply with such restrictions, terminated their franchise and resorted to becoming agents for American Federal Trucks. Clearly, the income potential compared to that as an associate of Opel was much reduced and the entrepreneur in Ben Pon was determined to rectify the shortfall.

Pon almost immediately pounced on the apparent opportunity of becoming involved with a new major force in motoring circles, the Nazi, or by association German government, backed people's car. Frustration must have mounted to fever pitch for the brothers as delays escalated. However, hope wasn't abandoned and gimmicks such as presenting Ferdinand Porsche with a gift of 10,000 tulip bulbs on the day in August 1939 when the KdF factory power station was officially switched on were perceived by the Pons as an appropriate way of keeping their name at the forefront of the Nazi regime's minds.

Whether or not Pon's first real contact with the *KdF-Wagen* came at the 1939 Berlin Motor Show, when a test drive was arranged for him, or whether actions equally unctuous to the presentation and planting of the aforementioned bulbs fast-tracked him into the arms of key Nazis, will no doubt remain a matter for speculation. According to Walter Henry

◄ Some pictures of Ben Pon are reasonably well known. This official-looking one, supplied by the Volkswagen Archive, betrays little of his exuberant personality.

Nelson in his book entitled *Small Wonder*, once considered to be the bible of Volkswagen history at least to the point of Heinz Nordhoff's death in 1968, Porsche appeared not only to have introduced Pon to Robert Ley, the particularly obnoxious Nazi in charge of the German Labour Front, and the man therefore holding the purse strings required to build the factory near Fallersleben and to bring the *KdF-Wagen* to fruition, but also to have driven the Dutchman around the Berlin Autobahn in just such a car. Pon is quoted as saying that the Beetle was 'terribly noisy', but of a likeable basic design. Nelson goes as far as to assert that the 'Nazis actually assigned him the Dutch Franchise', but of course whatever the effort on Pon's part, the imminent war eventually saw Hitler's regime, and any arrangements associated with it, swept away for ever.

Despite assertions that he wanted no dealings with Germany or German products Pon was soon on the Volkswagen trail once more. Now he declared his mission was to impress the British and not the Nazis. The various tales of how Pon went about his task differ, with by far the most entertaining one coming from the pen of Walter Henry Nelson. That the story includes the reminiscences of Pon himself would seem to imply utter validity, although Ivan Hirst's contradictory recollections of Pon arriving at Wolfsburg in a 'Dutch Army Medical Corps uniform – very ill-fitting', either at best casts at least a shadow of doubt on its total accuracy, or confirms that when the mood took him Pon's tales became ever more glamorously fictitious! Temporarily commissioned a full colonel in the Dutch army, Pon had a somewhat elderly Mercedes made available for his usage, and co-opted an appropriately forelock-tugging corporal as chauffeur, and, as he recalled later, 'drove into Germany in high style, puffing a cigar and waving at passers-by'. Throughout his visit – an occasion when he met not only Hirst but also Hermann Munch, the Berlin lawyer appointed to be the factory's custodian – Pon posed as a high-ranking Dutch officer on a friendly inspection visit, rather than as someone eager to acquire a franchise to sell the product. The ruse worked and Pon got his cars, as will be revealed below; but more important to the story of the Transporter is that both Hirst and his superior officer, Colonel Radclyffe, liked the man, trusted his expertise and were attentive to even his wildest ideas.

Undeniably, an alternative version of events told by Arthur Railton, sometime Vice President of Corporate Relations for Volkswagen of America, is equally worthy of repetition, as he too had a number of conversations with the ever theatrical Pon. 'On several occasions,' revealed Railton, Pon made it clear that 'he was never made a colonel, but that he merely borrowed a colonel's uniform from a friend.' 'With Pon,' declared Railton, 'who loved a great story, the line between

▲ Here is plain Mr Pon dressed in military uniform – no doubt set to invade Wolfsburg and the office of Ivan Hirst. *(BS)*

truth and fiction was a fuzzy one.' Typical of the man was the account of events he gave to Railton in 1963, when he recalled cutting 'some stiff plastic into strips' and then 'wrapped pieces of coloured skate strap around the plastic to make it look like campaign ribbons'. Pon joked with Railton that he 'had more ribbons on my chest than Montgomery'.

In his attempt to paint a full canvas Railton also spoke to another player from the days of British control at Wolfsburg. Wing Commander Richard Berryman was in charge of production operations, acting as Ivan Hirst's assistant. To him Pon was less of a loveable rogue and more of a thorn in the side of the British. Berryman's turn of phrase appears to have been Americanised by Railton, but casts a lengthy shadow on the Dutchman's reputation. 'This guy, Ben Pon, was a menace. He was tight whenever he was around the place. He would relate how the Dutch sailed up the channel with a broom at the masthead. Many is the time I could have kicked his teeth in. When I asked him what he did to fight for his beloved Holland, he would get abusive. He was supposed to have been a brigadier or something – he never smelled the powder. He was the first to get some export cars and, while I have no proof, I am pretty sure that some greasing of the palms took place.'

Conversely author Malcolm Bobbitt successfully unearthed yet another view of Pon, one of a talented individual who just happened to possess an

▶ Undoubtedly one of the most famous sketches of all time in the world of commercial vehicles – but was it really the pivotal point in the evolution of the Transporter, as has often been asserted?

▼ The Pon brothers – Ben to the left and Wijand to the right. Their air of prosperity belies the years spent establishing both the Beetle and the Transporter. The showman in Ben is demonstrable through his king-size cigar! (BS)

'effervescent attitude'. Bobbitt recalls the thoughts of George Pearson, a member of the REME inspection team at Wolfsburg, who suggested that Pon's outgoing over-the-top performances masked a strong regard for the Volkswagen, a clear understanding of its engineering prowess, and above all an admiration of Hirst's quest for perfection. His resultant 'amenable business relationship' with the Major was, according to Bobbitt, 'fundamental' to the development of the Transporter.

Whatever the percentage of accuracy of each and every tale, the cold, clinical facts are that at the beginning of October 1947, the Pon brothers imported five Beetles and in the process closed Volkswagen's first export deal. By this time Pon's Automobielhandel had been the authorised importer of Volkswagens for the Netherlands since 8 August of the same year.

However, despite Pon's undoubted pioneer status, any implication of a unique relationship with the factory was dashed permanently as exports multiplied from a total of just 56 in that year to 4,500 cars during 1948, necessitating the establishment of permanent contracts with operations in Switzerland, Belgium, Luxembourg, Sweden, Denmark and Norway.

With the appointment of Nordhoff as Director General, Pon had little option but to carefully switch his allegiance towards the new man. Nordhoff accepted Pon for the showman he was and their relationship blossomed, Nordhoff even entrusting the Dutchman with the important task of selling the Beetle to the Americans – a project in which, like others after him, he was less than successful. It is against this background that the traditional interpretation of the transition from *Plattenwagen* to Transporter is set.

Pon's initial plan foiled

Amongst his many reminiscences of those early days at Wolfsburg, Ivan Hirst confirmed that Ben Pon 'wanted these *Plattenwagen* for Dutch companies'. Pon had spotted the *Plattenwagen* on one of his trips to Wolfsburg and was struck by its simplicity; a basic nature akin to that of the three-wheel delivery vehicles in his home country, most of which were little more than pedal-powered runabouts. Pon saw a market for the *Plattenwagen* as an upgrade of this sort of workhorse and promptly applied to the Dutch Transport Authority for a street-legal certificate for such vehicles. Unfortunately, this status was instantaneously refused on the grounds that to control a vehicle the driver must be seated at its front; a principle that could only be considered as alien to the *Plattenwagen*'s design.

Down, but certainly not out, it wasn't long before Pon bounced back with a new idea, which came in the form of his legendary sketch already referred to. Following on from that simple drawing quickly pencilled during the course of a relatively casual meeting with Hirst at Minden, the Major was sufficiently impressed to recommend that Pon should discuss the vehicle with Colonel Radclyffe. Unfortunately for Pon, Radclyffe was more concerned about the struggle occurring to maintain even basic Beetle production, and when this was coupled to a lack of available manpower to rebuild bomb-damaged Wolfsburg the Colonel was clearly of the opinion that a second Volkswagen at such a stage was one step too far.

Theoretically, Pon's part in the creation of the Transporter was now played, as was Major Hirst's. The decisive steps on the road to production were made by Nordhoff, the ex-Opel truck plant manager, a professional who had benefited from training in the United States and understood fully what manufacturing was all about.

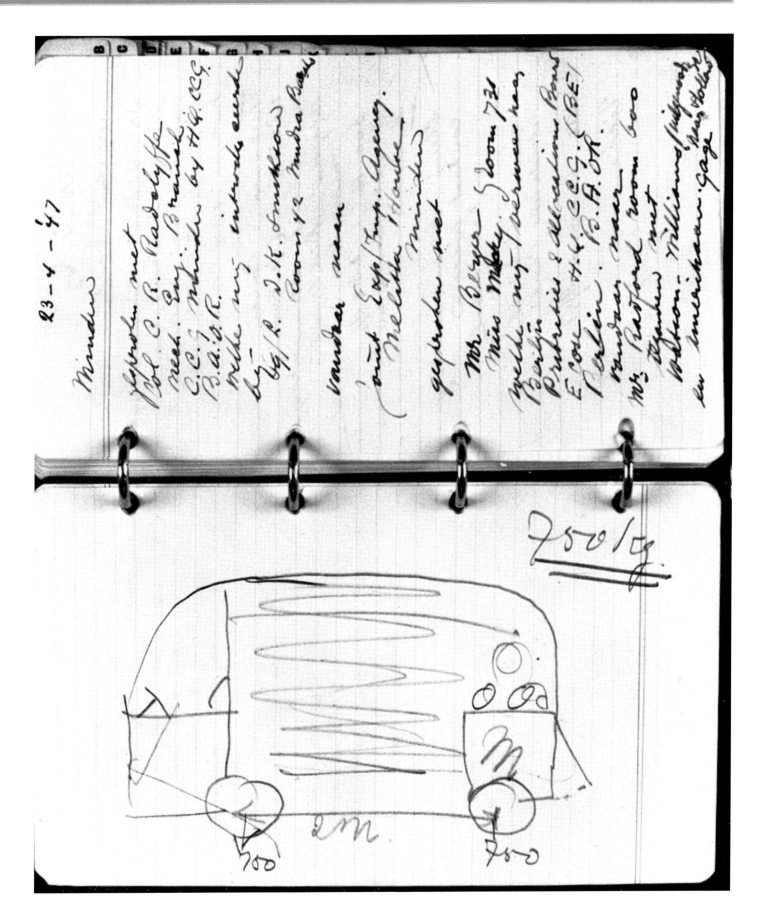

History interpreted

The cult of near hero worship that rapidly enveloped Heinz Nordhoff in his first years at Wolfsburg, and his swift elevation to semi-regal status as the key player in an operation that symbolised West Germany's economic miracle, in part at the expense of the reputation of the British and by implication Ivan Hirst in particular, must have galled the former major beyond measure. Although his career in the post-Wolfsburg years could hardly be described as a failure, Hirst didn't achieve the attributes of greatness afforded to the man he had not only specifically recommended for the top job at Wolfsburg, but to whom he then had little option but to hand over his authority.

There are those who argue with a reasonable degree of conviction that Hirst wanted the job of Director General himself and that his remarks of later years can be dismissed as the venom of an embittered and secretly jealous man. Conversely, an equally vociferous band, possibly including some of the historians employed by modern day Volkswagen to retell the story of the organisation's rise to its present world-embracing position, could argue that Nordhoff was a despotic ruler surrounded by lackeys whose brief was to promote him to the workforce, to distributors and dealers far and wide, indeed to anyone fool enough to be taken in by blatant propaganda, while the man himself would stop at nothing to achieve self-glorification.

For all those determined to confirm which cogs fit where in the Transporter story, clearing the truth-concealing mists of many a controversial year is not easy. During their respective lifetimes neither Nordhoff nor Hirst made it any easier, each accusing the other of over-glorifying their roles in Volkswagen's success in the first ten years after the war.

Speaking in 1954 Nordhoff lamented the state of the Wolfsburg factory at the point he first stepped over the threshold: 'I was faced with a desolate heap of rubble, a horde of desperate people, the torso of a deserted town – an amorphous mass which had never had any organising principle, no factory organisation in a real sense, without a programme or any rational work organisation. So something new had to be created because there was nothing there and never had been anything to build on at all.'

Despite an elapse of nearly 50 years since the events themselves and some 30 years since Nordhoff's death, Ivan Hirst's acidic remarks on the subject of the one-time Director General were particularly biting. 'I think you could have put anyone in there,' he said of the role of Director General, 'even a monkey and it would have been a success. There was a huge factory, a labour force, a building, a good management already in place, a car that would sell, huge demand all over the world for light cars, and it could not fail even if you put the biggest fool you could find in charge, it would still have worked…'

In a calmer moment Hirst admitted to a relationship with Nordhoff that was 'close, but cold', while suggesting that he was 'a distant figure to everybody'. Speaking to the author, Ivan Hirst described Nordhoff as 'a cat that liked to walk alone'. Others have jumped on the bandwagon. Respected author Laurence Meredith described him as a 'thoroughly unlikeable autocrat', while Ralf Richter's biography of Ivan Hirst paints Nordhoff as someone determined to deny others any part in the story of Volkswagen's meteoric post-war rise.

Original research at Wolfsburg has revealed a distinct twist in the accepted story of the birth of the Transporter. Several extracts from the speech Nordhoff made to the world's press on 12 November 1949 to launch the vehicle are reasonably well known, but the greater content certainly isn't. The successful campaign instigated by Nordhoff's immediate successor Kurt Lotz to tarnish his reputation in the face of Volkswagen's rapid slide into crisis after his death appears to have ensured, amongst other things, that his interpretation of how the Transporter came into being has been overlooked ever since.

Perhaps not surprisingly the Pon family have clung rigidly to the heartfelt belief that Ben Pon senior was the inspiration behind the Transporter. Writing to Wolfsburg in 1987 Ed Servaas, Public Relations Manager of Pons Automobielhandel BV, summarised as follows:

'During his visits to post-war Germany (see his notes in his diary from the 23/4/47) he sketched for his friends in the VW Factory a "no-nonsense" Box Van, along the same lines as the Beetle.

'…You can see the prototype of this Box-Van, which later came off the production lines in 1950. The starting points in Pon's deliberations were a wheelbase of 2.0m (it later became 2.4m), a loading capacity of 750kg, and a rear engine. The sketch is generally accepted by Volkswagen as the original idea of the Dutch Garage-owner, who had grown up with trucks (before the war he imported American "Federal" and German "Bussing" trucks). He was convinced that as well as the Beetle, the VW Factory should build a Van as soon as possible, in order to alleviate the transport problems in the aftermath of the Second World War.'

Heinz Nordhoff – the road to the Transporter

Just as with the potted biographies of both Ivan Hirst and Ben Pon, where detail is more or less restricted to information relevant to the birth of the Transporter, so it is here with that of Heinz Nordhoff.

Heinrich Nordhoff was born on 6 January 1899 in Hildesheim, Lower Saxony, where he spent the early years of his life. Following the failure of the bank his father worked for, the financially stricken family had no option but to relocate to Berlin, where Heinz was enrolled in a technical high school. Despite his youth, he had already decided on a career in mechanical engineering. From 1917 he saw service in the German army and was wounded in action. When the First World War was over, Nordhoff resumed his education, attending the Polytechnic academy in Berlin, from where he graduated as a certified mechanical engineer. In 1925 he joined the Bayerische Motoren-Werke in Munich as an aircraft design engineer. However, by 1929 he had left BMW to join Adam Opel AG, already by this time a subsidiary of General Motors, his heart being set on management and his attention directed towards automotive production and sales.

Nordhoff's 16-year period at Opel would probably have been greatly extended if it hadn't been for the Second World War, Germany's defeat, and his places of work falling severally into the Russian and American zones of occupation. Abandoning any thought of trying to pick up the pieces of his career in the Russian zone, he headed for Opel headquarters in Ruesselsheim. Although Nordhoff's association with both the Nazis and Hitler's government was, to say the least, tenuous, it was to cost him any chance of working at Opel in a management role. Never a card-carrying member of the Nazi party, Nordhoff had nevertheless been awarded the minor honour of *Wehrwirtschaftsführer* for his services to truck building for the war effort. As such, at least in the eyes of the Americans, Nordhoff was tainted and deemed unemployable. His career at Opel was over, once and for all. His interview with Major Hirst and appointment with Volkswagen has already been alluded to.

Nordhoff's first job at Opel back in 1929 had been the task of writing service manuals, a position that required technical expertise and an ability to work in a thorough and logical way. From here, Nordhoff was promoted to the role of department head in Opel's service organisation. Demonstrating a trait that was to be his hallmark at Volkswagen, he often worked a seven-day week and was known to spend his holidays on Opel's production lines. Almost inevitably his potential was spotted and Nordhoff, by now in his 30s, achieved a personal ambition of being despatched to America to study both sales and production techniques in Detroit. From the role of technical consultant to Opel's sales manager, the fully-fledged master automobile maker was quickly elected to the Board of Management, a position he relished, with effect from 1936. In early 1939 Nordhoff moved to Berlin to direct Adam Opel's office there, and then in 1942 he was appointed Director General of the Opel-Werke in Brandenburg, then the largest truck-making factory in Europe. Despite the deprivations of war he was responsible for producing 4,000 vehicles per month. There could be no sounder background than Nordhoff's when – once firmly ensconced at Volkswagen – he recognised the need for a second vehicle, a commercial.

Nordhoff's arrival at Volkswagen in 1947 proved to be something of a catalyst for concerted action. Gunter Hellman, who had joined the staff at Wolfsburg in 1945, and later became parts manager for Canada, spoke to Walter Henry Nelson of everybody being 'in a rut before Nordhoff appeared. We had no food

▼ An efficient publicity machine developed the cult of the King of Wolfsburg as far as Nordhoff was concerned. Here, the Director General is shown overseeing progress during further factory expansion. *(BS)*

▲ An official photograph taken on the occasion of Heinz Nordhoff's 65th birthday in January 1964. *(RC)*

previously exhibited when he was at Opel, Nordhoff took up residence within the factory, sleeping for a period of six months on a makeshift bed in a room next door to his office. While Nordhoff didn't demand the same of others, he did ask the seemingly impossible of his workforce. 'It still takes us 400 hours to build a car,' he told them. 'If we go on like this, we won't be doing it much longer.'

His personal drive was rewarded in the form of rapidly escalating production numbers for the Beetle, and an intensely gratifying increase in the quantity of markets keen to purchase any form of Volkswagen meant that during 1950 Nordhoff could openly express his life's aim of making 'this plant into the greatest car factory in Europe'.

Following Nordhoff's death at the age of 69 on 12 April 1968, shortly after the two-millionth Transporter had left the assembly line, Alan Dix, then Managing Director of Volkswagen Motors Ltd in Britain, wrote of the Director General's 'tremendous vision, outstanding courage and unbelievable ability'. Describing his death as 'an irreparable loss', Dix attributed his 'policies and products' as key to the post-war reconstruction of Germany, while confirming that all who came into contact with Nordhoff gained 'a sense of purpose and a feeling of inspiration'.

Dix summarised the significance of Nordhoff better than any other. Without him there would have been no Volkswagen organisation, just as certainly as if Porsche hadn't created the Beetle in the first place. However, if he had been present to write his own obituary Nordhoff would have added that without him there would have been no Transporter either. His background and his foresight suggests that he understood the needs of all sections of the potential market more than most. His time at Brandenburg confirms that his experience of commercial vehicles was second to none. Returning to the text of the special edition of the in-house magazine *Prospect*, printed shortly after Nordhoff's death, from which the words of Alan Dix have been taken, one paragraph more than any other confirms that until history was reinterpreted Nordhoff was seen as the father of the Transporter, whatever the respective importance of the contributions of Ivan Hirst and particularly Ben Pon might have been:

'In 1949 Nordhoff, recognising the need for a new concept of economic trucks which has since been widely copied by other car makers, led Volkswagen's engineers in developing the box-like panel truck which carried nearly a ton of cargo in 170 cubic feet of load space. The first eight Volkswagen "Transporters" came off the assembly line in 1949...'

That some of those eight prototypes weren't trucks but people-carriers is also highly significant, as will become apparent when yearly production statistics are analysed. The diversity within the Transporter range was of Nordhoff's making and nobody else's.

or materials to speak of and no one had any real idea where we were heading. When Nordhoff arrived and took charge he just quietly got everything moving. It wasn't anything specific that he did which changed the atmosphere. You just felt his presence, felt he was there and had taken firm command.'

The reality of the situation, however, was that Nordhoff's immense experience, plus his sense of both purpose and dedication to the job, were sufficient to galvanise Wolfsburg into productive action. Despite many initial reservations concerning the Beetle, Nordhoff told all who cared to listen that he was 'committed with my every fibre', while he knew within less then two months of joining Volkswagen that 'things could not continue in this way'. Replicating his style of devotion to his work

Heinz Nordhoff's speech to the Press 'on the occasion of the demonstration of the new VW Vans', 12 November 1949

'...Today is all about the baptism of the new Volkswagen Van.

'This vehicle was planned just over a year ago during a car journey I made with Dr Haesner. Together with his team, he deserves congratulations for having developed the new vehicle from first idea to production in about a year. As you will undoubtedly appreciate, we wanted to be ready earlier, but many thousands of kilometres had to be driven to test the vehicles; along the bleak roads to the north of here and towards the East German border, as well as on the steep inclines in the Harz Mountains. We wanted to be very thorough.

'Before we decided upon the basic specifications and purposes of this vehicle, we undertook careful market research. Due to our inevitable lack of official statistical material we carried out hundreds of individual interviews to obtain a clear picture of what is missing from the market, thus providing us with an ability to catch up on the lead that other European countries have in providing their people with vehicles of this kind.

'We arrived at the conclusion that it was not the typical half-tonner on a car chassis that was required, but a 50 per cent bigger three-quarter-tonner with as large as possible a load space; an enclosed van which can be used in many different ways. A half-ton payload is the largest that can be accommodated on a medium-sized car chassis, even with both stronger suspension and bigger tyres, and hence the 500kg payload of all vehicles of this type. The situation immediately becomes clear when you look at a schematic drawing of a typical example of this type of van on a car chassis. The load area lies completely over the rear axle, which carries practically the entire payload and therefore soon reaches its natural limit. It also causes a very undesirable distribution of axle load, with strong dependence on the distribution of the load, and therefore negative effects on the suspension.

'It didn't seem sensible to us to add a vehicle of our own to this kind of range. Just as our Volkswagen Sedan is a car without compromise, so our Van should also be without compromise. Therefore we didn't begin from the basis of an existing chassis, as this would have badly hindered the logical solution we wanted, but instead we started from the load area – actually much more obvious, and original. This load area carries the driver's seat at the front, and at the rear both the engine and gearbox – that is the patent idea, free of compromise, for our Van, and that is how it is built.

'The Van comprises a main area of three square metres of floor space plus, over the engine, an additional square metre and 45 cubic metres of volume. At the front there is a three-seat passenger and driver's area with very easy access and an unbeatable view of the road. At the back in a lockable, spacious and incredibly easily accessible space, there is the engine, fuel tank, battery and spare wheel. In short, neither the load area nor the driver's area is restricted by these items.

'All this is produced as a complete self-supporting steel superstructure, with a low and unobstructed loading area, while largely utilising the engine and gearbox of the Volkswagen Sedan, the 75,000th example of which recently left the production line. However, due to the Van's greater total weight an alternative gearing arrangement is employed, a set-up which has already proved itself under the most arduous conditions in thousands of vehicles used by the Army.

'This vehicle weighs 875kg in road-going condition and carries 850kg, thus representing a best-ever performance for a van of this size, with a weight to load ratio of 1:1. Fully loaded it has a top speed of more than 75kph, a hill-climbing capability of 22 per cent, and fuel consumption of 9 litres per 100km. Both its suspension and road-holding ability surpass anything so far achieved. It can also transport the most delicate load on the worst roads, without incurring the slightest damage.

'How does this happen? [Nordhoff makes use of a

▼ Nordhoff explains how the load area lay between the two axles on his new Transporter. (BS)

▲ Although clearly not taken on the same occasion as the previous photograph, a great deal of time and effort was spent on educating distributors, dealers, the press and many more regarding the merits of the new Transporter.

diagram of the Van at this point] *With this vehicle the load area lies exactly between the axles. The driver at the front and the engine at the rear match each other extremely well in terms of weight. The axle load is always equal, whether the vehicle is empty or laden. That allows for "spring-synchronisation" which is just not achievable if you have variable axle loadings. It also gives the best possible usage of the weight-bearing ability of the wheels, and the capacity of the brakes. As you will be aware, we are never afraid to turn away from what is normally accepted and think independently.*

'We didn't choose the rear engine layout in this Van because we felt morally obliged to do so. We would have unhesitatingly put the engine in the front if that had been the better solution. We are not tied to the general view of technology. The famous "cab over engine" arrangement gives such terrible load distribution ratios in an empty van, that it was never an option. You can tell from the state of the roadside trees in the entire British Zone how the lorries of the English Army, which have been built according to this principle, handle when they are unladen.

'Coming to the second point: with a standard van you are in the predicament that it has to have its loading doors at the rear; our quandary is that we

cannot do this. However, if I weigh these two scenarios against each other, then I am glad to be in our shoes, because the loading and access from the side is natural and normal – who would think of getting in to a limousine from the back? Our Van doesn't need any clear space behind when it parks to unload, and the next vehicle can be close behind it. With regard to the sill height of the loading area, this is close to the kerb height – it is incomparably easy to load and unload.

'I would now like to point out one other aspect which will become more and more important with the increasing number of vehicles: ie the degree to which the road area available to traffic is used. Normal vans made in the traditional way have a ratio of load area to total vehicle area of about 0.3; with our new Van we easily achieve 0.5, over 50 per cent more.

'Nothing in this vehicle has been left to chance, and in no aspects have we taken the easy way.

'In its first form this vehicle used 11 litres of petrol per 100km in general use. That was too high for us, as we are of the opinion it is not the purchase cost, but the running costs that decide the success of a vehicle. This will become even clearer after the expected rise in the price of petrol. Therefore we have done something that is a first with a Van. We went into a wind tunnel

with the vehicle with the result that, with only minor adjustments to the shape, we reduced the wind resistance factor to CW 0.4 and therefore the average fuel consumption to 9 litres per 100km.

'Of course, the VW Van is fitted with everything that should be in a good vehicle, with splinter-proof glass for all windows, driver area heating, windscreen defroster, double windscreen wipers, and all accessories. Today we are only showing you a few of the countless permutations that make it more user-friendly.

'With our new Van we have created a new vehicle the like of which has never been offered in Germany before. A vehicle which had only one aim: highest economy and highest utility value. A vehicle that didn't have its origin in the heads of engineers but rather in the potential profits the end-users will be able to make out of it. A vehicle that we don't just build to fill our capacity – that we can achieve for a long time with the Volkswagen Sedan – but in order to give the working economy a new and unique means to raise performance and profit.

'You, my esteemed Gentlemen of the Press, who have been the Godparents at this Christening of our VW Van, I ask that you send it on its way with a few kind and encouraging words.

'I am very grateful to you for your consideration and your interest. Please contact us whenever you feel it necessary. Publicity to date has not been one of our most urgent priorities, but from now on public relations will be an important consideration.

'A small formality at the end: the VW Van costs DM5,850 ex-works. I believe it will be a great success!'

Through his presentation of both vehicle and background Nordhoff achieved exactly what he wanted: an often cynical, sceptical press had been bewitched by the potential of the new vehicle. Joachim Fischer, editor of the Frankfurt motor magazine *Motor–Rundschau*, wrote: 'To be honest, I wasn't expecting too much from my trip to Wolfsburg to inspect and test drive the new van...The VW van must be the most stylish small load carrier with forward cab that I know – and I know a good many, including ones from abroad!'

Similarly the author of an article in the magazine *Das Lasauto* had been captivated by Nordhoff's new model: 'The good qualities of the Volkswagen, combined with the technical requirements for carrying loads and an entirely new shape have produced a van which the German market has been looking for, but until now, had yet to find.'

However, before taking the story further, a degree of interpretation of Nordhoff's speech is required.

Researchers and archivists at Wolfsburg all confirm that not only did Nordhoff wish to be minutely involved with all aspects of running Volkswagen, finding it impossible to completely delegate even seemingly trivial matters to members of his management team, but also that he meticulously prepared his innumerable speeches, carefully amending in his own hand the drafts typed by his secretarial staff. The speeches that have survived often total as many as 30 pages of closely typed text and none take the form of a report made after the event. While such a length makes it impractical to repeat every word spoken by Nordhoff when he launched the Van, no reference to its origins or design has been omitted. Likewise, while a totally literal translation of a 60-year-old document could well have left a modern-day reader perplexed, Nordhoff's meaning in each and every sentence has not been altered.

▼ A carefully-posed publicity photograph of Heinz Nordhoff, taken around the time of the launch of the VW Transporter in 1949. *(BS)*

The appointment of Alfred Haesner

In addition to the many problems experienced in the production of the Beetle in the days before Nordhoff's appointment, engineering capacity was severely restricted by the lack of personnel in Wolfsburg's drawing office. Ivan Hirst attempted to resolve the problem by holding a series of interviews. He thought he had found an ideal candidate in Rudolf Uhlenhaut, who at the time was working at the vehicle repair factory established by the REME at Hanomag in Hanover. However it was not to be; Uhlenhaut was determined to resume his pre-war career with Mercedes Benz and declined Hirst's offer. The Major then turned his attention to Alfred Haesner, an engineer who had been at Phänomen, a company who had specialised in the manufacture of commercial vehicles with air-cooled engines. Hirst was somewhat disappointed in Haesner, as he appeared only to be interested in the design of air-cooled engines and not the wider brief that would be demanded of any employee at Wolfsburg, and chose to let the matter lapse. However, Nordhoff realised Haesner's potential and he was duly appointed, his first task of any significance being to pick up from where he had left off at Phänomen and to work with Nordhoff on a commercial vehicle for Volkswagen, a van based on the chassis and running gear of the Beetle.

That Haesner knew his market and Nordhoff's goal is abundantly clear from remarks he made as the prototypes began to take shape. The vehicle, he said, was: 'Designed for town and country, short and long distances, motorway and field tracks, goods and passengers, retail and industry…This commercial van is suitable for all sectors of business, express delivery and freight transport, for example a minibus, special purpose vehicle, post van, ambulance or mobile shops.'

Design, wind tunnel and first prototype testing

Nordhoff's speech to launch the Van confirms that Haesner was duly briefed during a car journey made in the autumn of 1948. The path to production of a commercial vehicle was now an official one and was allocated the number EA-7, the letters standing for *Entwicklungsauftrag*, or 'development project'.

However, the Director General failed to mention in his press speech that the Van brief was not the only work demanded of Haesner; his other tasks included the highly important job of creating a de luxe or export version of the Volkswagen Sedan – a vehicle that would appeal to car-buying people across Europe and beyond, and as such a great revenue earner for the impoverished factory. Such was the pressure placed upon Haesner that by 11 November 1948 he felt compelled to send a memo to Nordhoff requesting additional staff, stressing that the 'available expertise' was insufficient to meet the workload. In spite of this cry for help, and consistent with the speed with which the Van project came to fruition, within another nine days Haesner had been able to present Nordhoff with a choice of two design outlines for his Van.

Haesner's twin blueprints were not that dissimilar and both bore more than a passing resemblance to Pon's sketch of a little over 18 months earlier. However, if Nordhoff's press launch speech is taken at face value, a similarity between the Dutchman's drawing and the emergent Van might well be regarded as purely coincidental; for the outlines presented by Haesner were, according to the Director General, a result of intensive market research and very little else. One design, known as Version A, had a flat front with a roof overhang; the other, Version B, which Nordhoff instantly preferred, had a slightly curved and raked cab.

Before work on a full-scale prototype of the vehicle known internally as VW29 was completed, the decision was taken to carry out wind tunnel tests. The report by the Institute for Flow Mechanics of the Technical College, Braunschweig, dated 9 March 1949, makes interesting reading. Van models were made of wood to a scale of 1:10 and fitted with three interchangeable nose shapes, or *bugformen*. The length of the models was 0.383m, the width 0.158m, the largest cross-sectional area 0.023m^2, and the wheelbase 0.23m. Two of the nose shapes were very flat; the third was described as 'highly streamlined'. Needless to say, the results indicated a CW of 0.75 and 0.77 respectively for the two flat-shaped noses and 0.43 for the 'rounded' version.

Perhaps it was naive of man like Nordhoff, with his background in engineering and design, and particularly Haesner, whose job it was bring the Van project to a successful conclusion, as well as everyone else involved, to believe that the Beetle chassis, widened to carry the box-like structure of the prototype Van, would be sufficiently sturdy to carry the 50 per cent larger loads demanded by market research, simply because in the case of the Sedan the body and framework were successfully bolted to each other. Seemingly unaware of what awaited him, Haesner pressed forward.

The first full-size prototype was ready for testing on 11 March 1949, but disaster beckoned. In order that an element of secrecy be maintained, the first tests were carried out at night-time. Ivan Hirst, still present at Wolfsburg but no longer a pivotal figure, recalled to American author Karl Ludvigsen what happened: 'When they came back to the works in the morning the van was six inches lower. The weight of the body and the load broke the back of the flat-section at the centre of the platform frame.' The date was 5 April 1949, and within less than a month of launching the prototype Haesner was more or less back where he had started, the project in tatters and the sands of time already running away from him. Reporting to Nordhoff, the Technical Director confirmed the now blatantly obvious by writing that 'the results clearly show that the task of the Van…cannot be performed by the Volkswagen Sedan chassis, as the load, and the torsion particularly, is simply too great.'

The race to production

Despite the setback encountered with the Beetle-based prototype, Nordhoff was determined that the Van would go into production before the year was ended, and on 19 May 1949 he set the start of production for 1 November or, at the absolute latest, 1 December of the same year. His objective was clear: the Van must be available for an official launch at the Geneva Motor Show to be held in March 1950, and by that time it must not only have been thoroughly tested at Wolfsburg, but also had to be sufficiently advanced for it to be made available for appraisal by Nordhoff's most valued customers.

The pressure on Haesner and his team was relentless, for not only did Nordhoff demand a fast solution to the chassis problem, but he also continued to look at ways of developing the Van range, while overseeing every detail of the project personally. Even in today's technologically advanced world it is barely conceivable that such a pace could be sustained, but Haesner achieved the near impossible and had an entirely new prototype available on the day that Nordhoff announced his production goals.

The new prototype was significantly different to its predecessor, which was carefully rebuilt, both vehicles now featuring a bespoke frame of a style that in future years would be generally known as being of unitary construction. Torsional rigidity was improved beyond measure by this means, for the floor and body were now welded together on a subframe. Five substantial cross-members were welded between the front and rear axles, while two strong longitudinal rails and a series of outriggers gave additional strength to the overall structure. By welding the steel floors in both the cab and cargo areas to the platform, as well as the one above the engine compartment, rigidity beyond need was achieved, taking the Van, like the Beetle before it, into innovatory territory.

Haesner's work, however, didn't end there. On the basis of the experience gleaned from the test of the first prototype, both the front axle and shock absorbers were strengthened. Although financial constraints prevented the development of a more powerful engine to cope with the loads the Van was expected to haul, this was not of primary concern to Nordhoff, who in later years proved himself to be reluctant to increase engine size for either the Beetle or the Transporter, even when the market apparently demanded it. It was his preference to combat the distinct lack of acceleration the Beetle's 25PS engine offered, when coupled to the heavier body of the Van, by adopting lower gearing. Wolfsburg's archive had the ideal mechanism at its fingertips in the form of the wartime *Kübelwagen*'s 1:1.4 reduction-gear rear hubs. Employment of such devices when coupled to an adjustment in the height of the front suspension also created the benefit of increased ground clearance, while dual torsion spring units were used for the back axle as a means of keeping costs down.

The second prototype was put on test in May 1949 and performed exceedingly well for a vehicle developed in such a short time. Apart from being subjected to gruelling testing on Volkswagen's own proving track the prototypes were despatched over some of the worst roads in Lower Saxony, accomplishing 12,000 more or less trouble-free kilometres in the process. Suitably encouraged, Nordhoff decided to give the go ahead for a further set of prototypes, although on this occasion he was looking to develop additional uses for the box–shaped vehicle. His demand was that a variety of vehicles should be available by 15 October. These were to include a pick-up and an eight-seater minibus, plus both an ambulance and a vehicle for the *Bundespost* to use. By the time production commenced eight prototypes in all had been built, the latter examples of which displayed numerous improvements over the earlier ones, while most significantly of all the need for a vehicle capable of making deliveries in the week and acting as family transport at the weekend had been recognised.

Nordhoff continued to oversee even the minutest detail throughout and must have made life for Haesner very difficult with his incessant demands for alterations and improvements, particularly when these were coupled to other amendments suggested by ongoing testing. Amongst Nordhoff's instructions were a requirement for stronger door hinges and lighter-weight doors, plus the lowering of the engine bay roof panel which would then make room for an extra layer of insulation to assist with the prevention

That this model is a prototype is evident from the vertical cooling vents, the external petrol filler cap and the rather indifferent nature of the bodywork finish.
(bottom left, BS)

▲ It has been suggested that this prototype – finished in striking two-tone paintwork – might have been either the sixth or seventh in the series.

of heat transmitting from the engine to the interior of the vehicle. Additionally, a wiper was fitted to the windscreen on the opposite side of the cab from the driver, while the heating and ventilation system was improved. Although apparently trivial, the external fuel filler was relocated to a position within the lockable engine compartment, which although nowadays would be seen as a somewhat lethal combination of potentially spilt fuel and heat from the engine, was preferable to making it too easy for valuable petrol to be siphoned off – a practice which was rife in post-war Germany.

On 9 September 1949 a second wind tunnel report was received from Brunswick Technical College. Once again a 1:10 scale wooden model of the Van had been made. On this occasion the model had a length of 0.4m, a width of 0.158m and a wheelbase of 0.24m. Its largest cross-sectional area came out at 0.252m². Not quite as streamlined as the previous 'Bugform 111', the CW nevertheless came out at a commendable 0.44, while the model

was tested at higher wind-speeds than on previous occasions. The maximum this time around was 56m/second, as opposed to 41.5m/second previously.

Although it might have appeared that Dr Haesner's difficulties were at last coming to an end, last-minute working around the clock proved unavoidable. In a memo dated 26 September he wrote to Nordhoff of the difficulties of maintaining the proposed date for the press launch. His latest problem centred upon the Van's roof panel, which if the schedule was to be adhered to had to be made available to him on or before 10 October: 'We are in need of four for the prototypes and a fifth one to try out beforehand. The roofs produced so far for experimental purposes have been made by hand and have not been pressed by a machine. As a result they can only be delivered as a flat form, not curved as is intended for the models to be presented to the press. Unfortunately, they lack the necessary tension, with the result that they have a tendency to flutter while driving. We have no option therefore but to obtain curved, machine-pressed roofs.' When the press works announced it was too busy, the only choice appeared to be to prepare the roof panels by hand, but this would have taken four long weeks – a period of time that could not be spared. The decision

▲ ◀ The prototype Micro Bus was later used as the model for the first brochure to feature passenger-carrying Transporters.

▼ Images taken from the first Transporter publicity brochure. *(BS)*

Klein-Omnibus (Innenansichten)

Klein-Omnibus

◀ The interior of either a prototype or a very early production Kombi.

was therefore taken to authorise overtime at the press plant, but even then the roofs were not ready by 20 October, painting having taken far longer than was anticipated.

6 November was next suggested for the planned launch, but a further week's delay proved inevitable as Nordhoff continued to make changes. Finally, it was determined that the press would be assembled on 12 November. Nordhoff duly made his speech and unknowingly created in the process the most significant date in the history of the vehicle which would eventually be officially named the Transporter.

▼ Photographed in front of the factory's central kitchen, this prototype probably saw service at Wolfsburg. Other pictures of the same vehicle exist in which the registration plate is replaced by a plaque bearing the simple designation of Type 29 – the official alias for the Transporter.

What's in a name?

Nobody would dream these days of launching a vehicle without a name or at least some meaningful number, and even in the immediate post-war years most manufacturers had the matter in hand. VW, of course, was somewhat different! Originally the concept behind the purpose-built factory was the manufacture of one vehicle – the Volkswagen, or in English the 'People's Car'. (The Nazi red herring term of *KdF-Wagen*, or 'Strength-Through-Joy Car' was more or less overlooked by all but Hitler's henchmen.) The arrival of a second model, clearly not a People's Car, but possibly a People's Van, presented a predicament. What was to be done about it? Could it still be simply a Volkswagen?

Although first used in an American magazine during the Second World War, the name *Käfer* – Beetle, or Bug – for the first vehicle wasn't yet official, and wouldn't become so for a long time. Instead, because it was the first model to be produced, in 1949 the factory simply designated it the Type 1, with 11 being the Standard model and 11A the Export, or De Luxe. Although many years later some stubbornly persisted in referring to the original car as the Type 1, this wasn't terminology that extended to Volkswagen's promotional literature. Instead, the company simply marketed its vehicles according to their trim level under the shared name of Volkswagens. Hence a flick through a 1950 brochure covering all products starts with the '*Export-Limousine*', followed successively by the '*Standard-Limousine*', the '*Sonnendach-Limousine*' and '*Das viersitzige Cabriolet*'. The next page depicts the '*Lieferwagen*' and the last one the '*Kleinbus*'. Although only referred to in the small print, for Nordhoff and his team the naming crisis was nevertheless over – the term '*VW-Transporter*' was there for all to see. A slightly later brochure even allocates a full page to a beautifully drawn Delivery Van and the two simple words '*Der Transporter*'.

The notional title of 'Van' disappeared from Volkswagen's vocabulary for many a year, only really resurfacing – and then with an appendage – for the American market, as 'Vanagon', before the 21st century and such T5 terminology as 'Window Van'. However, unofficial usage blossomed as the years passed by: who can overlook Europe's largest annual gathering of Transporters each September – the much emulated 'Vanfest' – for example?

Although it might appear that little time or thought had been given to allocating a name to the 'box on wheels', nothing could be further from the truth. Perhaps the fact that Auto Union's DKW delivery truck had been launched just a few months before without a name played a part in the decision, although Nordhoff hinted later that the key problem was either that the good names had already been trademarked, or were too vague to be allocated specifically to Volkswagen. One front-runner was dismissed due its similarity to the 'Bulldog' produced by Lanz – the 'Bullybus' might have been mistaken for something as agricultural as a tractor!

Fortunately, over the years the generic term 'Transporter' became synonymous with Volkswagen, even though some could be overheard referring to it as the Type 2; terminology that should be dismissed wherever possible due to its similarity to the letter 'T' and the numeral '2'. For when such a combination is adopted, as in the current Transporter, the T5 – still apparently in need of a nickname – all sorts of problems occur. To set the record straight, the first generation Transporter is the T1, the second the T2 and the third more often than not (as far as the British market goes) the T25. Across the water, fortunately, the third generation Transporter is the T3, the fourth is the T4, and the current model – hopefully for a few more years yet – is the T5.

When it comes to unofficial names life becomes fun, for the first generation Transporter with its happy smiling 'face' and split pane windscreen becomes either the 'Splitty' or the 'Splittie', depending on your preference. Due to its much larger front screen the second generation Transporter was quickly christened the 'Bay', while the slab-like proportions of the third generation model suggested to some people – rather unkindly – that the name 'Brick' was not inappropriate. Fortunately, others, noting the slope of the windscreen, thought the nickname of the 'Wedge' was more in keeping with the appearance of the vehicle. To date, it appears that both the fourth and current generation Transporters lack such terms of affection, even though both appear ever more popular.

One final name, 'Bulli', widely used in Germany and beyond and found in the name of probably the best-known enthusiasts' club, Bulli Kartei, requires a word or two of explanation. Although usually only really associated with the first-generation Transporter, as will be seen when its derivation is revealed, it is nevertheless just as pertinent to all subsequent generations. For Bulli is nothing more than an abbreviation of the words 'Bus' (as in *Kleinbus*) and *Lieferwagen*, with an additional 'l' thrown in for good measure.

1950-67

PART II

Developing a legend

▶ So instantly recognisable was Volkswagen's first generation Transporter that it was deemed unnecessary to depict the whole vehicle on the cover of several brochures, or to add text.

◀ One of Volkswagen's official photographs of the vehicle that became a factory workhorse in the 1950s. Believed to carry the chassis number 000010, dating it to pre-production days, this Transporter was used at Wolfsburg for many a year.

Although there was every indication by March 1950 that the Volkswagen Sedan was set to be an outstanding success (the 100,000th vehicle had rolled off the assembly line on the fourth of the month), this could not be said of the as yet nameless commercial vehicle summarily christened at Wolfsburg, somewhat unimaginatively, as the Van. The previous month had seen a tentative number of test-drive vehicles assembled and delivered to the company's most important customers, but when it went on sale officially at the Geneva Motor Show in March production had been set at a less than optimist limit of just ten vehicles per day. In addition to the *Lieferwagen*, the Delivery Van, being on display, there were also (although not quite yet available) the VW-Kombi – a vehicle that would prove to be the most significant of all models, and

◤ ▼ Now fully restored and resident in Wolfsburg's Stiftung museum, Wolfsburg's workhorse still bears evidence of 'modifications' (such as the addition of a rear window) which were made during its working life. *(RC)*

▲ ▶ Built in June 1950, the vehicle pictured here is now resident in the *Autostadt*, Wolfsburg, where it holds the honour of being the oldest known surviving example of a Transporter despatched from the factory in primer in preparation for the application of company logos and colours. *(RC)*

one whose name requires no translation – and the VW *Achtsitzer*, or Eight-Seater, which, at least in the United States as well as many other countries, would later be known as the Micro Bus, or even the Station-Wagon. While the Delivery Van would always account for more sales than any other individual model, Nordhoff's decision, and his alone, to develop a whole range of Van options was a crucial one in the creation of one of the most popular vehicles of its kind ever.

On 2 October 1962, just 12½ years after its sales debut, Nordhoff assembled the press once more, on this occasion to celebrate the arrival of the millionth Van, which by that time had been more formally named the Transporter. Extracts from his lengthy speech serve to indicate how he valued his product as an innovatory and highly successful revenue earner for his company.

From an image carefully stored in the VW archive, to two available for journalists and authors to use, the occasion of the arrival of the millionth Transporter was an event worthy to be recorded for posterity.

▶ Producing one million Transporters was so significant an achievement that distributors and dealers were invited to display this attractive three-dimensional stand in their showroom windows.

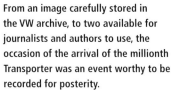

Extracts from Heinz Nordhoff's speech on the occasion of the production of the millionth Transporter

'In November 1949 I asked the representatives of the Press to Wolfsburg, to attend the unveiling of the VW Transporter. In those early days our daily production amounted to some 200 vehicles and we were very proud of that. In those days the VW Transporter was something completely new and original.

'No one foresaw that it would become the forerunner of a completely new type of vehicle, representing as it did an often near-slavishly imitated genre of utility vehicles.

'When one mentions vehicles, one usually thinks of cars, but production of these small Transporters of up to 1,000kg represents a considerable industry in its own right, probably the newest in the entire automobile industry, both in Europe and the USA.

'Although it also manufactures engines, it was thanks to the Transporter that we began to build our factory in Hanover, which now employs 20,000 people. Sixty-three per cent of all Transporters are exported, and their market share in this newly created sector is very high in many countries. It is 40.5 per cent in this country, but in Belgium, Holland, Austria, Sweden and Switzerland it is 50 per cent or more. Even in the United States it stands at five per cent, which is in fact a great achievement, taking into account the size of the US market. The VW Transporter is not only the original, but also remains the leader in its class.

'In the relatively short time of less than 15 years, something completely new has been created by the VW Factory, of which it can be said "Often copied, never equalled".

'Since that November of 1949 a million of these VW Transporters have been bought and sold, and even if we are now used to this million phenomenon, it seems to us to be an achievement of such fundamental importance that we have asked you to come again and celebrate this festive and meaningful day with us; to view the rapid development of our factories and to chat with us about the never-ending subject of automobiles.'

▼ Volkswagen took the opportunity to display each Transporter model available in the 'build programme' when journalists and invited guests visited Hanover for the unveiling of the millionth Transporter. The vehicle at the centre of proceedings in this picture appears to be a special model Pick-up fitted with an hydraulic lifting platform.

The original specification

While this volume is not intended to be a glorified specification guide, it would be wrong not to include a reasonably detailed outline of the Transporter as it was at its launch – otherwise readers may fail to appreciate why it proved to be such an outstanding success. For those whose lives have become forever intertwined with the first generation Transporter, there follow a couple of extracts from the first owners' manual that prove their love for the product wasn't blind:

'The VW Transporter is a vehicle with unbeaten road holding, high cornering and extraordinary acceleration.' However, 'do not be tempted into recklessness by the satisfying feeling of absolute safety which you will have after only a few miles in the Transporter'.

Recommended maximum long-distance speed was 47mph – but with a further warning: 'Do not forget that it would be completely irresponsible to charge your Transporter along the motorway at top speed for hours on end. No vehicle of this size can withstand such treatment undamaged.'

Although the Delivery Van as launched no longer merely comprised a different body on the same chassis as the Volkswagen Sedan, the two vehicles were surprisingly similar, at least in overall length. Early publicity material covering both models lists the Beetle as measuring 4,050mm and the Transporter as 4,100mm. However, as might be expected, the Transporter was wider than the car to the extent of some 120mm (Beetle 1,540mm, Transporter 1,660mm), and likewise had the greater overall height of a vehicle designed to carry all kinds of bulky objects. A 400mm difference between the Beetle's 1,500mm and the Transporter's 1,900mm probably did more than anything else to spread the illusion that the Transporter stood on much larger foundations than the Sedan.

To recap on the Transporter's mode of construction from the previous chapter, unlike the Beetle the Transporter didn't possess a separate chassis. Volkswagen suggested in their literature that the vehicle had a 'unitised, stiff all-steel box body', and most who have written about the Transporter, like Malcolm Bobbitt, make reference to a 'unitary arrangement'. The exception to this general rule is the somewhat pedantic Laurence Meredith, who writes of production bodies being made 'integral with the chassis', but adds that 'the unit is not in the manner of modern unitary construction', in which he is technically correct, although the welding of the body to the chassis has the same effect, a point he is prepared to concede. The essence of the new Transporter, however, lay not only in its 'unitised' construction, but also in five cross-members and their attendant outriggers, plus two longitudinal rails which were best described by such words as hefty, substantial, sturdy and robust. Surprisingly, some of the earlier brochures didn't emphasise this point. The relevant extract from a United States marketing brochure dating from 1953 simply notes that 'Volkswagen Transporters form an all-steel unit. Chassis and body are as cleverly engineered as a bridge'.

▼ Welds and blemishes were ground back, as the pile of sanding discs below testifies.

Virtually from the Transporter's inception and throughout the 1950s, Volkswagen relied on a combination of somewhat stilted photography and the magnificent artwork of Bernd Reuters to promote their products. The style of the day (when commercial artists were widely used) was to elongate the vehicle, making it appear more streamlined in the process; on occasion to add passengers, who were smaller in relation to the size of the vehicle than in reality; and to give an impression of speed by including movement-lines in many instances. Reuters reworked his imagery when modifications were made to the vehicle in question. Here are three of his Delivery Van portraits. *(BS)*

Body parts

Analyse any cutaway drawing of the first generation Transporter and it quickly becomes clear that the body had more metalwork lurking behind the external panels to add strength. Indeed, such was the basic nature of both the Delivery Van and the Kombi that a simple picture of the cargo space was enough to reveal all; a seemingly complicated mass of channel sections and box members. The load floor and metalwork over the externally accessed engine

was 'corrugated' for extra strength and to avoid dents when heavy items were thrown down. A short paragraph, sometimes even a sentence, summarises the story in many a piece of promotional literature. The following extract dates from August 1958: 'The load is completely protected by the strong steel body; steel ribbed floor and wall guards protect the interior.'

The roof section was unquestionably the largest single panel and reference has already been made to the reason why it shouldn't be entirely flat. The necessity of giving the metal a degree of shape, and the addition of a detail or crease mark that lined up with the division between the two halves of the windscreen, made the vehicle more rather than less aesthetically pleasing.

▼ Many a brochure included a cutaway drawing of the Transporter – primarily designed to indicate where the vehicle's strength lay. *(RC)*

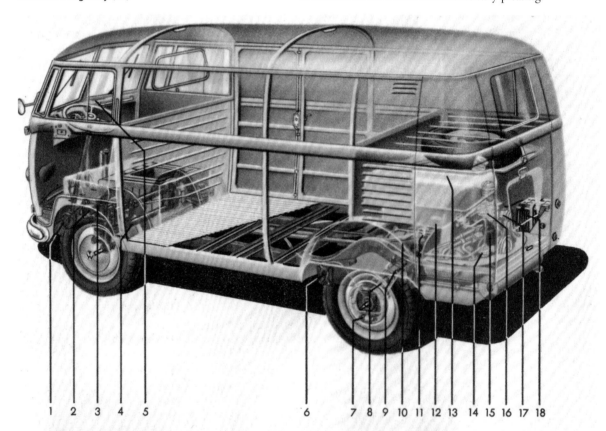

1 2 3 4 5   6   7 8 9 10 11 12 13 14 15 16 17 18

1. Steering gear
2. Brake master cylinder
3. Front shock absorber
4. Front axle
5. Defroster vent
6. Torsion bar mounting
7. Brake wheel cylinder
8. Spur reduction gearing
9. Rear axle
10. Transmission
11. Fuel tap
12. Starter
13. Fuel tank
14. Fuel pump
15. Distributor
16. Carburetor
17. Generator
18. Battery

A matter of expedience

The Transporter's distinctive split pane was more a matter of economy than a deliberate attempt to offer a vehicle with personality. Recalling that Beetles contemporary with the launch of the Transporter featured a completely flat glass windscreen but a two-piece rear window divided by metalwork, and that in 1953, as glass technology improved and became less costly, it was possible to fit the car with a single curved pane of glass at its back, all becomes clear. To offer the Transporter with a single pane windscreen complete with the necessary curve to its form would have been difficult to manufacture and prohibitively costly. Though as the 1960s gathered pace the first generation Transporter began, perhaps, to look distinctly out of date and there was a need to think about a newer model, to many 21st-century enthusiasts, besotted with nostalgia for the days when cars were made properly, the 'feel' of the first generation Transporter cannot be improved upon!

Suppose that the Transporter's stylists – both a term and breed that Nordhoff appeared to hate with a passion – had given the vehicle a plain flat or curved sheet of metal at its front. Would such a look, even with a split windscreen, have had the same level of appeal? The answer has to be a resounding 'no', for the partially double-skinned 'nose' is another make or break panel. Some argue that the near V-shaped swage lines were a deliberate move to replicate the look of the Beetle's front boot lid, and it could well be imagined that the Transporter's headlamps and those of the Sedan were similarly positioned with a view to each vehicle's overall frontal layout. But what can only be regarded as an over-the-top and massive VW roundel nevertheless adds further to what can best be described as a 'happy' appearance; a vehicle with a smile.

To complete these notes pertaining to the front of the first generation Transporter, it was only in later years that two successive styles of indicator housing broke the clean lines of the vehicle's design. The original semaphore-style indicator arms were located behind the driver's and passenger's side window respectively. Inevitably the sturdy blade-shaped bumpers were painted, in a shade known as Silver White to be precise, and when the range was expanded even the most luxurious models retained the same finish, albeit trimmed with a decorative strip.

▲ The distinctive flat-face look of the early first generation Transporter. This vehicle is parked outside part of the Wolfsburg complex.

Frontal postscript – ventilation or the lack of it!

As a postscript, a word or two about ventilation is important. The visual appearance of the Transporter would be changed in 1955 as a result of mounting pressure to do something about the poor ventilation offered to driver and passengers alike. For the moment, though, the crucial point to recall regarding the Transporter's frontal appearance relates to the lack of anything more than a simple rain gutter between the top of its split-pane windscreen and the roof panel. With effect from March 1953 owners had the official option of buying and fitting a Behr air ventilator, a device which gave the centre section of the roof panel a humped appearance, but nevertheless directed an effective flow of air into the cab.

One other feature of early Transporters that was to be amended in an attempt to increase air circulation was the hinging of the door quarter-lights. These were initially secured to the front of the doorframe by piano-style hinges, and while this allowed the window to be opened reasonably wide the glass acted as a barrier to the effective ingress of air. In January 1953, however, the old-style quarter-lights were replaced by pivoting vent windows which could be angled to direct a considerable amount of air into the stuffy, condensation-ridden cab.

Rearguard action

At the back of the vehicle, the Delivery Van – and for that matter its more luxurious brethren, as they were born – lacked a bumper, which would remain the case until late 1953. The only exception was the top executive Micro Bus De Luxe, launched in June 1951, which was initially fitted with an otherwise extra cost option of glorified rubbing strips. If the lack of a bumper was noteworthy, there were more startling features to come. Most outstanding was the enormous engine lid, which extended all the way up from the bottom of the vehicle to the swage line that ran all round the vehicle at a point approximately two-thirds of the way between its bottom and roof panel. Some describe this point as the vehicle's waistline, but realistically it was much higher. Not surprisingly, this gargantuan lid opened at the bottom (a top opening would have resulted in anyone wishing to work on the engine being some considerable distance from it), and a piano-style hinge was utilised for the purpose. Although the engine lid was single-skinned, it was fitted over a strengthening frame, the key pieces of which were drilled with holes to reduce their potential weight. Such was the size of the engine lid that it wasn't long before enthusiasts christened it the 'Barn-door', a term that was extended to define early Transporters in general. The massive lid was a casualty of a wholesale revamp of the vehicle in the early months of 1955.

The panel above the engine lid would probably have been passed by without notice if it were placed in a line-up of modern Transporters in Delivery Van guise, or amongst the products of other vehicle manufacturers. However, it was – at least initially – most unusual for the time, in that before April 1951 there was no hint of a rear window to improve the driver's visibility when manoeuvring the vehicle; a commonplace occurrence these days, when a window in any delivery van seems to act as an open invitation to lowlife elements of the population to remove whatever is visible inside at the first opportunity. From the Delivery Van's launch until 11 November 1950 the panel in question was adorned with a large VW roundel of similar size to that at the front. From then until the following April the metalwork was unadorned. That the adoption of a blind panel at the rear was extended to all other models introduced before April 1951 has to be the most extraordinary factor of all, bearing in mind that there was no shortage of glass employed in the side panels of both the Kombi and the Micro Bus. As for the window, when it did make its debut it was, in the style of the day, far from generous in size.

As, by modern standards, its rear light arrangements bordered on suicidal, the back of the Volkswagen Delivery Van looked very clean, verging on clinical. The lid contained a largish pressing in which the registration plate was located. In the top border of this there was a cut-out in which a housing sat to illuminate the plate at night, while above that was the single stop or brake light. The vehicle's diminutive night-lights and attendant reflectors were positioned in the rear wing panels, the whole arrangement following the style determined by the Beetle.

Despite the ease with which it was possible to work on the engine, the crossways section attached to the two rear quarter panels – metalwork to which the term rear valance might be loosely allocated – could be removed by the simple expedient of undoing two bolts and a single screw on each side. Removal of the engine as a result was incredibly easy, as it was possible, with the 'valance' out of the way, simply to ease the engine back and out on a trolley jack.

▶ **The enormous VW roundel dates these three images to pre-November 1950, while the lack of a rear bumper and window, plus the exceptionally large engine lid, are all characteristics of the earliest Transporters.**

Entering by the side door

The lack of access to the interior of the Delivery Van from the rear – a situation that would prevail until the aforementioned revamp of 1955 – was turned to advantage by those whose job it was to promote the product, ranging from the Director General downwards. The following extract is from one of the first brochures to be produced for the English-speaking market:

'Most … firms told us they wanted the loading doors on the side next to the pavement so as to speed up and facilitate loading and unloading. That was sound advice, so we followed it. The doors of the Volkswagen Transporters have been so designed and located that the driver can reach every part of the interior without having to move about inside. Thus full use can be rationally made of every inch of loading space. Volkswagen Transporters save the driver a lot of work. The double doors are so wide that he has no difficulty in handling even the bulkiest articles and the floor is so low that he has to do little lifting of heavy ones. Furthermore the driver does not have to leave the sidewalk in loading and unloading and never has to stand in the gutter.'

Although certainly not at odds with acceptable norms for the time, the fact that the first generation Transporter featured outward-opening double doors has since become a subject for criticism, at least in certain circles. Although access was easy once the doors

were open, the argument runs, their outward-opening nature prevented their use – or at least caused the vehicle owner inconvenience – when any work had to be carried out in a reasonably tight space. This claim, however, is undermined by simply looking at any Delivery Van brochure, for while inevitably the door would open outwards it's clear to behold that it was capable of folding right back on itself, and only the dull-witted wouldn't think to open the doors before backing or driving into a narrow loading space. With effect from 27 June 1951 the Delivery Van could also be specified with loading doors at both sides, a move which theoretically weakened the overall strength of the vehicle, however convenient it was to the would-be owner. Volkswagen, though, hardly ever missed a trick and introduced underbelly floor plates at the same time, restoring strength both to vehicles with additional doors and with sliding roofs. Perhaps the ideal solution to the door question would have been to include a sliding door in the specification, but Transporter owners would have to wait 17 years from the launch of the Delivery Van before such a feature became standard with the advent of the second generation Transporter. However, for those with a pressing desire to upgrade from the standard specification, from 16 April 1963 a sliding door could be specified at extra cost on the first generation model.

As an aside, but nevertheless a very important one, having only a side door opening (at least until 1955 – and, in reality, for much longer, unless a scramble over the engine compartment was to be contemplated) rendered the Transporter the ideal medium for a leisure vehicle. By creating the potential of a summerhouse on wheels Volkswagen had inadvertently germinated the seeds of a camping vehicle in some fertile minds.

Reference has already been made to the protruding swage line that ran along the Delivery Van's sides and across its back panels. At the front this connected with the V-shaped line that has also been described. These lines helped to break up the slab-like nature of the Transporter's side elevation. The cab doors followed the same lines, almost curving over the front wheelarches, the swage line falling slightly to line up with that on the vehicle's front. The only other intrusions, at least as far as the Delivery Van was concerned, were the recesses created for the door handles, and the two sets of eight horizontal outward-facing louvres, one on either side of the vehicle, designed to allow cool air to enter the engine compartment. Although not present on the very first Delivery Vans, with effect from 11 September 1950 three air vents were cut into the upper panels in order that the cargo area be better ventilated, an issue that became increasingly important to Volkswagen in the years and months before March 1955.

▼ The advantages of double side-opening doors were heavily promoted to possible buyers. The interior of a Delivery Van lacked creature comforts, offering nothing more than cold metal throughout.

Wheels and tyres

The Transporter ran on 16in steel wheels, which until 1955 were of a solid design, and were shod with 5.50 x 16 tyres. The Delivery Van's wheels were painted Silver White, although some other models in the range as it developed could be found with part body-coloured arrangements. Like the Beetle, the Transporter featured domed hubcaps, which in the case of the Delivery Van were normally painted in Light Grey, while the V over W emblem at the cap's centre might well have been picked out in white.

Under the lid

Having outlined the external appearance and merits of the Delivery Van as launched, the next stage has to be items of a more technical nature, the hardware of (in alphabetical order) braking, electrics, steering, suspension and transmission, but starting with the most important element of all, the engine.

When the Transporter was launched it had to be taken into account that Volkswagen was far from endowed with immeasurable wealth with which to create the ideal product for its customers. The launch of the Export model Beetle in the summer of 1949 was one of Nordhoff's schemes to generate both volume and satisfactory returns so that he could build adequately for the future. Clearly, under such circumstances it was out of the question that the Transporter should be fitted with its own air-cooled engine; a unit that, no doubt, in ideal circumstances would have been capable of more power than the Beetle's 25PS unit, with which the Transporter was destined to be mated.

Conversely a much more powerful engine would have been at odds with the norm for the time. For example, DKW's ¾-tonner, branded as the *Schnellieferwagen*, or fast delivery truck, offered owners no more than 20PS when it was launched, while Tempo borrowed none other than Volkswagen's ubiquitous flat four for use in its Matador. They also offered a smaller vehicle, the Tempo Viking, which they described as 'economical', but offering 'high performance' from its 450cc, 17PS motor. Later, Tempo offered the Viking Rapid, a vehicle which embraced a 32PS Austin engine – but it has to be borne in mind that by this time the clock had ticked forward to 1957. The Gutbard Atlas featured nothing more than a couple of two-stroke engine options, 800 and 1,000cc motors that developed 16 and 18PS respectively. The Goliath GV, which was introduced in 1951 and considered to be another potential rival for Volkswagen, came with either 450 or 600cc engines, which turned out a modest 16 or 21PS respectively. The next Goliath out of the pod was the GV 800, by which time there had been progress in the power stakes. This vehicle, which was discontinued in 1961, was offered with the choice of a 29 or 40PS engine. Within Germany, the Transporter's nearest rival was probably the Ford

Transit, an offering which emerged from the Cologne factory in March 1953. From the beginning, Ford manufactured engines that could easily outstrip the Transporter in terms of performance, as not only was a 38PS unit available but also one developing 60PS. Needless to say, the Transit sold well, but it is a credit to Volkswagen that even with its more powerful engines it took Ford's model 12 years to break the quarter-million barrier.

Turning to the first reviews of the Transporter following its appearance on British soil, Laurence J. Cotton, writing in *Commercial Motor* on 2 April 1954, was suitably enamoured. It is worth noting, however, that the Transporter's original 25PS engine, just like that of the Beetle, had been upgraded with effect from 21 December 1953 with a 30PS unit:

'There are few power units, for light commercial vehicles, that can compare with the efficient operation of the Volkswagen … engine. … Having previously driven a Volkswagen in Germany, its

▼ The 25ps engine pictured had simply been lifted out of the Beetle and placed in the Transporter. The cavernous engine compartment of early years was accentuated by the location of the spare wheel by the side of the engine – a practice which would be amended in October 1950 (the wheel then being positioned horizontally on a platform above the engine). *(BS)*

liveliness with light load was not surprising, but trying the van with a 15-cwt payload on home ground confirmed that it is speedy and economical, and well equipped, in its lowest ratio, to soar over the 1-in-4¼ gradient of Succombs Hill with power to spare.'

Volkswagen's 25PS engine had first seen the light of day in March 1943, Beetles and their attendant military incarnations having previously been fitted with a 985cc unit capable of developing a maximum of 23.5PS at 3,000rpm. The bore and stroke stood respectively at 70mm and 64mm, while the compression ratio was quoted at 5.8:1. For the 25PS four-cylinder, air-cooled flat four engine the bore had been increased to 75mm.

Most early brochures included a page headed *technisches*. Although reproduced in German, the details given are intelligible to all:

Motor

Bauart	*4-Zylinder-4-Takt-Vergasermotor im Heck des Fahrzeuges*
Zylinderanordnung	*Je 2 Zylinder gegenüberliegend*

Mahe

Zylinderbohrung	*75mm*
Hub	*64mm*
Hubraum	*1131cm²*
Verdichtungsverhältnis ...	*5.8:1*
Ventile	*hängend*
Höchstleistung	*25PS bei 3300 U/min*
Kolbengeschwindigkeit ...	*6.42 m/s bei 3000 U/mon*

The Transporter's top speed in 25PS guise was somewhere in the region of 55mph or 86kph. Volkswagen preferred to err on the side of caution and announced that they considered 50mph as the engine's natural limit. However, as with the Beetle there was something to boast about, as maximum speed and cruising speed were always considered to be one and the same. Acceleration between 25 and 50mph stood at a very leisurely 80 seconds when a full load was on board. Although some doubted it, Volkswagen's claim that the heavily laden Transporter was capable of coping with a 1 in 4.3 gradient proved realistic. When it came to petrol consumption, although in the region of 30mpg at a steady 50mph might appear no better than average, while the near inevitable drop to below 20mpg round and about town could be interpreted as thirsty, in comparison with its contemporaries the Transporter was deemed to be highly competitive and notably fuel-efficient. Perhaps, after all, the generous 41-litre fuel tank, complete with three-way fuel tap which included a reserve switch, wasn't

entirely necessary, particularly as the internal fuel filler prevented petrol siphoning, which was rife for a time before the German economy began to forge ahead in leaps and bounds.

Volkswagen's two-piece, vertically split, magnesium alloy crankcase, coupled to cast iron cylinders that were finned on the outside in order to aid cooling and to reduce weight, was the basis of an engine designed specifically for longevity. It also benefited from flat-topped aluminium pistons (manufactured by Mahle), which were secured to entirely conventional forged connecting rods. The four-bearing, forged steel crankshaft drove a single camshaft, which was mounted within the crankcase. At the top of the crankcase and bolted to it was the sheet steel fan housing, which was painted black and mounted vertically. Within this were a rotor cooling fan to the right, which was driven by the dynamo, and an oil-cooler to the left. The fan was driven at twice the speed of the engine by means of the fan belt at the other end of the armature shaft. The air drawn in through the louvres in the body was forced over the engine in order to cool it and then utilised to heat the interior of the vehicle. Metal painted black, and invariably referred to as tinware – at least by those in the know – encased both the cylinder head and barrels in order to stop heat generated by the engine from escaping into the cooling fan and becoming a cause of overheating. Although apparently trivial, a black rubber seal positioned around the border of the engine compartment was in reality vital in creating an airtight bond between the tinware and the rest of the body.

Volkswagen's engine lacked a sump in the traditional sense of the word, as the oil drained to the bottom of the crankcase whenever the engine was switched off. A single type 26VFIS downdraught Solex carburettor was fitted, which was topped by a simple domed metal oil bath air cleaner. 2.56 litres of oil prevented the engine from seizing.

Halt!

Many have noted that, unlike the Beetle, the Transporter benefited from hydraulic braking from its inception. In reality the Transporter had only been on general release for a month when all but the Standard or base model Beetle were allocated hydraulic brakes. Considering the weight of the Transporter, it is likely that the design team thought it inappropriate to fit cable brakes anyway. The Transporter's brakes consisted of single circuit 230mm drums with two leading shoes on the front wheels and a leading and trailing shoe on the rear. The handbrake operated on the rear wheels and was activated mechanically by two cables which ran partially through conduits.

Steering

It was decided to endow the Transporter with the worm and peg principle of steering, in essence mimicking that of the Beetle. The mechanism comprised a transverse link and unequal length tie rods, while king and link pins coupled the steering gear to the front hubs. Thanks to the large diameter of the three-spoke steering wheel the Transporter's steering felt light, while compared to many other vehicles offered at about the same time there was hardly a hint of vagueness.

Suspension

Volkswagen was rightly proud of its all-independent torsion bar system of suspension, invented and utilised by Porsche in the Beetle and logically adopted by the team behind the Transporter. At the front it consisted of two transverse steel axle tubes positioned one above the other and held in place by substantial uprights, to which they were welded. Within each tube the torsion leaves, five in the lower and four in the upper, were held securely together by a sturdy, centrally located block. At the rear the bars were positioned just in front of the rear wheels, a single bar being located in each tube. Independent suspension at the front was achieved by two parallel trailing arms on the outer ends of the torsion bar beams, whilst at the rear the structure veered away from the trailing arm arrangement towards a straightforward swing axle system. For some, such a set-up threatened the characteristics that would allow the wheels to tuck under when the vehicle was driven at full pelt, but as acceleration could only be described as leisurely at best – even if completely acceptable in comparison to the offerings marketed by other manufacturers – there was little chance of this happening.

Gears

The Transporter's gearbox, a rudimentary crash box, was borrowed from the Beetle, and as a result might therefore be said to have been designed by Porsche. Comprising a two-piece light alloy unit, the starter motor sat on the top of the right side, while the box was driven by a cable-operated Fitchel and Sachs 180mm single-plate clutch. Oil-filled housings containing reduction gears were carried on the outer ends of the rear axle tubes. The system was derived from the wartime *Kübelwagen*, both vehicles needing aids to acceleration, particularly when hauling heavy loads. As the gearbox was obviously located towards the rear of the vehicle many noted with surprise that, despite the distance between the box and the cab linkage, gears could be changed smoothly and with a more than acceptable degree of alacrity.

Six-volt

Like the Beetle, the Transporter was supplied with a six-volt Bosch battery, which was located within the engine compartment close to the right-hand rear quarter panel. While Volkswagen was one of the last manufacturers to switch from six to 12-volt technology – the change, as far as the Transporter was concerned, came in August 1966 for the '67 model year (the last that would see the first generation model still in production) – there was no criticism of the arrangement at the Transporter's launch, nor, at least as far as the press were concerned, for many a year thereafter.

The essence of the Transporter

Much more closely linked to the essence of the Transporter was its revolutionary design, which afforded both plentiful loading space and excellent handling characteristics. Taking the latter first, Nordhoff not only recognised its importance but was the driving force behind ensuring the concept became reality – recall some of the key elements of his speech at the press launch quoted in the previous chapter. Volkswagen had recognised the urgent need for a commercial vehicle with acceptable handling characteristics. '[The] load area carries the driver's seat at the front, and at the rear both the engine and gearbox – that is the patent idea, free of compromise, for our Van, and that is how it is built,' proclaimed a triumphant Nordhoff. Subsequently Volkswagen

▼ Throughout its early years of production the Transporter was built at Wolfsburg. This delightful image depicts the power station, while an elderly gentleman fishes in the Mitteland Canal. *(RC)*

◄ A varied production line at Wolfsburg. Note the vehicle second from the right, which because of its lack of a rear window and an apparently small engine lid must be an ambulance. The fifth vehicle from the right appears to be a Delivery Van.

▼ This aerial photograph was taken at a time when the Transporter would still have been built at Wolfsburg. Fifty years and more later, the factory and township have expanded greatly.

▷ The bodyshell is prepared for paint more or less by hand.

▽ These fully painted and trimmed bodies appear ready to receive their front axles.

laboured the point in the deluge of promotional material they meticulously prepared:

'"Ride amidships for comfort" is as true on land as it is at sea and has become a principle of modern automobile engineering. Volkswagen Transporters not only incorporate this feature but go one better: they are counterbalanced. That is to say the weight of the vehicle is perfectly distributed since the weight of the engine in the rear counterbalances the weight of the driver in front. That is why goods are given a smooth ride even when driven over rough roads, if they are delivered in a Volkswagen Transporter.'

The creation of a vehicle with appropriate handling opened the door to what market research demanded of the design: a 'three-quarter-tonner with as large as possible a load space'. To appreciate fully the groundbreaking nature of Volkswagen's endeavours it is necessary to turn to the vehicle's interior.

The view from inside

Nordhoff spearheaded the advance at the press launch in a no-nonsense way: 'The Van comprises a main area of three square metres of floor space plus, over the engine, an additional square metre and 45 cubic metres of volume. … In short, neither the load area nor the driver's area is restricted by these items.'

Shortly afterwards the brochure copywriters told the same story in their own rather more flowery style. The following atypical extract comes from a slightly later brochure of 1955 vintage, designed for the American market at a point when the original Transporter had undergone something of a cross between a makeover and a transformation:

'The spacious van has a floor extending unobstructed from the cab panel right to the engine compartment; furthermore, it is fitted with four wide doors – two cab doors for driver and co-driver, double doors for loading from the side and a top hinged rear door for loading from the rear. Both features – the unobstructed floor and exceptional accessibility of the Volkswagen Transporter ensure speedy loading and unloading. … Does it not drive home the fact that a converted sedan must of necessity have a very restricted load space and just cannot compare with a car designed as a van right from the beginning?'

Few present-day authors make such a big deal of the interior space as the key players in the Transporter story did when it was launched. This is somewhat odd, as without such a generous loading capacity there is a distinct possibility that the Transporter wouldn't have taken off as a delivery van.

▲ ▼ These additional images of the Wolfsburg factory at work, supplied from the VW archive, illustrate the cavernous (but incredibly neat and tidy) Spare Parts Department, while the *Plattenwagen* appears to have had a rival in the fleet of battery-powered load-carriers.

Against a backdrop of images depicting the difference in available loading space in the average van and the 4.6m^3 afforded by the Volkswagen, confirmed by a diagram showing the difference in load stability between one where the weight is counterbalanced by an engine in the rear and a driver at the front and a vehicle with its load always bearing down on the rear axle, Volkswagen had this to say:

'Volkswagen Transporters are all trucks and not just converted sedans offering relatively little load space for freight in lieu of passengers. Utility dominates every feature of Volkswagen Transporters. Two-thirds of the entire volume of these fast and handsome vehicles is load space ... Volkswagen Transporters can haul a larger load and take care of a longer delivery route, thus cutting down delivery costs and increasing profits.'

As the improvements made to the Transporter specification in 1955 have been briefly alluded to, it's worth noting that one result was a further increase in available loading space, from an admirable 4.6m^3 capacity to 4.8m^3. Volkswagen's message remained constant, still concentrating on 'weight distribution', with 'driver in front, motor in back, the load in the middle, in the best sprung space. Now 4.8 cubic metres of storage space...'.

Just as the launch model Export or De Luxe Beetle dating from the summer of 1949 appears spartan in the extreme compared to even the base models of today, so too does the first generation Transporter when parked alongside not only the T5, but also the T4, T3 and even the second generation model. However, before decrying it as an economy model beyond belief it's worth taking a moment to consider other manufacturers' products. Their cabs were generally uncomfortable with the most basic of seating, and in many instances the engine, possibly a diesel, sat by the side of the driver, so that not only was the noise horrific but there were also trying vibrations to deal with. In comparison, then, although austere, the Volkswagen Transporter sat on a pinnacle, ahead of its competitors in this as in all respects.

At launch the bulkhead between the cab and the load area only came to roughly the height of the seat backrests, but with effect from 16 June 1950 this changed with the addition of a fibreboard panel to roof height.

Although Nordhoff had suggested a separate seat for the driver, for once a deaf ear was turned, presumably on grounds of both cost and practicality. The result was that for many years the Transporter was offered with nothing more than a firm bench seat capable of accommodating three people. Most Beetles of 1950 or thereabouts vintage were offered with cloth upholstery. As fashions changed, vinyl – a feature of the Transporter's interior – became nearly universally accepted, certainly amongst family or smaller saloons. The key became the complexity of the vinyl's 'weave' pattern and conceivably the use of more than one shade of material in the vehicle's interior. The Transporter, at least in Delivery Van or workhorse guise, never indulged in such frivolities. Plain and crucially practical, easily cleanable vinyl was the order of the decade.

The bench seat wasn't adjustable; to be frank, few would have expected such luxury in a commercial vehicle. The cab door panels were completed in plain fibreboard, with a cut-out in each for oddments, while the headlining was made out of nothing more plush than hardboard. The metal floor was covered by a single-piece, longitudinally ribbed rubber mat. The load space, roof panel and all the other interior areas were simply painted metal.

Apart from a grab-handle for the passengers and a foot-rest bar positioned across the floor, there was only a single instrument binnacle, and of course the rather attractive three-spoke black steering wheel already beloved by Beetle owners, albeit of a slightly larger diameter in the Transporter.

Just about everything the driver needed to do or react to was contained within the confines of the body-coloured binnacle. The speedometer, calibrated to a realistic 80kph, had a black face with white letters, and conveniently offered advice to the driver when a gear change was recommended via a series of red markings. Unusually, the needle indicating the vehicle's speed ran from 10 past the hour, rather than 20 to the hour, giving the impression that it was going backwards. Warning lights for the indicator semaphores (red), main beam (blue), ignition (red) and oil pressure (green) surrounded the speedometer. The wipers and headlamps were operated by rudimentary switches, while the ignition sat between them. The starter button was a separate item, mounted on the left-hand side of the binnacle, while a simple toggle switch positioned at the top operated the semaphores.

The pedal arrangement was in line with that of the Beetle, which meant that heeling and toeing was impossible due to the pedals' angle in relation to the floor.

Vehicles with air-cooled engines are invariably criticised when it comes to heating and the Transporter was no exception. Controlled by a rotary knob positioned on the metalwork below the seat, what hot air was available was channelled through a circular tube positioned behind the front panel.

Finally, and undoubtedly for cost reasons, the side windows in the cab were of the sliding variety rather than the more conventional and convenient wind-down type.

More models equates to more sales

▼ Elegant with its two-tone paint, the Micro Bus initially led the field in passenger-carrying terms. See page 64 for a fascinating rearward shot of the same vehicle.

Addressing the press in October 1962, more than 12 years after the events that are about to unfurl, Nordhoff made what can best be described as one of those off-the-cuff comments that stay firmly wedged in the mind. 'Cars are bought from money earned,' he said, 'and Transporters are bought in order to earn money.'

The two models that followed the Delivery Van into production fitted Nordhoff's words precisely.

15 April 1950 had seen the prototype Micro Bus delivered to a valued customer for testing, and production of the Kombi started in earnest just over a month later, on 16 May. Fast-forward just six more days and on 22 May the Micro Bus joined the Kombi, its evaluation period having proved that it too was potentially a worthwhile addition to the range.

The Kombi

In the Kombi, Volkswagen had developed a true forerunner of the MPVs that were to represent a large chunk of total sales several decades later. For as the name implies, the Kombi could one minute be a delivery van, and the next a passenger carrier capable of transporting up to eight people. Indeed, it was this degree of flexibility that gave rise to the notion of a vehicle that could be used for weekends away by the addition of a removable camping box – an idea generally, but not exclusively, credited to the Westfalia stable. However, for the moment at least that's another story.

For someone used to today's levels of luxury, casting an eye over a first generation Transporter in Kombi guise would leave them in a state of shock, such was the basic nature of the vehicle. The differences between the Kombi and the Delivery Van were not that great. Three rectangular window spaces were cut into the panels behind the cab side-windows, which of course meant that on the side where the loading doors were evident they too received window glass. Inside, the partition was only of seat backrest height, the load area was covered in rubber matting of the same style as that fitted in the cab, and there was removable seating. The Kombi lacked a headlining of any sort in the rear 'load area', and no attempt was made to line the painted metal side panels.

The Kombi's additional seating was far from luxurious, both in its design and in the way it was fitted and removed. Taking the latter first, wing nuts were deemed sufficient to secure the seats or, when undone, to allow them to be removed. Essentially finished in the same manner as the bench in the

▼ Reuters captured the essence of the Kombi to perfection through his tactic of including two vehicles in his picture, one with passengers and the other with goods. *(RC)*

VW-Kombi

cab of the Delivery Van, the Kombi's seats sat on somewhat spindly and certainly exposed frames.

That being said, it was an ingenious set-up, as Volkswagen's literature made abundantly clear, albeit in somewhat turgid language by today's standards. The following extracts are typical of the message preached by the company's publicity department in the early years:

'[The Kombi] embodies all the best features of a roomy eight-passenger car with that of an extremely practical and economical truck for deliveries. Indeed it is even better than an ordinary panel truck. Its six side windows can be easily made into as many attractive and extremely effective show windows to display your merchandise. Every Volkswagen Transporter is in itself excellent advertising as it attracts the attention of all eyes. Arranging displays in the windows permits full exploitation of its great advertising power ... The Kombi is ... particularly well suited for the conveyance of livestock or for use as a service utility truck in which work can be performed in peace and quiet. There is not a vehicle in its field that can serve so many purposes. Using the entire 162cu ft of load space for freight, the cab still seats three persons, or you can use half of the load space for freight and seat six persons including the driver. With all the seats installed you can use the Kombi to convey 8 to 9 persons back and forth on the job or on a trip.'

After the modifications made to all Transporters in the spring of 1955, someone at Volkswagen thought it fit to itemise the advantages of Kombi ownership in numerical form. The following is taken from a home market brochure and translated into English:

'Many VW Kombis are put to good use in the following ways: 1 – as a delivery vehicle with a large, bright loading space and all the advantages of the VW Delivery Van. 2 – as an eight-seater, for with the flick of a wrist the two comfortable upholstered seats are installed. The large space at the rear, accessible from outside, is reserved for bigger items of luggage. 3 – as a combined vehicle – for simultaneous transportation of people AND goods in the interior. The decor is deliberately simple and entirely suited to changing usages – for the loading space must be quickly and easily cleaned.'

By the summer of 1966 and the last year of first generation Kombi production, the message was considerably slicker in presentation, but nevertheless told a similar if more sophisticated story:

'The VW Kombi is three different cars in one. That means you save buying ten [sic] wheels, two engines, two transmissions, tax and insurance on two vehicles. And lots of other things. First of all you can use the VW Kombi as a delivery van, which has 170ft³ of load space and takes a payload of 2,183lbs. With smooth sides, floor and roof. With large double wing doors and a rear door that facilitate easy loading and unloading. With windows that give a lot of light. And turn the van into a mobile service station once it's fitted out. Or a mobile workshop which covers a large area. Or a laboratory or an office. Moreover with the VW Kombi you have a small bus which transports eight persons. Both padded seat benches in the centre are easily installed – and you have converted a practical delivery van into a comfortable passenger car. With lots of room for everybody. And plenty of luggage space.'

Those in the know would recognise the style of the text above as the work of the American advertising agency DDB, Doyle Dane Bernbach. Their role in boosting sales of Volkswagens generally and the Transporter in particular follows later, but an extra snippet of text serves to indicate that the agency never missed a trick:

'You can convert your VW Kombi into a camping car. No need for a tow-bar. It's motorised! ... Removable equipment. Which can be installed easily. And taken out just as easily. If you think about it, it's little to pay for a lot of pleasure. With the VW Kombi as a camping car you have no worries about sleeping accommodation or luggage. No reservations to make, no tipping. You can go where you wish and stop when you have found the best place. Wouldn't you like that?'

▼ **To load the Kombi with goods the seats were of necessity removed, having been held in place by nothing more complicated than simple wing-nuts. With the doors open, as in this picture, it is clear that the Kombi provided only basic passenger facilities.** *(RC)*

VW-Kleinbus

The Micro Bus

To potential buyers in Germany the next variation on the general Transporter theme was *Der Kleinbus*, literally the 'Small Bus', or the VW-*Achtsitzer*, a term that can be quickly worked out to mean 'Eight-seater'. For the UK market, though, the vehicle was given the name of the Micro Bus, while in the United States it was referred to as the Station Wagon. However, whatever name was proffered, this was the vehicle that broke the mould established thus far. To utilise the title of the brochure in which the many purposes of the Kombi were listed, such a vehicle offered 'transport efficiently'; the Micro Bus, though, presented its purchasers with the means to 'travel comfortably'.

Inside, the latest variant came with a soft cloth headlining throughout what had previously been described as the load area, the material of which extended around the side windows. Additionally, the bare metal of the Kombi below the vehicle's interior waistline was covered with fibreboard panels suitably clad with vinyl. The seat upholstery was more luxurious in that it was pleated rather than plain and featured piping around its edges. At least initially, the

▲ If the reproduction of Reuters' Micro Bus appears dark, this is due not to an error on the part of the printers but to the seemingly gloomy way in which the artist chose to portray his subject. Note nevertheless the disproportionate size of the vehicle's occupants. *(RC)*

▼ The conservative nature of this Reuters image is carried through to the rest of the models depicted in the brochure. *(BS)*

AM FOR PASSENGER AND GOOD

Compared to the Kombi, an abundance of Micro Bus images are available from the VW archive. This attractive series of photographs of Volkswagen's 'oversize passenger car' are most likely to have been taken to coincide with the start of series production in the spring of 1950. As the VW emblem on the rear was discontinued in November 1950 the pictures were certainly taken before then.

rubber floor covering was of a raised square design rather than being ribbed, while towards the back of the vehicle and above the metalwork separating the engine from the interior – at least until a rear window was added – there was a sliding partition designed to conceal any luggage stored within the enclosed area. Generally, the level of fittings was more generous, the addition of ashtrays for a generation of confirmed smokers being one such example, the 'modesty boards' that disguised the framework of the middle row of seats being another.

Externally the Micro Bus could be distinguished by its paint colour, being available in either Brown Beige over Light Beige (the notion of two-tone paintwork being a first for the Transporter) or straightforward Stone Grey, a shade not available to owners of Delivery Vans or Kombis. The options for the workhorse models developed from the sole choice of ubiquitous Dove Blue, through to both Pearl and Medium Grey, to Chestnut Brown and Brown Beige. The only complication to muddy the waters came in the form of vehicles delivered in primer. Significantly, the first ever sale of a Transporter was of just such a vehicle, a Delivery Van to convey the products of the 4711 Perfume Company. Not surprisingly, the owners thought it advantageous to personalise their vehicle in the company livery, a package which included their logo. Vehicle quantities delivered to the home market in primer during the first year of Transporter production were significant, and this would continue to be the case for some years to come. Compared to the 2,356 Delivery Vans finished in Dove Blue,

and the 919 Kombis in the same shade, 1,989 of the former and 264 of the latter left Wolfsburg with nothing more than primer to keep the rust at bay. Even more significantly, and despite the option of both an exclusive colour and the only two-tone paintwork available as standard, 145 unpainted Micro Buses, compared to 789 painted ones, were despatched to the distributor and dealer network in Germany. Even when it came to exported vehicles the same situation prevailed, with 142 painted Micro Buses heading either overland or overseas to find owners, compared to 62 in primer.

In order to distinguish the Micro Bus from the decidedly more basic Kombi, early sales literature tended to refer to the vehicle as a car, rather than as anything else:

'The Volkswagen Micro Bus is in reality not a bus but an oversize passenger car accommodating eight persons. Every passenger has more head, leg and elbow room than he needs. There is not another car of its kind so easy to get in and out of as the Volkswagen Micro Bus and no other in which the passengers are so comfortable, seated well between the axles … The vehicle is astonishingly fast. It has such a fast get away, it handles so easily and the driver has such a deep angle of vision in front of him that it is a joy to handle in traffic. … The deeply upholstered seats are so well cushioned that travelling hundreds of miles is a pleasure. The Volkswagen Micro Bus is a new type of eight-seat passenger car for inexpensive travelling. It will pay for itself in savings before you know it.'

VW-KLEINBUS „SONDERAUSFÜHRUNG"

The Micro Bus De Luxe – icing on the cake

Recalling the feverish days when Nordhoff was demanding of Häesner and his team that no time at all should be lost in bringing the Van into production, at least two other options were under consideration besides the Delivery Van and the Micro Bus. These were some sort of public amenity vehicle, suitable for use by the Post Office or conceivably by the ambulance service, and a Pick-up. In reality neither came next after the Micro Bus. Perhaps the limited market for such a vehicle as an ambulance was a deterrent, while the expense involved in reshaping the Transporter into a Pick-up was

considerable. Instead Volkswagen decided to provide a luxury version of the Micro Bus in direct response to the rapidly improving fortunes of Germany and its economy. Only through sales of such a vehicle, together with the other Transporters already launched, could Nordhoff guarantee the considerable sums of money required to create all the options originally planned.

The new model, branded in Germany as the VW *Kleinbus 'Sonderhausführung'*, or special model, and in English-speaking countries as the Micro Bus De Luxe, made its debut on the production line on 1 June 1951, over a year after its less well appointed sibling. Here was the Export Beetle of the Transporter world, not merely personified but improved upon. The vehicle known today as the Samba had a plethora of both luxury trim fittings and exclusive items. No wonder, then, that when an American dealer came to scribble prices on one of the many brochures he undoubtedly handed out, the Samba topped the bill. After 1955 the Delivery Van would have set its new American owner back by $1,930, the Kombi $2,130, the Micro Bus $2,230 and the Samba $2,685. If the inclusion of seats and fixings added up to $200, and a full headlining and better seats with additional trim equated to a further $100, the additional $455 to buy a Samba must have added up to some considerable package – and it did.

Externally the Samba could be distinguished by several features. Working from the roof panel downwards, a full-specification Samba featured a near full-length canvas fold-back sunroof which was manufactured for Volkswagen, just like that fitted to some Beetles, by the German firm of Golde. However,

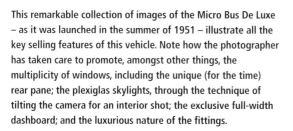

This remarkable collection of images of the Micro Bus De Luxe – as it was launched in the summer of 1951 – illustrate all the key selling features of this vehicle. Note how the photographer has taken care to promote, amongst other things, the multiplicity of windows, including the unique (for the time) rear pane; the plexiglas skylights, through the technique of tilting the camera for an interior shot; the exclusive full-width dashboard; and the luxurious nature of the fittings.

a note of caution, for concurrently with the start of Samba production the Micro Bus could also be purchased with a sunroof, albeit at extra cost, while a handful of Samba owners specified a version without either a sunroof or another exclusive and endearing Samba feature, namely eight skylights. Glazed with plexiglas, a perspex-type material most frequently used in the manufacture of aeroplane cockpit canopies, four skylights ran down each side of the Samba's roof, starting at a point over the cab doors and culminating in a line parallel to the third out of four side windows. Plexiglas was also used to form wraparound windows on each upper rear quarter panel, these windows meeting with both those on the sides of the vehicle and that at the back. Those unfamiliar with the Samba's make-up may nevertheless have already worked out that the De Luxe model featured one additional window on each side, bringing the total up from the three on the Micro Bus to four on the Samba. Apart from further adding to the light and airy nature of the vehicle, the additional side windows had the effect of changing three rectangles to four essentially square pieces of glass. Even without the benefits of a tape measure it was obvious that the rear window was larger than fitted to other models. The overall result of the stylists' work was to create a particularly light and airy vehicle, entirely in keeping with the executive

feel Volkswagen were trying to engender. Nobody, but nobody could offer a comparable 23-window car!

As might be expected, the Samba had its own unique paint combination in addition to the Stone Grey which it shared with the Micro Bus. This was the delightful mix of Chestnut Brown over the appropriately named Sealing Wax Red. It was also the only model in the range to feature a host of brightwork, starting with chrome domed hubcaps – an extra cost option for other models – and extending to a magnificently shiny chromed VW roundel on the vehicle's front, plus chunky bright trim strips which ran around the De Luxe's waistline to meet at the tip of the 'V' on the front panel. These were examples of the stylists' craft in themselves, for instead of being simply one hefty lump of polished metal, two more delicate bands were separated by an infill coloured to match the shade of the lower panels.

The design of the Samba's front bumper at the time of the De Luxe's launch was such that it appeared to have a separate centre section. In reality this was an illusion created in the pressing of the metal, but in the case of the top-of-the-range model there was indeed an additional section in the form of a rubber trim insert secured by a brightwork surround. No other Transporter in 1951 was fitted with a rear bumper and while the De Luxe too lacked what might be termed a

full bumper in the true sense of the term, it benefited from trim strips which at least softened the impact of a nudge when parking.

Having highlighted the main distinguishing features of the Micro Bus De Luxe from the outside, one feature immediately caught the eye on opening any of the doors to look inside. Again unlike any of its siblings, the top-of-the-range model featured a full-width dashboard instead of a single binnacle. Although the instrumentation was still limited by later standards, at least a large mechanical clock was offered, while there was ample space to insert a radio. In contrast to the other models, and very much in the mould of the Export Beetle, the fixtures and fittings were finished in an ivory colour rather than the more austere shade of black. This luxury extended from major items such as the steering wheel and instrument surrounds to such details as the window-winder handles, gear-knob and the grab-handles on the seat backs. Upholstery by definition was of the finest quality Volkswagen could produce, with both piping and pleats being a part of the package, while at the rear the luggage area was not only carpeted but also sported both chromed rubbing strips and protective restraining rails.

At the time of the De Luxe model's launch it seemed that travel by aeroplane was something the citizens of Europe and America aspired to. Still largely

the province of the rich and famous, the notion of ferrying airline passengers from their penthouse suites at a nearby hotel to the airport in a Volkswagen Micro Bus De Luxe added a certain credence to the company's claims regarding their vehicle's standard of luxury:

'This airline uses Volkswagen Micro Buses De Luxe because it wants to give its passengers maximum comfort and economy of transport. No words or pictures can properly convey to you the beauty, comfort and numerous advantages of this remarkable eight-passenger vehicle. You have to see it and drive it yourself to appreciate all its qualities. The Volkswagen Micro Bus De Luxe equips you to meet any competition. Its stream lines and handsome colours attract the eyes of everyone. Its interior is equally inviting with its eight comfortable seats affording each passenger a panoramic view. Side windows in the roof afford an upward view as well.'

Two further extracts from the wealth of words written about Volkswagen's intended showstopper serve to illustrate how the same message could be repeated over and over again without detriment to the vehicle's cause:

'A harmonious two-colour scheme and a double chromium-plated ornamental band enhance the beauty of the Volkswagen Micro Bus De Luxe. Comfortable deep-cushioned seats and handsome fittings make the vehicle a miniature luxury bus for travel and comfort.'

'"Attractive and luxurious", these are the attributes reflecting the first and lasting impression which people gain of the Volkswagen Micro Bus "De Luxe". An exquisite colour scheme, rich chromium mouldings and tasteful interior appointments produce the perfect blend which is characteristic of European styling.'

Although the Micro Bus De Luxe was an important member of the Transporter family, its level of sales paled into relative insignificance when compared to the big players in the range. Price undoubtedly played its part, but perhaps the slightly more cynical might venture to suggest that despite its luxury trim level it was, after all, still only a glorified van. In the Samba's first full year of production 1,142 vehicles were produced, little more than a quarter of the number of 'ordinary' Micro Buses which left the Wolfsburg factory. Today, though, ask most enthusiasts which model of first generation Transporter they would most like to own and the answer would undoubtedly be the Micro Bus De Luxe.

◀ An early interpretation of what would become a recurrent theme – luxury transport for those fortunate enough to be able to jet across the world for business or pleasure! *(BS)*

VW-Krankenwagen

▲ Without question the Ambulance's biggest talking point was the creation of a rear entry point, making the handling of a patient on a stretcher much easier. Reuters captured the scene to perfection. *(RC)*

▼ Direct from Volkswagen's archive, this picture represents the Ambulance as it was launched in the last month of 1951.

VW-Krankenwagen

1951 saw the launch of a second addition to the Transporter range. Although this vehicle had an important role to play, its debut on the Wolfsburg production line on 13 December stirred little in the way of journalistic curiosity. Indeed, it would be a rare find if a test review of the new vehicle was to be unearthed today. Furthermore, throughout the remaining 16 years that the first generation Transporter remained the current model, production of this particular variant never exceeded an all-time high of just 883 vehicles in a 12-month period, this event occurring in 1961. When it is considered that in the same year Delivery Van production totalled 45,121, the apparently trivial nature of this latest addition to the range appeared to be unquestionable. Yet here was a variation on the theme that had been planned from the earliest of prototype days, and one that was not only included in many a Transporter family brochure, but also qualified for its own promotional literature and superb artwork from the pen of Wolfsburg's then resident artist, Bernd Reuters.

The vehicle was, of course, the Ambulance, and its significance lay not in the paraphernalia of stretchers, frosted glass, or even the special rear-loading arrangement – which pre-empted this general improvement to the range by several years – but in its ability to demonstrate that the design of the Transporter was so versatile that it could be adapted to suit a multitude of purposes. Here indeed was the forefather of, and the ambassador for, what were known in Germany as *sonderausführungren*, or in English a catalogue of 'special models'.

What exactly Volkswagen hoped to gain from the text accompanying the Ambulance in their early generic brochures is hard to imagine. Surely if subtlety was the plan, in terms of reference to the Transporter's flexibility as a vehicle of many varying uses, the text was so obtuse that it would be lost on all but those who had the benefit of many years' hindsight?

'The Volkswagen Ambulance is the ideal means of conveyance for ill or injured persons. Every feature has been carefully planned to give patients maximum comfort. Standard equipment for Volkswagen Ambulances includes two stretchers mounted at the same level on each side of the ambulance, an upholstered removable seat for carrying patients up and down the narrow stairs, a further well-upholstered seat for patients and a folding-seat for the medical attendant next to the patients. The cabin seats the driver and two stretcher bearers.'

Der VW-Pritschenwagen

Following the Samba's debut there was a gap of some 16 months before the introduction of the next Transporter model (if the 'specialist' Ambulance is overlooked, which it surely must be in this context). That there was a gap was not because Volkswagen's flow of ideas had dried up, for what did emerge on 25 August 1952 was another vehicle that had been planned since the earliest days of development, just like the Ambulance. This was the Pick-up, and the reason for its apparent delay was straightforward: sufficient finance had to be amassed to pay for the expensive design work and re-tooling required to produce a flat-bed vehicle.

Apart from the obvious need to organise a new pressing for the vehicle's truncated roof panel, considerable ingenuity had to be employed to relocate both the petrol tank and the spare wheel, each of which sat above the engine in all other models. The easier of the two tasks was the creation of a special well behind the driver's seat to house the spare wheel, while the positioning of the fuel tank to the right of the gearbox was more complex. In the process, almost by accident, Volkswagen had made an overnight improvement, as the petrol filler was no longer concealed within the engine compartment but was instead easily accessible on the right-hand side of the body. The final change, although undoubtedly of far less significance, related to the engine cooling louvres, which sat behind the cut-out for the rear wheels.

The key players at Volkswagen undoubtedly appreciated the significance of the Pick-up as a jack of all trades. Not only could it be used to ferry heavy loads such as those associated with the building trade, but it also provided an ideal platform to which a special body or equipment could be added, examples of which might include a mobile shop in the former case or a turntable ladder in the latter. However, ingenuity didn't end with possible uses for the vehicle, for the basic design contained at least a couple of innovations worthy of Volkswagen at its best. First and perhaps most obvious was the creation of a low-height loading platform, further aided by the ability to drop each and every hinged side-flap completely down. The stroke of genius, however, came in the inclusion of

▼ Potential owners wanted to know that the Pick-up would be easy to load and that it had the added advantage of dry, secure storage space. Reuters illustrated both top-selling points admirably. *(RC)*

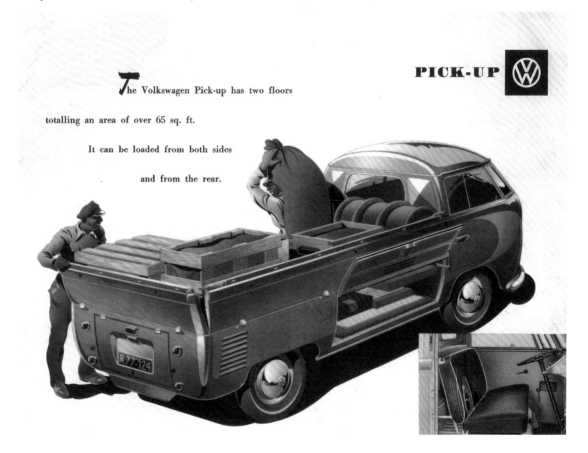

The Volkswagen Pick-up has two floors totalling an area of over 65 sq. ft.

It can be loaded from both sides and from the rear.

PICK-UP VW

a secure storage area below the loading platform and between the cab and the area reserved for the engine. Accessed by a top-hinged door, this 'locker' afforded secure storage on a platform of 1.9m². Another thoughtful move was the availability of tilt and bows to support a canvas roof, thus ensuring that when there was a need to keep goods dry, the means were available, albeit at extra cost.

Although this late addition to the range cost Volkswagen dearly in terms of its development, the rewards were there for all to see. In its first full year of production 5,741 Pick-ups left Wolfsburg, only slightly fewer than the total of Kombis and certainly more than for the Micro Bus and its De Luxe counterpart combined. Volkswagen quickly sang the Pick-up's praises:

'Yes, indeed, the Volkswagen Pick-up Truck does have two floors. The upper floor has an area of 45sq ft and the lower 20sq ft. The upper floor is at the proper international standard for loading with a hand truck from a loading platform. It is convenient for loading anything anywhere, as a Pick-up is required to do. Easily damaged goods can be stowed on the lower floor which forms a closed compartment where the goods are thoroughly protected from the elements, dust and even thieves, for the compartment can be locked. Both upper and lower load spaces are unencumbered and free of shafts or wheel wells. Both sideboards and the tailgate of the upper loading space can be let down'.

▲ ▼ **Although these two photographs weren't taken at the time of the Pick-up's launch – as evidenced by the inclusion of a rear bumper, an addition dating from late December 1953 – they are sufficiently early to depict the model before the significant changes made in March 1955, a restyling exercise which affected the appearance of all Transporters.**

Late arrivals to complete the first generation family

Turn to any brochure covering the entire Transporter range that dates to later than 1961 and the family of vehicles so far encountered will have two further members. For starters, there was the Double Cab Pick-up, an extra model that dated – at least as far as production was concerned – from 3 November 1958. Then from September 1961 and the early days of the '62 model year the High Roofed Delivery Van became an option.

Officially, with the addition of these two models Volkswagen's line-up was complete. The problem, however, was that for those whose concern was marketing and ever-increasing sales, it wasn't enough! There were more storylines to tell, additional businesses that could be catered for, and people with money in their pockets who couldn't be overlooked. Using as a typical example of Volkswagen's literature a brochure dating from July 1963, up pops the 'quick loading' Delivery Van, a vehicle with sliding doors not only on the passenger's side but on the driver's side as well. Then there's 'The VW Pick-up with Enlarged Platform', because – as the copywriter is quick to note – 'some businessmen need an even larger load surface'. However, nobody at Volkswagen saw such vehicles as models in their own right. But the overlap with optional equipment – defined by the inclusion of one or more 'M' codes (standing for *Mehrausstattung*) – was clearly becoming more difficult to define. Add the already alluded to Special Models, classified by an 'S' code, and Volkswagen's

range slowly but surely became all-embracing. The Double Cab Pick-up, an all-time favourite for many an American owner, had itself started life as an 'S' model, manufactured by the German coachwork firm of Binz from around 1953 to a standard acceptable to and approved by Volkswagen.

The Double Cab Pick-up was exactly what Volkswagen stated it to be. Again, as with the single-cab Pick-up before it, a reasonable degree of re-tooling was required. However, what had been accomplished in the process of creating the first Pick-up didn't have to be reinvented; this time it was a simple task of re-jigging presses to work on the new panels. These consisted of a larger roof to accommodate a bigger cab, a side door allowing entry to the second row of seats in the cab – note that only one extra door was offered and that this was on the passenger side of the vehicle – plus the means to produce a truncated load bed. A victim of the redesign was the lower storage area, but someone cleverly created a new hideaway under the rear bench seat. Although the load area was smaller it still measured 1,755mm x 1,570mm and there was still the option to pay for bows and a tarpaulin, thus creating a dray storage area for items bordering on 1,200mm in height.

By the time the *VW-Pritschenwagen mit Doppelkabine* was introduced Volkswagen Transporter sales had taken off in America as well as in Europe, and in a country where pick-ups were generally big

▲ The Double Cab Pick-up was a popular and worthy addition to the Transporter line-up and was undoubtedly created on the back of the success of the 'S' model manufactured by the Binz coachworks.

◀ The original Double Cab Pick-up as manufactured by the coachbuilders Binz. Note the 'suicide' style door, plus the non-opening window, and then compare these features with those of Volkswagen's own model.

▲ In 2008, the concept of a Double Cab Pick-up produced by Volkswagen was 50 years old. This image depicts a first generation model dating from the mid-1960s and, with its 'face' away from the camera, the latest T5 Chassis cab with loading platform in place.

'Like many great ideas, it seems simple once you've hit upon it. You can take half a Kombi and half a Pick-up, put them together and presto, you have a completely different type of utility vehicle with many special, nay unique advantages. As a matter of fact, it's a vehicle with many applications. For example: It can take six persons and 980 pounds of cargo … or three persons and 1,411 pounds … or one driver and 1,698 pounds. It's merely a question of arrangement. The VW Double Cab offers room for six persons, three in front and three in the divided part of the cab in the rear. It takes a full maintenance crew plus all their tools and equipment … The 30 square-foot platform in the rear takes a payload of 981 pounds … When more cargo space is needed, you can remove the rear seat bench and the tool chest beneath it, and get 65 cubic feet more of weather-tight, lockable load space for valuable goods. Bows and tarpaulin are also available at an extra charge, making it possible to convert the platform into an all-weather van. Now you see why we consider the VW Double Cab Pick-up so practical – need we say more?'

business this multi-seater load carrier was bound to be a big hit. As far as promoting the product went, an early device was to describe the new introduction not as a Double Cab but rather as 'The VW 6-passenger Pick-up'. However, initially for Volkswagen of America, and not long after for the rest of the VW Empire, a promotional revolution was about to take place. The world of advertising would never be the same again. Try the following, which dates from 1963, as an example of the new approach and intensely lively sales pitch for the Double Cab that supplanted the politely informative and somewhat turgid text of the past:

The High Roofed Delivery Van introduced in the autumn of 1961 and during the second month of the 1962 model year inevitably also featured in the same brochure, with the subheading: 'spacious – because inside it is five and a half feet high'. However, it's from copy which first saw the glint in the VW salesman's eye in August 1965, and a British salesman too, that the next extract is taken:

▲ An attractive mid-'60s picture of a High Roof Delivery Van in the livery of the *Deutsche Bundespost*. At first glance the other vehicle appears to be a straightforward Delivery Van, but closer examination reveals that this too has an extended roof section.

◄ The High Roof Delivery Van, although never Volkswagen's most popular version of the Transporter, was invaluable to those who needed additional height to move their goods about. *(BS)*

'You have still longer, wider or higher objects to transport? Well then, this is the van for you. It's 14 inches higher than the normal delivery van. The mean height inside is 66.1". And the load compartment has 212 cubic feet of space. Therefore you have more room to move in this van and it's easier to get at things. There's really room to swing the proverbial cat. In addition it has even larger doors and an even larger side area for advertising.'

Beloved particularly by members of the clothing trade and the likes of furniture shops needing to deliver bulkier, taller items such as wardrobes, the High Roofed Delivery Van was definitely not a cheap option. A straightforward Delivery Van purchased

in Britain in 1967 would have cost its owner £680, or if fitted with doors at both sides an additional £30, bringing the total for such an option to £710. However, the High Roofed Delivery Van would have commanded £910, which seems to be a lot of additional money for an extended tin top. For Volkswagen the task of manufacturing the High Top was relatively straightforward, so presumably the much higher asking price related to the amount of material used. The essence of the vehicle was extended body panels above the vehicle's waistline and taller side doors. Possibly the most complex panel to add was the curved one above the windscreen and cab doors. At the back, as the standard size tailgate was retained, there was little to do.

Factory-fitted optional extras

Delve into any Beetle specification guide and it won't be long before an array of extra-cost options or extras materialises. Bolt-on or built-in goodies were available almost from the start and would remain a feature through the years of German production and beyond. Consider the scenario nowadays, and deny if you dare that Volkswagen offer a myriad of extras if you choose to order them rather than buying a vehicle, commercial or otherwise, straight from the local dealer's showroom. Nothing different was to be expected when the Transporter was launched in 1950, safe in the hands of one of Europe's most experienced managers, Heinz Nordhoff.

The aim here is not to itemise every single option, but rather to highlight some of the more interesting ones as a prelude to tackling a subject which was unique to the Transporter, at least until other manufacturers realised there was money to be made out of copying what Volkswagen had already done. One further

observation is, however, essential – not all the extras were available in 1950 by any means, and a percentage of those noted didn't last the course through to the end of first generation production in July 1967:

M035   Reinforced sides for the Pick-up.
M053   Tailgate with window (available until March 1955), perhaps a recognition of the fact that not everyone wanted to load everything through the side doors.
M054   Full-width dashboard, available for a few years following the introduction of the Micro Bus De Luxe for anyone wishing to avoid the embarrassment of a single instrument binnacle.
M055   Rotary fan in the roof – was this extra recognition of the fact that the ventilation was inadequate in the Transporters built before March 1955?

M066   Rubber mat for the load area – almost an upgrade to Kombi status for Delivery Van owners.

M070   Tilt and bows – an essential for any Pick-up owner wishing to keep their load dry.

M093   Behr air ventilator. This curious metal box sat incongruously above the windscreen and facilitated air circulation on pre-March 1955 Transporters. Condensation and misting were a big problem with the Barn Door model.

M113   Opening windows at the front. Undoubtedly a more drastic means of controlling condensation, this popular accessory was particularly useful in countries where the climate was either particularly hot or predominantly sultry. Many a modern-day owner of a first generation Transporter will add such windows (now known as Safari Windows) to their wish list!

M130   Micro Bus De Luxe without either a canvas sunroof or plexiglas skylights.

M161   Sliding Door – on one side for the Delivery Van (M162 had sliding doors both sides).

M181   Chrome hubcaps.

M200   Pick-up with extended steel platform – from October 1958.

M201   Pick-up with extended wooden platform – from October 1958.

M620   12-volt electrical system – standard for the last year of first generation Transporter production.

During the 1960s Volkswagen of America went more than a little way to promote the optional extras available for the given model in whatever range it was promoting. The following extract taken from a 1964 brochure luxuriating in the single title word of 'Spacious' concentrates mainly on the 'De Luxe Station Wagen':

'Whitewall tires; Hinged side windows; Electrically operated roof ventilator; Split front seat; Retractable step; Wing doors on both sides; Sliding sunroof available on Standard model; Sliding window in the roof-high driving cab partition; second outside mirror; Both models also available without seats in the passenger compartment; 12V System.'

▲ **Delivery Van with sliding doors both sides.** *(RC)*

▼ **Pick-up with extended wooden platform.** *(BS)*

From optional extras to *sonderausführungen*

Just for a moment ignore the rise of the Micro Bus and its De Luxe counterpart, and the valuable contribution these models made to overall Transporter production. Instead concentrate on the *sonderausführungen* or special models and their determining role in the commercial vehicle story. Nordhoff may have had his mind firmly fixed on creating an all-embracing range of everything from delivery vans through to large passenger carrying 'cars', but he didn't overlook the needs of the few. Special packs, altogether a different beast from items listed as extra equipment (which could, indeed, also be added to a special model in many instances), made their debut as early as 1951. A decade later the variety was nearly infinite, with Volkswagen listing over 130 options for buyers in the Fatherland and as many as 80 for right-hand-drive markets, principally Britain. Such diversity was undoubtedly particularly important in the Transporter's success story, even though it would have been impossible for Volkswagen to build each and every variant alongside the mainstream models. Yes, some specials were developed and built in-house – the Ambulance, for instance, not classified as a special but nevertheless a typical niche market product, was first put together by the coachbuilders Miesen until the point was reached where Volkswagen wished to produce it in-house. Many options were simply too specialist in their nature to go anywhere other than a coachbuilder.

One special more than all others deserves a fleeting mention at this juncture. Volkswagen didn't build Campers in the lifetime of the first generation Transporter, or for that matter the second, third, or fourth generations, but it didn't take long for the German firm of Westfalia to partner-up with Wolfsburg to produce such a vehicle. When brochures were printed promoting the Camper, only those in the know would have appreciated that another special was being referred to. However, that's a tale worthy of its own chapter in the Transporter story. Instead, spare a moment to indulge in the inventiveness of the 1950s copywriter charged with the task of making businesses aware of what was on offer:

The VW Pick-up Truck is particularly adaptable to different trade requirements. Here are some ideas:

'Glaziers' Pick-up – with one type of pane carrying frame.
'Mobile store and exhibition truck: brings your shop to your customers.
'Pick-up with swivelling extension ladder – for street lamp servicing, tree trimming, checking overhead cables, bill-posting, fixing neon advertising and many other overhead jobs.
'Pick-up truck with jinker – for trailing loads: pipes, scaffolding, lumber masts, boring rods, ladders.
'... just a few of the thousand and one conversions that will meet your special needs just the way you want. Your dealer will be pleased to advise you.'

More succinct, and, let's be honest, considerably more truthful when it comes to the little matter of the number of 'conversions' on offer, was the following observation:

The VW Pick-up Truck is particularly adaptable to different trade requirements. Every dealer has a file of practical variations...'

And so they did, while the British version of the in-house magazine, *VW Transport*, allocated space in a 1963 edition to list everything that was available under the heading 'Special Models – Special Bodies – Special Equipment', which, accompanied by a cavalcade of photographs illustrating some of the models listed, told Volkswagen's story particularly well:

'VW Commercials for every purpose – just the right size – 80 versions too, well conceived and well-made – special vehicles of proven excellence for speedy transportation of articles of every description – tested hundred of thousands of times in practice – and praised accordingly.
'VW Commercials à la carte – Which type would you like? Here is a "menu" giving you 80 possibilities – from the standard models produced by the factory – to the special models produced in Germany by firms recommended by us.'

Although to list all 80 variations might be considered the task of a specification guide, such is the importance of the special models in the success of the Volkswagen Transporter that a reasonable percentage are worth mentioning. For instance, the Delivery Van could be requested from any British dealership as a Mobile Shop and Delivery Van, with shelves, counter and folding awning; a Display Van; a Cinema and Loudspeaker Van; an Insulated Van; a Refrigerator Van with compressor refrigeration unit; a Mobile Workshop; a Fire Truck (with German equipment); with special equipment for carrying meat etc; with Dry Powder fire-extinguishing equipment; with special fittings for carrying blood plasma; and so on.

Continued on page 98 ▼

It has been possible to collate a pictorial treasure-trove of special models from various sources, from mainstream *sonderausführungen* to the decidedly obscure! The inclusion of material from an early brochure dedicated to the variety of purposes to which a Transporter might be put has increased the scope of this section considerably. Note, however, that the preface to this extremely rare document runs as follows: 'The Volkswagen Company does not deliver the special bodies and equipment shown in this folder, as modern and efficient Volkswagen mass production must be based on the needs of many, not of the few. Your local Volkswagen Dealer and his specially trained personnel will be only too glad, however, to give you practical suggestions as to how you can increase the efficiency of your VW Transporter for your individual needs and to give you the names of reliable firms that can make the alterations for you.' *(below BS)*

▶ The signwriting on the side – 'Volkswagen, Porschewagen – Spare Parts Service' – indicates that this is a mobile spares vehicle. The Delivery Van is racked out to hold a large stock of parts, and has a wonderful extending canopy, presumably designed to keep the customers/mechanics dry whilst waiting for the right spare to be located. *(BS)*

◀ **Pick-up-based livestock carrier.** *(BS)*

◄ Mobile Kitchen – the sign on the left-hand door reads: 'Liquid Gas, economical, cheap, clean, quick, and safe'. *(BS)*

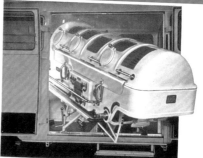

▶ Red Cross 'Iron Lung' vehicle. *(BS)*

▲ Delivery Van-based livestock carrier. (BS)

◀ Pick-up-based Furniture Transporter.
The signwriting reads: 'Hausmann Brothers,
Cologne. Piano and furniture transport',
and, sure enough, the two men depicted are
manhandling a piano. (BS)

◀ Pick-up with extending ladder and Delivery Vans fitted with 'radio' communications. *(BS)*

▶ The vehicle at the top left of the image is a mobile workshop orientated to the farming industry. The information board indicates that for every farming co-operative, here was a proven way to repair farming machinery either in the farmyard or in the field, as the Transporter was both 'Cheap and Fast'. The other two pictures are of a Transporter designed as a promotional vehicle for the sale of electric milking machines – 'freely at your disposal', proclaims the accompanying board! *(BS)*

▶ Kitchenware salesman's
mobile showroom. (BS)

◀ Pick-up cleverly adapted
to carry ladders without
impinging on the load
platform. Clearly intended
for use in the construction
industry. (BS)

▲ A combination of signwritten promotional vehicles used for deliveries, and a mobile projection room and cinema. (BS)

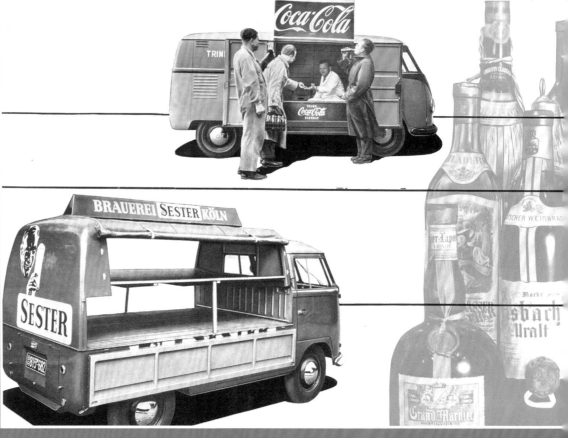

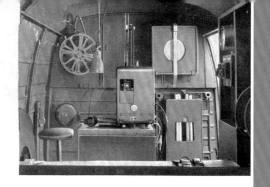

◀ Delivery Vans and Pick-ups adapted to carry soft drinks for sale. Note how the Coca-Cola vendor has to serve from a seated position. It appears that the Pick-up conversions simply bolt onto the platform. The anomaly of the retention of rearward vision from the cab may be explained in terms of the driver needing to see his stock. (BS)

▲ Delivery Van adapted for use by surveyors. The roof rack houses their ranging rods and other kit. Note how it has a tray underneath, shaped to the roof. (BS)

▶ Pick-up adapted to carry sheets of glass. (BS)

▶ Delivery Vans and Pick-ups designed for bakers. (BS)

◀ Mobile milk sales vehicle and inspection/testing Transporter for agricultural produce: it would appear that the milk van had a carrying tank at the back, and that milk could be bottled as required through the machinery that can be seen. Although the true purpose of the other van is unclear, it is emblazoned with Germany's official crest, while the visible lettering reads 'German Agricultural…' . (BS)

◀ Mobile radio transmitter. Obviously the mast could be raised or lowered by the winding handle. *(BS)*

▶ A variation (with awning) on the mobile grocer's shop theme. *(BS)*

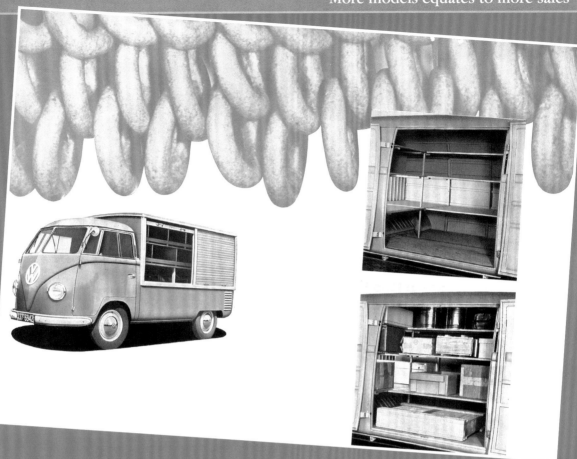

▶ Storage unit built onto a Pick-up. *(BS)*

◀ Another storage unit, plus what looks like a butcher's van – a vehicle which certainly wouldn't meet current EU regulations! *(BS)*

◀ Accident Investigation unit. The most interesting features of this vehicle, fitted with a ladder and platform to make walking on the roof practical, is that it has been allocated the Micro Bus De Luxe's full-width dashboard (MO54) and a tailgate with a rear window (MO53). *(BS)*

▶ This adapted Kombi might best be described as a mobile incident room for police or other official usage. *(BS)*

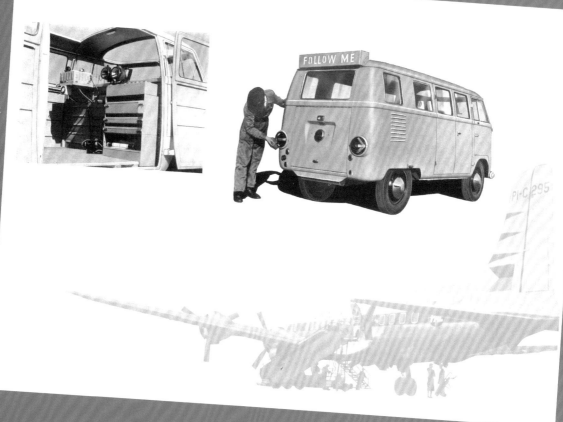

▶ Airport runway vehicle – a 'Follow Me' truck. Note the rear lights with big arrows, presumably so the pilot could see them. Also note large areas of glass roof, presumably so that the driver could manoeuvre his way under wings etc and also see any planes that might be above him. *(BS)*

◀ Aircraft maintenance support vehicle. The Esso logos give the game away that the vehicle's primary purpose was oil replenishment. Note the particularly neat storage arrangement for the ladder. *(BS)*

Volkswagen-Transporter
für jede Branche, für jeden Zweck

1   VW-Neunsitzer „Sondermodell"

2   VW-Neunsitzer

3   VW-Campingwagen

4   VW-Krankenwagen

5   VW-Feuerlöschfahrzeug TSF (T)

6   VW-Kombi als Verkehrsunfallwagen

7   VW-Tiefkühl-Transporter mit Kältemaschine

8   VW-Großraum-Verkaufswagen

11   VW-Pritschenwagen mit Drehleiteraufbau

12   VW-Pritschenwagen mit hydraulischer Hebebühne

Reise, Camping, Zubringerdienst, Krankentransport, Erste Hilfe, Brand- und Katastrophenschutz, Polizeieinsatz, Tiefkühlkette, Lebensmittelhandel, ambulantes Gewerbe, Neon- und Gebäudereinigung, Straßenbeleuchtung und Baumpflege, Langmaterialtransport: Es gibt fast nichts, wofür es einen Volkswagen-Transporter nicht gibt

VW-Pritschenwagen mit Doppelkabine und Langmaterialanhänger

9   VW-Pritschenwagen mit Kippeinrichtung

10   VW-Tieflader

VW-Pritschenwagen mit Langmaterial- und Stückgutanhänger

▶ Mobile Post Office.

▼ Special shelving and storage for bakers.

▲ Volkswagen's own archive of images also includes an array of special models: Pick-up with trailer to carry long pipes or poles.

▶ Double Cab breakdown vehicle. The full wording on the side reads '*Schnell zur Stelle: VW-Kundendienst*', which literally translates as 'Quick to the place – VW Customer Service', and is probably best interpreted as 'We get there fast'. Research indicates that in the early 1960s at least, Volkswagen supplied these vehicles to main dealers fully equipped and signwritten.

▶ Nine Pick-up-based display buses suggest an exhibition of some significance. Enthusiasts would delight in seeing such a line-up today. *(BS)*

◄ Post Office Kombi with large parcel rack.

▼ Delivery Van fitted with loudspeakers and lamps.

▲ A new and a slightly older signwritten mobile service unit. The older Transporter is bringing up the rear. Note the bullet-style indicators. *(BS)*

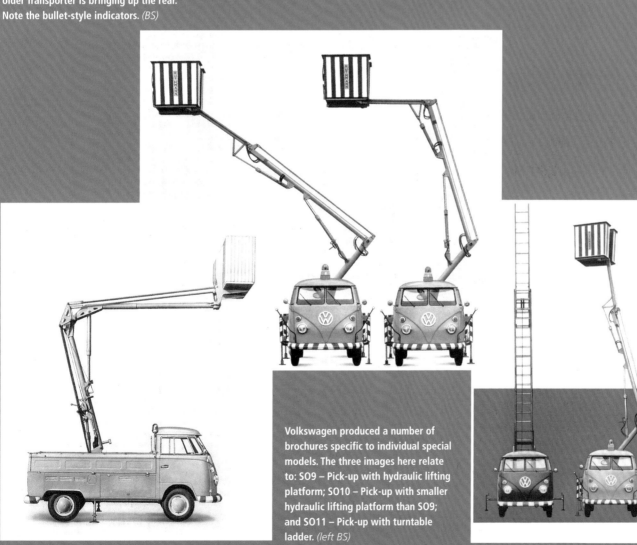

Volkswagen produced a number of brochures specific to individual special models. The three images here relate to: SO9 – Pick-up with hydraulic lifting platform; SO10 – Pick-up with smaller hydraulic lifting platform than SO9; and SO11 – Pick-up with turntable ladder. *(left BS)*

The first generation Transporter Ambulance: these images are readily available from Volkswagen for modern-day journalists and are not necessarily the period pieces they appear to be.

▶ A wide variety of vehicles were produced for the emergency services, which might be described as special models but are nevertheless worthy of a class of their own. This Ambulance is fitted with river or sea rescue equipment.

▲ **continued from page 77**

Highlights of the Pick-up specials included versions without side boards; with an hydraulic service tower; with a swivelling extension ladder; with hydraulic tipping gear; with a box body; with a jinker; and with a box-type jinker.

Amongst the Kombi options were some real gems, including a workshop; one 'with removable camping equipment Mosaic' (a term used in Germany which in Britain would be rendered as 'kit'; see below); a crew truck for firefighting; a Police Van (for accident response, traffic control, radar equipment, special investigation or prisoner transport); a mobile office; with special equipment as an emergency ambulance; an emergency service truck, an expedition vehicle; and so on.

▼ An official Volkswagen publicity shot of an Ambulance dating from after March 1955 and before June 1960.

Two images of the Transporter in Police service. The component parts of optional equipment pack M160 – Bosch siren and blue flashing light – are easily discernible in the colour picture.

Curiously the Micro Bus could be specified with some seemingly workaday fittings. Perhaps the fact that one version, with special equipment, was a mobile bank demanded full headlining as part of the package! Others included a version with a glass partition between cab and passenger compartment; versions without seats as either a cable repair van or a radio detection van; a school bus; and a control vehicle for firefighters and civic authorities.

The Micro Bus De Luxe could be specified with the same glass partition between the cab and passenger compartment, undoubtedly a device to separate chauffeurs from the rich but not necessarily famous. Otherwise, the list was somewhat limited and restricted to gizmos such as 'two electric fans in special ventilation system'.

In Germany the special vehicles were designated with an SO code during the course of 1956/7, and dealership catalogues not only listed all the SO options available but also provided full details of what they entailed, together, where appropriate, with the pedigree of the *Karosserie* authorised to carry out the work on Volkswagen's behalf. Eager to accommodate all enquiries, Nordhoff's team provided dealers with a list of 'possibilities', vehicles not yet constructed but which could easily be prepared should the occasion arise. Again, to give every SO variant would be inappropriate, but it is well worth listing a selection of the more interesting ones, which included:

SO1   Mobile Shop
SO2   High Roofed mobile shop
SO7   Frozen food transporter with refrigeration unit
SO9   Pick-up with hydraulic lifting platform
SO11   Pick-up with turntable ladder
SO14   Pick-up with carrier for long pipes or poles
SO15   Hydraulic tipper truck
SO19   Exhibition and Display Bus
SO22   Westfalia camping kit, first described as a Camping Box and later as the Camping Mosaic
SO25   Pick-up low loader
SO29   Emergency van

A particularly fascinating action-packed image of the SO3 – Police Mobile Incident Room – produced by Westfalia. (BS)

An array of images depicting Transporters adopted for use by the fire service. Note particularly the Kombi, which would normally be carrying the pump motor laid out in front of it, and the use of a Double Cab Pick-up too. *(p103 bottom both BS)*

Advertising success

Although Volkswagen enthusiasts far and wide praise the work of Volkswagen's resident artist of the 1950s, Bernd Reuters, as exquisite, the sad truth is that other manufacturers were employing similarly talented individuals to produce stylised images of their latest offerings. Although highly collectable today, Reuters' work was typical of his age; that it is in vogue now and has been for a good number of years only puts it ahead of others by virtue of the vehicles he was presenting – equally desirable Volkswagens. This is not to belittle the artist's talent in successfully transforming the Beetle and Transporter into far more elegant vehicles than any camera ever could.

In the case of the Transporter, he elongated the vehicle, making it look sleeker in the process; he carefully restyled any sharp edges (an essential requirement when, for example, promoting the top-of-the-range Micro Bus De Luxe); he reduced the size of the occupants in relation to the vehicle, suggesting that it was larger than it really was; he added 'speed' lines, implying that the Transporter was no sluggard; and, when the occasion arose, he set the vehicle against a backdrop that all would wish to share in, suggesting that purchasing a Transporter would lead to a lifestyle

▼ Perhaps not the most exotic of Reuters' brochure covers, but a useful example of his work in illustrating not only the Transporter but also the Beetle. *(RC)*

unimaginable with other brands. When the Transporter was improved, Reuters incorporated the latest developments into carefully reworked images. The importance of his work is such that no book about the Transporter can ever be complete without portraying examples of his finest drawings – but there is no evidence that Reuters' work generated additional sales.

Whether or not it assisted sales when it was written in the 1950s, the text accompanying Reuters' pictures would undoubtedly deter purchasers today. The adjectives stilted, contrived or simply dull spring to mind when reading this opening gambit taken from a brochure dating from 1954:

'Firms the world over have long needed economical light-duty trucks perfectly fitted for the job at hand so that the delivery costs can be drastically reduced. Following closely the advice of users of light-duty trucks, Volkswagen engineers have designed a line of commercial models that fill this need to perfection. Volkswagen Transporters – a model for every type of job – offer you more than you ever dreamed of. Well over 100,000 of them are already in service.'

Transition – paintings in preference to photography remained in vogue throughout much of the 1950s, although commercial artists other than Reuters chose to portray their subject matter in a manner more akin to reality. (BS)

 VW-TRANSPORTER-SONDERSCHAU

sehenswert · aufschlußreich · lohnend

As the decade came to an end Volkswagen of America, under its new leader, former personal aide to Nordhoff and future Director General in his own right, Carl Hahn, decided to do something Volkswagen hadn't done before. There had been no need, for although it had taken a few years to establish the Beetle in the USA, once established sales had spiralled to unprecedented levels. Where the Beetle led the Transporter followed. 1958 had seen close on 150,000 Beetles sold and the prediction for 1959 was that this figure would rise by at least 10,000. However, by this time the big Detroit car manufacturers – Ford, General Motors and Chrysler – were all poised to fight back, with compact models due for launch in the autumn. Hahn thought it expedient to advertise; not only to pre-empt the counterattack from the home market, but also in the belief, mistaken or otherwise, that the time was rapidly approaching when the Beetle and the Transporter would peak on the back of personal recommendation from owners and localised dealer promotions.

Hahn met numerous ad men during an intense three months of interviews, but remained singularly unimpressed. All seemed to be of the same mould, besotted with research before, during and after the event. That is until he came across Doyle Dane Bernbach – an agency formed less than ten years previously – who had successfully completed work for the VW Distributor Arthur Stanton. Hahn was impressed with what he saw. Instead of presenting a series of proposals, the agency offered him a selection of their work from their existing portfolio – unusual, highly creative promotions for companies such as Polaroid and El Al. Hahn appointed DDB to handle the Beetle account almost overnight, but granted the work on the Transporter to Fuller, Smith and Ross, an agency specialising in industrial advertising. Within 12 months such was the dynamism of DDB's activity that they became Volkswagen of America's only advertising agency. Within two years DDB's track record was proven once and for all. The Detroit companies had indeed made an impact on foreign car imports. In 1960 sales had totalled 614,131 cars, but by 1962 this figure had plummeted to 339,160. Volkswagen, however, stood apart from this trend, its sales now being in the region of 200,000 vehicles annually.

More room.

More brrmmmmmm!

Our '63 truck has two (2) engines.

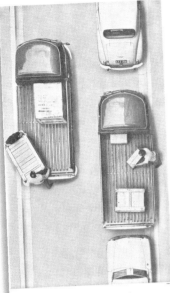

One-way traffic, 3-way tray.

One cab

Two cab

One side

Two sides

Most utilities you load or unload from the rear only.

Not a Volkswagen Pick-up.

If a close-parked vehicle blocks one loading to the rear you need to the side.

Either side. Even when you park on the right-hand side of a one-way street, you'll still load or unload.

Also with a VW Pick-up you never have to unload goods at the rear to get at the ones in front.

Even though you carry twice the load of a car-type utility.

And longer loads.

And wider loads.

So why not join the growing list of businessmen who use Volkswagens and save money.

VW Pick-up, £1198 tax paid. VW Double Cab Pick-up, £1266.10.0 tax paid. VW Delivery Van, £1198.10.0 tax paid. VW Kombi Van, £1199 tax paid. (Additional seats, a low cost extra.) VW Micro-Bus, £1336.10.0 tax paid. (Prices for State Capital Cities.)

Volkswagen Pick-ups and Vans are tough and reliable in all kinds of trades.

What you get is low-cost running, lots of space, and high-speed loading and unloading.

Take the Pick-up. You can seat three, or six, and in the six-seater still carry the goods, tools and equipment you would get on a hydon utility. Goodness there's an extra lock-up compartment.

At three sides drop. So do your costs.

The VW Van has two sides loading doors so two 136-cubic feet of load carries even small loads profitably.

Both models have non-hunting for long things, low-loading for heavy things, and a large stand-up cargo space to you can shift things quickly, easily, smoothly.

Reliable "Durable" They're Volkswagens, independent suspension on all four wheels, too, so they're gentle with drivers as well as cargoes. Synchromesh on all four gears. A wide three-seater split bench seat and a heater, too. The fresh air system ventilates the cabin and can cargo space as well.

Who not get at the facts?

(only have catalogues and like to hear them anyway)

Any questions? Just ask.

VW Pick-up, £1198 tax paid.

VW Double Cab Pick-Up, £1266.10.0 tax paid.

VW Delivery Van (7 seat), £1198.10.0 tax paid.

VW Delivery Van (4 door), £1199 tax paid at Kombi-Van £1198 tax paid. (Additional seats are a low cost extra.)

VW Micro-Bus, £1336.10.0 tax paid. (Prices for State Capital Cities.)

It may not be much, but to many it's home.

Our little house on wheels is called a Volkswagen Campmobile.

It's for knocking around in the brush, or for playing house away from your house.

The VW Campmobile comes with all the simple comforts of home.

You get an icebox, bed, mattress, water tank, hand pump, clothes closet, dining table, seats, windows, and curtains.

Or you can sink a little money into it and make some home improvements.

You can add a stove. (And be perfectly at home on the range.)

On the inside, you can bed down two 6-footers and a couple of kids.

And if you're having weekend guests, we have a 4x8 tent for the top that sleeps two more 6-footers.

You can own a Volkswagen Campmobile for thousands and thousands of dollars less than the house you're living in now.

And the house you're living in now doesn't even have wheels.

Come in and go for a test walk.

That's a Volkswagen Station Wagon, with an aisle like a real bus.

You can walk between the front two seats, past the middle seats, to the back seats.

Without stopping or opening doors.

And if you take trips with children, it makes a big difference. In fact, the longer the trip, the bigger the difference.

You'll be able to get to things you couldn't get to before.

Not only the kids, but anything else you happen to have along.

Even to the 16 pieces of luggage behind the back seat.

Our high roof makes it all possible. (Or-dinary, low-roof wagons couldn't even consider an aisle, never mind a flock of people and 16 suitcases.)

Of course, to get an aisle you have to give up something.

Instead of the usual 9 seats, you get 7.

Only Volkswagen offers this optional minus at extra cost.

Introducing the 2 family car.

The population explosion hasn't caught us sleeping.

We made the Volkswagen Station Wagon big enough to hold about twice as much as a regular station wagon.

So why not two families?

There'd be seats enough (9). And luggage space enough (13 pieces). And enough windows to go around (21).

Also, you'd be able to split fuel bills. (It averages 23 mpg to begin with).

And you could park our 2 Family Wagon in 4' less space than a 1 family wagon.

The problem, naturally, is to find another family with the same tastes in drive-in restaurants and movies, and such.

However, maybe you already have enough people and belongings around your house to fill two wagons.

Then all your problems are solved.

Can it really carry as much as we say?

Ask the man who borrows one.

The man on the right owns a conventional station wagon.

It's got twice the style of a Volkswagen Station Wagon, but only about half the carrying space.

So when he has more to carry than his wagon can handle in one trip, a trip next door can save him a trip.

Or, if he has something extra big to bring home, like an upright piano, he can bring it home in his neighbor's Volkswagen. Upright.

(Our wagon has an unusually high roof, and an unusually wide 4' door in its side.)

But then maybe you don't live next door to a Volkswagen Station Wagon. In that case, you might want to buy one.

The Deluxe Model has 21 windows and a sliding sunroof. It seats 9 comfortably. It gets around 23 miles to the gallon. Its tires will last for about 35,000 miles. And it parks in 4' less space than most conventional wagons.

Of course, if for some reason you can't buy one, there's always the next best thing . . . talk your neighbor into buying one.

If you can sell her on this, you can sell her on anything.

"Me? In that?"

When you take your wife to see the Volkswagen Station Wagon don't be surprised if you have to drag her.

"But it looks silly."

That's your first problem: you have to explain the flat face and square shape.

The front is flat because the engine is in the back. This eliminates a long hood and makes our wagon almost as easy to park as our Sedan.

(There's only 9 inches difference.)

And the square shape holds almost twice as much as an everyday wagon: 170 cubic feet.

Once you coax her behind the wheel be ready for something like this:

"But it's like sitting in a fishbowl."

She's right, it is. There are 21 windows. And if she handles the family checkbook, you might show her a few numbers:

23 mpg on regular. 35,000 miles on tires. 4 pints of oil, not 4 quarts.

If you can sell your wife on the VW Station Wagon, consider yourself a star salesman.

We certainly will.

There are some gaping holes in our theory.

The theory behind the Volkswagen Station Wagon is simple: the box.

Inside the box there is almost twice as much room as there is in a regular wagon.

Now. What kind of dumb theory would give you all that extra room and no extra way of getting to it?

So we punched our theory full of holes. One on the side is 4 feet wide.

(That way, you won't lose your mind trying to angle a rocker around a doorpost.)

And our back door is too big to fit through the back door of a regular wagon.

If you'd like to just sit back and enjoy all the extra room, there are 21 windows of assorted sizes, and one very large sunroof.

And that can turn a very routine trip to a supermarket into a picnic.

If you measured it, you'd find that there are more holes than theory.

That's the theory.

What DDB did for the Beetle and Transporter, for Volkswagen, and by default all other vehicle manufacturers, was to revolutionise the way the product was advertised. Out went the practice of selling a vehicle on the basis of something it wasn't; out went exaggeration. In came simple imagery, often without a background, and one clear message per advert. Honesty, clarity and simplicity were the bywords of the DDB style. Self-congratulatory smugness was no longer on the agenda, but would a self-deprecatory style work on occasion? Indeed it would.

The images and strap-lines reproduced each tell a great story. The text from a couple of ads that haven't been reproduced demonstrates just how clever the copywriters' words were:

'A beautiful day to own a Volkswagen.
'On Monday January 24, 1966 an estimated 262,825,033.74 tons of snow fell upon the United States of America. In Fraser Colorado, a VW Station Wagon that stood for days out in temperatures of 25 below, started up without a tremble. In Scarsdale, a lonely VW was blazing a trail to the commuter station. In Albany, a VW took 8 angry neighbors down to the local service station for 8 sets of chains. In Moline, a VW woman was first in line at the A&P Steak Sale. Up in Boston, a group of college kids were finding out how many toboggans they could stuff into 170 cubic feet of VW space. A Milwaukee junior hockey team won its game by default. On Monday, January 24, 1966, not too many Volkswagens were sold in the United States. On Tuesday, things picked up.'

'Should you pay twice as much to get it washed?
'A Volkswagen isn't any bigger than other station wagons … it just carries more. That's because a station wagon shaped like a box can hold about twice as much as a station wagon shaped like a station wagon. So it will cost you exactly the same to get it washed, but that's about all that will cost you exactly the same. Our VW Wagon gets around 23 miles to the gallon. You'll pay Volkswagen prices for parts. Some 35,000 miles should go by before you have to go buy new tires. And come to think of it, maybe you should pay less for the wash job, too. A Volkswagen is actually shorter than other station wagons. (It'll park in 4' less space.) So next time, why not ask the man at the car wash for a discount. Don't tell him we sent you.'

How to lose money more profitably:

He's a good customer.
It's a small order.
(Your profit is maybe a dime.)
If you sent it 5 miles in a conventional truck (at 5.5¢ a mile) you'd lose more than you'd gain.
So you ask your customer to pick it up.
Maybe he understands.
But if you sent it 5 miles in a Volkswagen Truck (at 2.3¢ a mile) it wouldn't be costing you very much.
It would certainly make your customer very happy.
And that's a more profitable way to lose money.
Isn't it?

The box in front holds all the boxes in back.

We built this pile to show you just how many boxes you can fit into a VW Truck.
(The VW Truck is the box in front.)
Each little box measures 1 cubic foot. There are 170 boxes in all.
You could put every one of them into a Volkswagen Truck.
But suppose you only had one box to deliver.
You could send it one mile in a Volkswagen for about 2½¢. (Our average cost for gas, oil, tires and all maintenance.)
The same mile in a conventional truck would probably run you closer to 6¢.
A difference of 3½¢ a mile.
In fact, one owner put 24,000 miles on his VW and only spent $300 for gas.
The same 24,000 miles in his old truck cost $600.
Another reported 15,000 extra miles on his tires. The VW average is 35,000 miles a set.
No owner has ever paid for anti-freeze, or flushings. The engine is air-cooled.
So what you have is a truck that runs for pennies, and holds a pile.
That's some heap.

Takes pennies only.

Volkswagen Truck owners tell us maintenance usually runs them half the cost of their other trucks.

For example, the VW Truck doesn't need anti-freeze. Or flushing. Or draining. Or hoses. Or hose connections. (The engine's air-cooled.)

The VW Truck hardly ever needs oil between changes.

It gets 35,000 miles and more on a set of tires. (20,000 is thought good on most other trucks in our class.)

Even VW's boxy shape is economical. After all, it isn't every 14-foot truck that has 170 cubic feet of space. Or can carry a 2,205-pound steer. Or deliver a profit on a 1-pound package of hamburger.

Loading and unloading is economical and fast, too, through the 4-foot-wide hole-in-the-side.

Then, there's the gas.

Suppose you drove your VW 2,000 miles a month, and saved 2¢ a mile. (Which isn't at all unusual from what VW Truck owners tell us.)

That's $40 a month to the good.
Or $480 a year.
Or $1,440 in three years.
(Just on gas alone.)
That's a lot of pennies.

When do the tires give up?

Some owners never find out.

We advertise 35,000 miles to a set. Some get closer to 60,000.

You can safely expect 15,000 miles more than you get with a regular truck.

The tires on a Volkswagen aren't loaded down with heavy fenders, or frame, or hood.

VW welds its truck into one solid hunk to make it light and solid.

This takes nearly a half ton off the tires. (Which is also one half ton you don't buy gas for.)

Even the engine saves you weight. It's made of aluminum-magnesium alloy. (Lighter and stronger than aluminum itself.)

And you never need water or anti-freeze. So you don't even have to haul a radiator.

When you load the Volkswagen, the cargo sits in the middle because the engine's in back.

The tires share the load equally.

Even at that, though, some VWs won't get 35,000 miles.

A lot depends on the roads.

Volkswagen doesn't build those.

DDB's authority wasn't simply restricted to adverts placed in a wide variety of magazines which would have attracted an equally broad spectrum of readers. More than mere influence was to be found in all Volkswagen's promotional literature. Two examples, both from the days of the first generation Transporter naturally, set the scene perfectly. From *Meet the Volkswagen Truck*, 1961, published by Volkswagen of America:

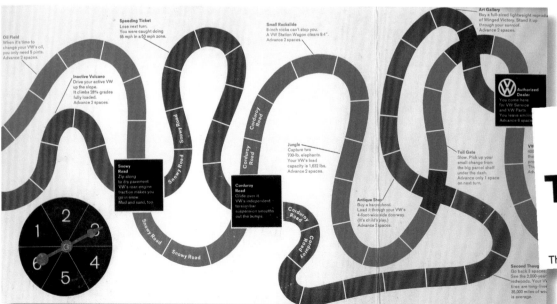

Tourismo – the Volkswagen version of snakes and ladders – almost!

'The Anatomy of a Volkswagen.
'How to design a truck which will carry a big load
yet be light and manoeuvrable, that will be tough
enough to do a job, yet economical to run and
maintain, that will provide comfort for the driver
and make loading and unloading efficient?

'Eliminate dead weight and you solve your
problems with a new idea in truck design. Cool
the engine with air: no water, no radiator. Use
magnesium-aluminium alloys, the lightest made
today. Make the body of unitized construction: no
bolts, 13,000 spot welds. Put the engine in the
rear: no heavy driveshaft. Result: 1,600 lbs less
dead weight.

'An engine in the rear will balance your truck
and provide superior traction (when others are
stuck in mud, sand or snow, you go). To design an
economy truck, start with a new idea.'

From *Can you afford to drive another commercial?*,
1967, printed in Germany for the British market:

'There are very few commercials to beat it as far as
economy is concerned. Can you afford to drive one
which is less economical?

'One of these days you should take the trouble to
work out what a VW Commercial costs. Including
depreciation and loss of interest. And then do the
same with the commercial you're using at present.
(Unless, of course, you're already using a VW
Commercial!) It could be worth your while. You
may find that you would have done better with a
VW Commercial. Or would do better with one in
future. Because it's not what a commercial costs
to buy that makes all the difference – although
naturally that's important too. It's what it costs to

run. But don't just blow your top if you find you've
been paying more for your present commercial. Do
something about it instead.'

To the avid collector of Transporter memorabilia
a hoard of DDB-originated brochures is treasure
indeed. While Reuters' artwork commands significant
sums of money and is more suitable for display on a
sitting room or study wall, it's the DDB material that
can entertain for hours.

DDB's influence extended rapidly across
all aspects of Volkswagen's promotional
material – from what might be loosely
termed as promotional brochures
to fascinating calendar images. 12
quirky Transporter images per year –
undoubtedly the annual VW Calendar
was awaited with due eagerness. *(BS)*

First generation Transporter chronology

Although the range has been outlined and both optional equipment and special models have been referred to, the story of the first generation Transporter is far from complete. In its 17½-year production run the vehicle inevitably evolved – little else was to be expected with anything that came under Nordhoff's watchful eye. He might abhor the way many manufacturers chopped and changed models on a whim, and he referred to stylists as 'hysterical' (albeit in the context of the Beetle), but Nordhoff didn't want to see any of his own products stand still. It's worth stressing once again that this book is not a specification guide and amendments to widgets won't be included; instead, its purpose is to demonstrate why the Transporter stayed ahead of its competition for so many years.

This section also affords the opportunity to embrace a wide variety of first generation Transporter images which have been included either because they depict examples of vehicles that have been painted in a firm's colours, with their logos or other artwork added; they demonstrate a change to the specification or depict how Volkswagen decided to illustrate such modifications; or simply because they have a great period feel, which, for enthusiasts at least, possibly matters more than anything else. Space is also allocated to work in progress at both Wolfsburg and Hanover.

▼ New-look Kombi, taken direct from Volkswagen's archive at Wolfsburg.

▶ Double Cab Pick-up belonging to Karl Meier, whose company Kamei produced a wide range of accessories primarily for the Beetle.

▽ This well-known vehicle now resident in the Stiftung Museum at Wolfsburg is painted in the livery of the Lufthansa airline.

▲ Coca-Cola – it's the real thing!

◀ A particularly early example of a signwritten vehicle – note how the Wolfsburg factory building in the background is partially covered in scaffolding.

◀ The majority of the signwriting is obscured by the open side-doors.

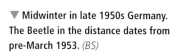
▲ The Midland Electroplating Company. (BS)

▶ Some vehicles had very little lettering, but were painted in the 'house' colours of the company. (BS)

▼ Midwinter in late 1950s Germany. The Beetle in the distance dates from pre-March 1953. (BS)

▲ 'Dallmayr Caffee' – a fleet that Volkswagen must have been very proud of. *(BS)*

◀ 'Jacobs Kaffee' – an equally impressive fleets of Volkswagens. *(BS)*

▶ Promotional signwriting extended across the world, as this Canadian mobile radio studio demonstrates. *(BS)*

We'll Weather the Weather — So Have a Happy Day

Abracadabra – and a VW Micro Bus is transformed into a Mobile Studio in a flash. This is what C.F.P.L. Radio did in London, Ontario. To be more specific it was the idea of Mr. Dave Wilson and his colleagues who looked for the best and quickest method of covering events.

The VW was eminently suitable for this and the Mobile Studio is fitted out with all the usual equipment and a plastic window giving allround vision has been fitted on the roof. Broadcasts can take place in all weathers, and whether it rains or shines it is always a happy day where they are concerned.

◀ Perhaps this 'refrigerated vehicle for meat products' should have been included in the section dedicated to special models. Its attractive horizontal stripes indicate otherwise. Note the tailgate lacks a window, for rather obvious reasons. *(BS)*

▶ In the fruit trade! *(BS)*

▼ One highly satisfied customer! *(BS)*

▲ 'Fire extinguishers – Sales and Service' – a trick sometimes employed today was even used in the 1960s. (BS)

◀ At a quick glance the artwork on this pre-March '55 Delivery Van could have been applied in the 21st century. (BS)

▼ Another signwritten vehicle with a 21st-century look! (BS)

1950

June
Partition added between the cab and load areas of the Delivery Van.

October
Spare wheel mounted flat above the engine rather than to its right-hand side as previously. Micro Buses now heated throughout – previously just the cab was.

November
Large VW roundel discontinued on rear of all models.

1951

April
Small rear window standard on all models, previously blank metal.

June
Delivery Van available with loading doors on both sides – underfloor strengthening plates fitted to this model and to vehicles fitted with a fold-back canvas sunroof.

1952

July
External mirror arm altered to point downwards, rather than upwards as previously.

1953

January
Quarter-light design changed from piano hinge opening to pivoting movement on pins top and bottom for more effective airflow.

March
Syncromesh now standard on all models on second, third and fourth gears. Rear bumper fitted to Micro Bus De Luxe.

December
One key for door and ignition. Rear bumper fitted to Delivery Van, Kombi and Micro Bus.

Engine upgraded to 30PS, this change taking place on 21st of the month. The design was, as might be expected, the same as that of the 25PS engine with differences restricted to only a few apparently minor details. However, the increase in power made a world of difference.

Capacity: 1,192cc
Bore: 77mm
Stroke: 64mm
Compression ratio: 6.1:1 (from Dec '53 to April
    '54 only – then 6.6:1)
Maximum power: 30PS at 3,400rpm
Maximum torque: 76Nm at 2,000rpm

A *Road and Track* review of the Transporter dating from December 1956 concluded that it was 'easy

◀ **The spare wheel was stored above the engine from October 1950.**

to see that the VW, in any of its commercial forms, is no fury on wheels. On the other hand it gives reasonable and sensible performance with remarkable economy and utility'. The magazine also noted the Transporter's acceleration times with its 30PS engine. sometimes Volkswagen referred to such figures – but never the set reproduced here!

Acceleration	Seconds
0–30mph	9.6
0–40mph	16.8
0–50mph	30.6
0–60mph	75.0

Of course, it should be pointed out that Volkswagen stated on a warning sign placed where the driver couldn't fail to notice it that 'The allowable top speed of this vehicle is 50 miles per hour.'

▶ ▼ **The arrival of a rear window in April 1951 was clearly a talking point worthy of supportive imagery!**

◀ As this Delivery Van has both a rear window and, more importantly, a rear bumper, but the 'barn-door' engine lid, it can be dated to a point between December 1953 and March 1955. *(BS)*

▼ 9 October 1954 was a memorable day in the history of the Transporter, for it was then that the 100,000th such vehicle rolled off the assembly line in Wolfsburg. Nordhoff made his customary speech (as the photograph serves to indicate), while, no doubt to the surprise of many, the vehicle chosen to take the honours was nothing more than a straightforward Delivery Van.

1954

April

Fuel gauge standard for the Ambulance. Pick-up allocated a rear bumper.

1955

The near unprecedented rush to push the Transporter into production during 1949 had meant that a few issues which might have been improved on during a further 12-month period of prototype testing were either not considered to be crucial, or simply lay dormant waiting for experience to tell its tale.

For example, although the brochure copywriters made great play of the market research which indicated that people preferred to load their goods from the side of the vehicle rather than its rear, the truth of the matter was somewhat different. That the niche market Ambulance required an opening panel at its rear so that stretchers could be manoeuvred into it, and that this could be accommodated with relative ease, is significant.

Similarly, the fact that money had been spent on reducing the size of the engine compartment and relocating the fuel tank during the development of the Pick-up's ideal height load-bed is of considerable importance.

Then there was the question of ventilation; the addition of the Behr air scoop as a service part in March 1953 and the changes made to the quarter-lights indicate that all wasn't well in this respect.

Inside was a single instrument binnacle, even though, unlike the Beetle, there was no policy to produce a Standard model, a no frills and no nonsense version at a reduced price.

Clearly, all these aspects of the Transporter had to be looked at and a development strategy established. As the Beetle had been given a total revamp in October 1952, with changes ranging from a new dashboard and additional brightwork trim to sturdier bumpers, it was logical that more fundamental improvements could be made to the Transporter if one of the overriding considerations was to generate additional sales. Behind the scenes Nordhoff's boffins were fabricating all the changes necessary, and on 1 March 1955 a redesigned Transporter was launched on a largely unsuspecting public.

Working from the front of the vehicle backwards, the 'new' Transporter was transformed by what might best be described as a peak above the windscreen. While some argued that the result was an aesthetically more pleasing vehicle, others

▶ **The new-look Delivery Van.**

suggested that the loss of the stylish crease in the roof panel did nothing to improve its appearance, However, such observations were academic when compared to the purpose of the peak. Underneath were air intakes that created far superior interior ventilation at a stroke. Although not affecting the shape of the vehicle, the cab roof area was now home to a substantial air distribution box. Almost inevitably Bernd Reuters was charged with redrawing the Transporter to depict this change, a task he performed with consummate ease, pointing his vehicles skywards as if the ascent of a hill was being accomplished and, of course, showing off the peak to perfection in the process. Surprisingly, the brochure for this new-look Transporter was far from devoted to extensive coverage of it being condensation free. Text specifically devoted to this innovation, accompanied by a small illustration, was apparently limited to no more than the following: 'Apart from the Volkswagen Transporter, there is no other vehicle in this range fitted with roof-mounted ventilation as standard equipment.'

However, delving further into the details of the Delivery Van revealed a further paragraph of

informative text: 'Fresh air is admitted through the inlet above the windscreen – well above the dusty road – and directed into the cab, the loading compartment, or into both. This air conditioning system allows the amount of incoming air to be renewed once every minute while the vehicle is in motion.'

A little later the message was put over somewhat more strongly at the start of a brochure, albeit conceding that the heating and ventilation systems were inextricably linked. Fair enough too, as many a commercial vehicle of the 1950s lacked adequate heating: 'The adjustable built-in heater provides ample warmth. In addition fresh air is circulated by a specially designed ventilating system. The stream can be regulated in five steps.'

Or, the same message padded out into a few more words: 'The adjustable built-in heater provides

▲ View of the new-look Kombi, taken direct from Volkswagen's archive at Wolfsburg.

▶ The Micro Bus as presented to the motoring world in March 1955.

Although the new-look Micro Bus De Luxe was less affected by the changes made in March 1955 than its more lowly brethren, Volkswagen's archive contains a wealth of images of the vehicle. Of particular interest is the image which shows the new dashboard – applicable to all models – as, more or less by accident, this also reveals the new ventilation system above the windscreen.

whatever temperature is needed. Besides, there is the special-type air conditioning system that directs fresh air into the cab, the loading compartment, or into both – the stream of air being regulated in five stages.'

For would-be owners of the Micro Bus De Luxe one element of the vehicle's exclusivity was removed at a stroke in March 1955, when a full-width dashboard was introduced in all vehicles. To make matters more democratic still, the new version also replaced the old full-length dashboard in the De Luxe. Text specifically allocated to the new dashboard was virtually nowhere to be seen in promotional literature except in a brief reference to an 'attractively styled dashboard' as a prelude to announcing 'a full-width parcel tray to hold smaller items'. General references to cab comfort were, however, numerous, while even those determined to criticise any form of change recognised that the instrumentation layout was both more convenient for the driver and modern in design. Like the Beetle dashboard introduced in the summer of 1957, the March 1955 arrangements remained unaltered for many years, indeed in reality to the end of first generation Transporter production at the end of July 1967.

At the back of the Transporter there was plenty for brochure compilers to write about and for Volkswagen salesmen to sell. Utilising the technology gleaned from the production of both the Ambulance and particularly the Pick-up, the Barn Door was a thing of the past, as was struggling with a petrol filler in the engine compartment, while the key benefit was that it was now possible to load the vehicle from both the traditional side position and the all-new rear hatch, a substantial door measuring 900mm in width and 730mm in height. Volkswagen covered the advantages of the redesign immediately and comprehensively:

'Two-thirds of the van is available as loading space. Whatever goods are to be carried – you can load them with ease and speed either through the wide double doors, the large rear door or through both at the same time … Wide double doors help the driver stow bulky goods. When it is a matter of loading, say, pipes, carpets or similar items of unusual length, the top-hinged rear door will prove to be very useful – whilst the assistant – well out of the driver's way – starts loading from the side doors. … See how much easier and speedier the van can receive the goods when loaded straight from a loading platform through the large door in the rear. … The tank filler is readily accessible from outside and sheltered by a lid.'

Although there was no mention of the spare wheel in the text of the brochures, this found a new home – one it shared with the only mainstream model

not to have had a cavernous engine compartment previously – in a specially created compartment behind the cab bench seat. Likewise the Transporter's wheels were reduced in size from 16in to 15in, while chunkier 6.40 x 15 tyres replaced the spindly 5.50 x 16 ones. There was also a new design of steering wheel, with two spokes instead of three.

That the overall load space was increased by reducing the size of the engine compartment is fairly obvious and the new capacity of 4.8m³ has been mentioned previously. That said, the increase served to add further fuel to Volkswagen's claim that their product was way ahead of its rivals.

April
Although semaphore indicators would be part of the package for European market Transporters for a further five years or more, American and Canadian vehicles were now fitted with bullet-style flashing indicators.

1956

February
A seven-seater version of the Micro Bus was launched.

August
Instead of the VW logo on each hubcap being painted in the vehicle's body colour all were now painted in black.

1958

May
Single central brake light replaced by new larger tail lamps which incorporated the braking function. Engine lid modified to take account of this change.

August
Stronger bumpers without ribbing, but with slash end. American market Transporters receive two-tier bumpers linked by overriders. The purpose, as it had been with the Beetle, was to align the vehicle's bumpers more accurately against those of US home market products, thus avoiding minor scrapes and scratches when parking. This type of bumper became increasingly popular, with many European owners paying extra to have them fitted when ordering their Volkswagen Transporter.

▶ European market Micro Bus De Luxe with the new stronger bumpers introduced in August 1958.

◀ Vehicles destined for America alongside those being produced for the European market. Note that the vehicle in the foreground not only exhibits two-tier bumpers, dating it to a point after August 1958, but also has bullet indicators – a feature of US-destined Transporters built on or after 1 April 1955. The European models still relied on semaphore indicators.

1959

May

30PS engine redesigned, instantly recognisable by a detachable dynamo pedestal. Bore and stroke as before, but compression raised slightly to 7.0:1. Stronger crankcase halves, sturdier crankshaft. Modified cylinder head with wedge-shaped combustion chambers and barrels slightly further apart, which improved cooling. Crankshaft pulley to fan ratio changed from 1:2 to 1:1.75, the reduction in speed giving the impression of a quieter-running engine.

▼ ▶ Although the vehicles depicted in these two pictures from the late 1950s are sufficiently small as to make identification of specification details difficult if not impossible, their respective charms lie in the period feel they encapsulate. *(BS)*

All-synchromesh gearbox of design similar to the one fitted by Porsche to their 356 sports car. Essentially tunnel-type cast in one piece, rather than a two-piece box split vertically and longitudinally as previously.

1960

June

Anticipating the upgrade the Beetle would receive at the end of July, the Transporter was endowed with a 34PS engine on 1 June. Essentially the same as the engine introduced 13 months earlier, the welcome increase in power came when the Solex 28 PCI carburettor was replaced by the 28 PICT. The new carburettor was fitted with an automatic choke which was thermostatically controlled. Oil bath air cleaner now with pre-heating. The ratio of the reduction gears in the axle hubs was adjusted to 1.39:1 – previously 1.4:1. Optimistically the Transporter's speedometer was recalibrated, being marked up to 120kph compared to previous 100kph. The ignition/starter was fitted with a non-repeat lock.

At long last, European models were endowed with flashing indicators of the same style that the American market had enjoyed since 1955.

November

Number of blades on the cooling fan increased to 28 – previously 16.

▲ Perhaps this bustling image of Frankfurt airport – taken at a point in the late 1950s – should have been included in the section allocated to special models, but its inclusion here reminds us of the Transporter's basic specification before the introduction of bullet-style indicators during the course of the 1960s.

▶ These two publicity images of the Kombi clearly show that semaphores were a thing of the past with effect from the summer of 1960.

1961

July

Column-mounted starter switch applicable for all models. At long last a fuel gauge became standard.

Larger tail light clusters, divided into sections, with indicator lens in orange (European market) or red (American market). American market Transporters receive a large and flatter front indicator housing and lens. Due to its shape this quickly became known as the 'fish-eye' lens.

OVERLEAF Taken from a brochure produced in the early 1960s, this image of the Kombi illustrates just how basic the vehicle was – although the family pictured seem to think nothing of such austerity! *(BS)*

1962

July

Spare wheel recess became larger, while both front and rear arches were enlarged and included a protruding lip intended to strengthen the metalwork.

Inside, Nordhoff finally got his way and the bench seat was replaced by a separate but close-set single seat for the driver and a bench for two passengers. Driver's seat now adjustable.

October

Volkswagen badge added on the rear of the vehicle, above the engine lid.

Whether it's a Micro Bus De Luxe transporting its occupants to a relaxing day at the seaside, an extended family with their Micro Bus enjoying the tranquillity of a nearby lake and more distant mountains, or a Micro Bus De Luxe without plexiglas skylights about to ferry a number of air-hostesses back to base; the imagery commissioned by Volkswagen in the early 1960s has a great period feel, while still demonstrating the sales pitch for which it was originally created. *(below and right BS)*

1963

January

With effect from 7 January American purchasers could specify the Transporter with a 1500 engine. The general feeling is that this engine, borrowed from the latest Volkswagen saloon, the VW 1500 (or Type 3), was rushed into the Transporter to counteract Ford's and Chevrolet's move into traditional Transporter territory with their respective models, the Econoline and Greenbrier.

As ever, Director General Nordhoff had a few words to say on the subject; the following extract is taken from a speech made on 19 October 1962 to New York businessmen:

'As convincing evidence of the fact that we in Wolfsburg take this market – the American market – most seriously, I am pleased to announce that a test programme for the new 1500 truck engine will begin here ... [in] November. This test will be on American roads, under American conditions in American traffic. VW engineers will supervise the test programme but the trucks will be used and, I am sure, abused by typical American truck drivers. By doing this we are guaranteeing that when the VW engine becomes available, as it will shortly, it will already have had a thorough testing at the loading docks of America.'

The 1500 engine became an option for passenger-carrying Transporters elsewhere with effect from March 1963 and for all models from August and the start of the new model year. The 1200 engine was still available but sales of the lower-powered model inevitably declined until October 1965, when it was deleted.

For the VW 1500 saloon, with one of its two storage areas being right over the rear-mounted engine, it was important that the cooling fan could be mounted directly onto the nose of the crankshaft at the back of the engine. The resultant modifications to the cooling trays, the dipstick arrangement and the inlet manifold worked together to create a seemingly more compact and certainly flatter engine, with the result that in Volkswagen enthusiast circles the engine was nicknamed the 'suitcase' unit. Thanks to an alloy covering over the fan, the 1500 engine couldn't be simply eased into the Transporter. As a result, the traditional Beetle and Transporter fan and its housing were fitted on the top of the new block, while both the standard trays and dipstick were reinstated.

Essentially the 1500, or 1,493cc, engine was little more than a bored out version of the trusty 1200. The bore and stroke were increased to 83 x 69mm respectively, while the compression ratio was raised to 7.5:1. Maximum power of 42PS was achieved at an accommodatingly low figure of just 3,800rpm. An intentionally restrictive narrow-bore inlet manifold ensured longevity, as did retention of Volkswagen's 28 PICT carburettor. Ever conservative, Volkswagen claimed a top speed of 65mph and no more for the new engine.

Although an increase of 8PS would be considered marginal by other manufacturers at the time and by just about everyone today, it was sufficient to warrant an important increase in payload from 750kg to a promising 1,000kg.

Although a postcard used by Volkswagen dealerships proclaimed the message '25% more horsepower available', the brochure copywriters didn't really do the improvement justice. The following is an example of what was said to the US market in 1964:

'The Volkswagen's new air-cooled engine has a 25% larger displacement, produces 25% more horsepower than the engine it replaces. It can push a fully-loaded VW wagon up 28% grades. Or drive along the highway at a top speed of 65mph. A single-throat downdraft carburettor with an accelerator pump gives you quick pickup when you need it, yet keeps fuel consumption low. And the new engine still averages about 24 miles to a gallon of regular gas.'

▼ European-specification Transporters were fitted with larger front indicators from August 1963, these units previously having been the sole preserve of the North American market. *(BS)*

March
The nine outward-facing air intake vents were replaced by ten inward-facing ones. (The original eight louvres had been increased by one to nine in March 1955.)

April
Vinyl replaced woollen headlining in the Micro Bus and Micro Bus De Luxe.

August
Wider rear window in enlarged tailgate results in increased visibility for the driver. However, the Micro Bus De Luxe lost its two rear quarter panel windows as a result and became known in enthusiast circles as 'the 21-window bus' as a result. Press-button lock instead of T-handle. Volkswagen badge relocated to left-hand side of tailgate. European models now fitted with fish-eye indicator lenses. Driven gear shaft in reduction gearbox increased in diameter from 30 to 35mm.

December
Cab door-handles changed to press-button type, replacing pull-out type. 14in wheels shod with 7.00 x 14 tyres became universal, replacing the 15in wheels introduced in March 1955. VW emblem on hubcaps no longer picked out in either body colour or black paint by the factory.

▲ ▼ Compare these two images of the Micro Bus De Luxe. The cutaway dangling enticingly above visitors to an exhibition illustrates the look of the model before the tailgate and rear window were enlarged. Note particularly the rear quarter panel with a curved window, bringing the total number of panes in such a vehicle to 23. The grounded cutaway dates from August 1963 and features a larger tailgate and rear window, making visibility much clearer in all models, including the Micro Bus De Luxe. Sadly, with this model it was no longer possible to include the curved rear quarter glass, as the image demonstrates, the revised De Luxe therefore having just 21 panes in total. *(above BS, below RC)*

1964

April

Cab heating arrangements amended with vertical pipe of old replaced by two louvred vents. Heat regulated by lever-operated flap between defroster and footwell vents.

August

More powerful self-parking wipers and larger blades. Carburettor throttle governor fitted on 1,500cc engine as a direct result of it being brought to Nordhoff's attention that people were exceeding the quoted 65mph top speed by anything up to 10mph. The prospect of a Transporter crashing out of control due to excessive speed so concerned him that the governor was fitted. Overtaking instantly became trickier, while hill climbing was more difficult. Fortunately help was at hand in just 12 months' time.

1965

August

To improve the 1500 engine's breathing, larger inlet and exhaust valves were fitted, the diameter of the former increasing from 31.5 to 35.5mm and the latter from 30 to 32mm. Coupled to the use of a more efficient carburettor, the Solex 28 PICT 1, maximum power went up by 2PS to 44PS. However, this wasn't the crucial factor, for the revised 1500 with its new carburettor was able to breathe throughout its entire rev range, pulling far better than of old.

Two-speed wipers introduced. Headlight flasher switch moved from floor to steering column. Headlight and wiper switches now rotary rubber-edged knobs.

Larger rear window for Pick-up and cooling louvres increased from original outward-facing eight located in rear quarter panel, to nine inward-facing positioned over the rear wheelarch.

1966

August

All vehicles supplied with 12-volt electrics – previously an M-pack option. Tailgate fitted with press button and finger grip instead of push button. Frustrating system of different keys for locks to ignition replaced in favour of one key for all purposes.

▶ **This publicity picture, taken in the final years of first generation Transporter production, conveys the message that many different models were available. However, cynics and admirers of the products of other manufacturers might be tempted to count the duplicates to vindicate their disdain!**

The Transporter on the move

Opinion seems to be a little divided concerning the reasons why the manufacture of Transporters at Wolfsburg was brought to a halt in favour of a brand new facility at Hanover some 75km distant. Although Beetle production had escalated beyond all expectations, the vast Wolfsburg plant was not at full capacity. Perhaps recognition of the fact that sales of the saloon would continue to spiral ever upwards, with a continuing inevitability of lengthy waiting lists both at home and abroad, demanded that Nordhoff plan ahead.

Some would argue that the total output in 1954 of a relatively trivial 40,119 Transporters, compared to 202,174 Beetles, couldn't possibly have triggered

▼ Parts of the assembly line at the Hanover factory.

Nordhoff to make the decision he did in the first month of the following year. Others suggest that with a production level of 170 Transporters per day and a demand for twice that number something had to be done. Nordhoff recognised that the momentum behind the Transporter was gathering pace, the 100,000th having rolled off the assembly line on 9 October 1954. Wolfsburg's predictions for future years undoubtedly showed consistent growth.

Historian Walter Henry Nelson, who wrote the first edition of his Beetle book *Small Wonder* at a time when Nordhoff was not only alive but also able and willing to be interviewed, suggests that it was the lack of available manpower that precipitated the Transporter's move to a location where a ready workforce awaited it. Of the 35,000 residents of Wolfsburg in the mid-1950s over 24,000 worked at the Wolfsburg factory in some capacity or other. Amazingly, despite the distance involved and the lack of a fast road system between the two locations, but no doubt due in part to the relatively high level of unemployment in the area, quite a number of people also made the journey from Hanover to supplement the Wolfsburg workforce.

Whatever the real motive behind Nordhoff's declaration, once he had taken the decision, on 24 January 1954, that Transporter production should be moved from Wolfsburg to Hanover, rather than to any other location, his expectation was that the undertaking would be completed quickly. Although, as usual, he wished to be involved in every detail of the project, responsibility for the move was placed in the hands of Otto Hoehne. Previously Hoehne had been responsible for Volkswagen's smaller factory at Brunswick, which supplied Wolfsburg with materials and sundry parts, and as such he was a highly capable manager whose talents extended to efficient working practices.

The new site at Stöcken on the outskirts of Hanover was acquired officially on 4 February. It was an excellent location in terms of road, rail and sea networks, and in addition had a ready pool of employable people. Covering some 112 hectares, 40 of which were specifically allocated to assembly halls and the other buildings required in a modern vehicle factory, construction work began on 1 March following the laying of the foundation stone by the Director General. After a string of inevitable interventions from Nordhoff the completed building closely resembled the plant at Wolfsburg. Progress was rapid, and the first vehicle – a Dove Blue Pick-up – left the new factory on 8 March 1956, just over

▶ Construction work on the Hanover plant began on 1 March 1955, long before the harshness of the German winter was guaranteed to be over.

▲ With the foundations laid, work moved at a pace over the summer months of 1955.

▶ 9 March 1956 saw the first Transporter leave the new Hanover production line. Otto Hoehne, as head of the factory, marked the occasion by handing over the keys of the model, a Pick-up, to the VW Distributors Dost, from Hildesheim.

12 months after building work had started. Mass production began on 20 April.

Recalling the atmosphere of those now long distant days, Carl Hahn – future VW Director General and, at the point when he was interviewed by author Henry Walter Nelson, *Volkswagenwerk Vorstand* member in charge of worldwide sales – spoke of the lack of any form of rigid plan. 'We didn't even have a detailed budget for it,' he told Nelson. Nordhoff instructed Otto Hoehne to build the factory and get it going, and Hoehne, adding whatever was needed as he went along, soon had it running as smoothly as a Swiss watch.

Volkswagen's copywriters saw fit to tell all potential purchasers of the Transporter what they deemed to be the good news about the Hanover factory for at least the next few years. What follows, written in 1958 at a time when Nordhoff had decided to add additional engine production to Hanover's tasks, is a typical example:

The Volkswagen plant in Hanover – which went into production in 1956 – is considered to be the most modern and beautiful automobile factory in Europe. Here, the finest machinery combines with automation and traditional German craftsmanship to achieve the

precision and dependability of Volkswagen Trucks and Station Wagons. This is a plant that was truly built by popular demand. Year after year, the great demand for Volkswagen constantly increased production. It became imperative to build a new plant. Today, the famous Wolfsburg factory produces sedans only. Over 2,000 roll off the assembly line each day. At Hanover, the daily production of trucks and station wagons exceeds 400.'

Nordhoff, dare it be said, had been proved right to split production of the commercial vehicle from his beloved Beetle. Hanover had only been open for a few months when the 200,000th Transporter rolled off the assembly line on 13 September 1956. Less than a year after the brochure copywriter wrote of 400 vehicles being constructed at Hanover every day the 500,000th Transporter was produced. That

was on 25 August 1959, and in just over three years Nordhoff would be speaking to the world about the millionth Transporter.

By the end of Nordhoff's life daily production at Hanover had risen to a figure in excess of 800, while the factory had grown to employ in the region of 23,000 workers. Hanover also manufactured all VW engines. Shortly after opening Hanover, Nordhoff had added pre-war premises at Kassel to his growing empire, sending 25 workers from Wolfsburg to start production there in 1958. Within two years the factory had been rebuilt, employed a workforce of 9,000 and was capable of reconditioning 10,000 engines and axles a month. By the mid-1960s the workforce had risen to 11,000, while tasks specific to the Transporter added to its portfolio included transmissions and vehicle front ends.

▼ Although production had already begun the first stage of the factory was only completed in the summer of 1956. Suitably impressive, the western elevation and administration block extended some 378m.

▶ The work completed at Hanover in 1956 was only the start of a massive undertaking for an increasingly confident Heinz Nordhoff. In this picture, a second hall is nearing completion. One day this would be attached to the first hall by means of a connecting bridge. This image was taken on 7 August 1958, only two and a half years after building work began on Hall One!

▼ During the work of expanding the final assembly area, Hall One developed to the west. The second extension – which included the press shop – extended existing buildings by 24m. The area in front of the factory was allocated to parking for members of the despatch department. This aerial picture was taken on 3 May 1960.

This sequence of images, depicting the Hanover factory at work, is bound to fascinate both Transporter enthusiasts and those with a general interest in the look and feel of the 1950s. Many of the images, but not all of them, were taken in July 1957.

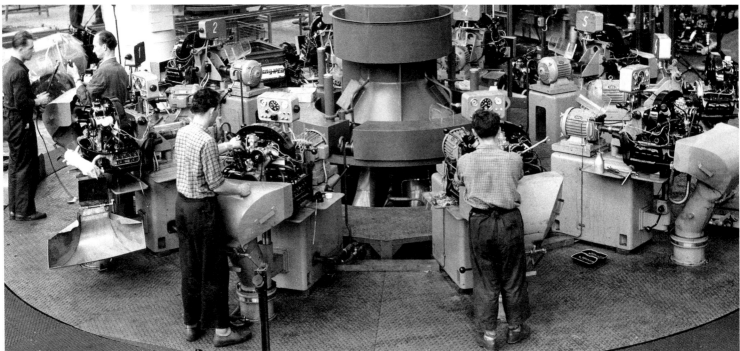

First generation Transporter production numbers

Having emphasised the escalation in production numbers of the Transporter from its early days through to the decision to build a factory dedicated to its production, clarification of the actual figures is required. Mention has also been made of the popularity of one model against another, while surprise has been expressed at the inclusion of the Ambulance in Volkswagen's publicity material. Consequently a year-by-year breakdown of production, model by model, makes interesting reading.

Year	Total	Delivery Van	Kombi	Micro Bus	Micro Bus De Luxe	Pick-up	Ambulance
1949	8 prototypes	6	1	1	–	–	–
1950	8,059	5,662	1,254	1,142	–	1	–
1951	12,003	6,049	2,843	2,805	269	1	36
1952	21,665	9,353	5,031	4,052	1,142	1,606	481
1953	28,417	11,190	5,753	4,086	1,289	5,741	358
1954	40,119	14,550	8,868	5,693	1,937	8,562	589
1955	49,907	17,577	11,346	7,957	2,195	10,138	694
1956	62,500	22,657	16,010	9,726	2,072	11,449	586
1957	91,893	30,683	23,495	17,197	3,514	16,450	644
1958	101,873	36,672	21,732	19,499	4,342	19,142	486
1959	121,453	41,395	25,699	22,943	6,241	24,465	710
1960	139,919	47,498	30,425	22,504	7,846	30,988	658
1961	152,285	45,121	35,950	25,410	8,095	36,822	883
1962	165,774	47,237	38,506	29,898	11,280	38,118	728
1963	174,866	47,891	40,882	31,196	14,764	39,458	675
1964	187,947	48,481	44,659	40,115	14,031	39,832	829
1965	176,762	43,723	44,331	37,933	12,467	37,444	864
1966	176,275	43,084	46,284	30,767	18,790	36,534	816
1967	68,100	–	–	–	–	–	–

These figures do not include Transporters built in countries other than Germany, Brazil being a prime example, and exclude completely knocked down kits (CKD), or in other words vehicles put together at Hanover and exported in boxes for assembly at a Volkswagen plant overseas. Worldwide production figures in the 1960s were reasonably significant. Compare, for example, the total for 1961 listed above with the overall figure including all the factories involved in CKD or local manufacturing, which runs at 168,600. In 1964, the best year of all for the first generation Transporter, total production topped the 200,000 mark by 325 units.

When first generation Transporter production ceased in Germany at the end of July 1967, 1,833,000 vehicles had rolled off the assembly lines at either Wolfsburg or Hanover. However, it wasn't the end of the road for the original Transporter, despite the introduction of a new model, for the Brazilian factory continued to manufacture and export it until

1975, producing 400,000 vehicles in all over a 17-year period.

As with the Beetle, Nordhoff's driving ambition to ensure Volkswagen conquered the motoring world was a contributory factor to the Transporter's success. Few networks of dealers were prodded and poked to the extent that Nordhoff agitated his sales people. However, the dividends of such prodding were there for all to see in the figures. Typical of his style were the words spoken at his traditional New Year's reception, on this occasion held on 5 January 1960 and just after it would have been revealed that production for the previous year had risen to 121,453, an increase of over 19 per cent on the figure achieved in 1958:

'There is simply no reason why Transporter sales should be good in one country and meagre in a neighbouring country. I know that increasing sales isn't always easy, but I repeat what I said to you two years ago – that the period for really high growth in Transporter sales hasn't even arrived yet. Anyone clever will take the opportunity now to prepare himself. I've asked our sales department for years whether or not we should increase Hanover's capacity. I know that I have been irritating about this, but I ask once more and with increasing urgency, for it takes at least two years to implement such a decision … The VW Transporter still has no real competition. … Today we produce 530 Transporters a day, and I am certain that even this figure isn't enough! We must move forward, not in some wild optimistic way … but with the courage to do what has never been done before. We must take what the Americans call a calculated risk.'

One other message apparent in the figures requires analysis. It has often been said that Nordhoff was so besotted with the Beetle that his approach to a possible replacement was blinkered. During the recession that hit West Germany and the rest of Europe in 1966 and for much of 1967 Nordhoff criticised the newly elected coalition government for their lack of positive action to protect the motor industry. Inevitably the politicians fought back and none more so than the ebullient Finance Minister, Franz Josef Strauss. Volkswagen had been immovable for too long, he roared. Following Nordhoff's death in April 1968, his successor seemed to lead a growing army of opinion that blamed him for Volkswagen's downward spiral as the company endeavoured to find a car to replace the Beetle. Yes, Nordhoff's caustic observations about 'hysterical stylists' were well known, as was his abhorrence of change for change's sake. But his belief in a product went much deeper than that, as

his remarks at a gathering of the International Press Institute in 1959, dutifully reported in the in-house magazine, *VW Information*, serve to indicate. Inevitably Nordhoff's thinking related to the Beetle and not the Transporter, but had the question been specific to the commercial vehicle and station wagon the answer would have undoubtedly been the same. Models produced by other firms 'had gone through four or five basic changes during the past few years, while the Volkswagen had stayed the same. "What would be the advantages of a new model at this point? I cannot see any," replied Professor Nordhoff. The aim of any manufacturer was to sell his product and make money with it. "It would be irresponsible to bring out a new model each year just for the sake of novelty. We considered it our duty to increase the quality of our car continually."'

A little over 12 months after these remarks were made the first steps were taken towards producing a replacement for the first generation Transporter, and a prototype, given the development number EA114, was built during 1960. As production and sales were still increasing at a particularly rewarding rate, and as Volkswagen continued to make money with the first generation vehicle, Nordhoff, having given the matter due consideration, put a stop to further work. The policy of improving rather than replacing the model would prevail.

All was well in 1963, Nordhoff declaring at a company meeting held on 7 March that 'on this occasion we should all show the Transporter a mark of respect. It has again proved in an amazing way the unique stability of this business which is still capable of expansion. My special thanks goes to all those who work in this area. They have proved that they understand their craft.'

A year later, however, the situation was a little different. For the first time since its introduction Transporter production had fallen; not by an enormous amount, but nevertheless there was a fall. It was at this point that Gustav Mayer, then head of the development department for the commercial vehicle, was charged by the Volkswagen board and its Director General with the task of producing a new Transporter.

Few of Nordhoff's critics when it comes to his policy regarding the Beetle care to recall that the second generation Transporter was not only initiated by him, but also successfully launched during his lifetime. The success of the first generation Transporter was in no small part due to his determination that Volkswagen would prove itself as the key representative of West Germany's economic revival and that the letters VW would be known throughout the world. Its demise also took place at the hands of Heinz Nordhoff; a new model was needed if even greater heights were to be achieved.

Although this sequence of pictures was taken not just on different days, but in reality at least a couple of years apart, the story is complete. A string of Transporters emerge from the factory to be propelled along an elevated driveway, before they descend to ground level. After a short drive, they are loaded onto rail transporters. The first two photographs were taken in 1962, at a time when the factory was producing in excess of 750 Transporters a day, as well as 5,000 engines. The Hanover plant employed around 20,000 people. *(left BS)*

Transporters around the world

Flick through the pages of many a piece of promotional literature produced for and by Volkswagen in the 1960s and the probability is that it won't be long before something like this extract from August 1966 is spotted:

'What's so special about the VW Commercial?
'...It's backed by 16 years' experience. No tiresome teething troubles to bother you. ... There are more than 1,600,000 on the roads. And 760 more come off

the line every day. ... Just like the VW passenger cars it's backed by a fast reliable service organisation. In 136 countries ...'

Elsewhere in the same brochure there is reference to 'more than 8,000 workshops all over the world.' From humble beginnings – Nordhoff's early days at the helm, despite pre-war Nazi pretensions, cannot be described as anything else – Volkswagen had

▼ **Never manufactured in America, Transporters were exported en-masse...** *(BS)*

▲ The Volkswagen Transporter made its way to the Far East... *(BS)*

◀ ...and to the Middle East... *(BS)*

▼ ...and to the West Indies. *(BS)*

WITHOUT VW SERVICE — 60,000 MILES WITHOUT REPAIR

In Bridgetown, capital of the West Indian island of Barbados, this VW transporter has covered 60,000 miles without the engine being overhauled, cleaned or repaired. As an experiment this is, of course, a remarkable performance, but don't forget — we built up the worldwide VW Service Organization so that all our cars can receive the specified maintenance

▲ ...and on arrival in the United States were quickly unloaded as potential purchasers eagerly awaited their arrival in the showrooms. *(BS)*

mushroomed into a multinational organisation. If Nordhoff planned the Beetle to be an ambassador for German industry, as well as a valuable revenue earner for company and country, which he most certainly did, it goes without saying that where the Beetle led, his creation – the Transporter – was bound to follow.

Ample evidence has already been proffered in the form of extracts from literature specific to US customers to confirm that the country was initially a prime target for Volkswagen expansion and subsequently a mainstay of both Beetle and Transporter sales. Such was the importance of the American market that it is possible to catalogue a whole series of developments made to the Transporter specifically for US buyers, at least initially. Included in this list are two-tier bumpers and attendant overriders, bullet-shaped and fish-eye indicators, and even something as major as the 1500 engine.

Before and during the course of 1952 no more than ten Transporters had made their way across the Atlantic to America. When in 1953 only 33 examples were sold, followed in 1954 by a languid 271, the prospects for Volkswagen looked bleak verging on hopeless. However, up to this point the Beetle too had struggled. With the right personnel behind the wheel targeting locations and driving sales, all was

set to change. In 1955 as many as 2,021 Transporters were sold, more than seven times the number of the previous year, and this pattern was set to continue. 1956 saw 5,233 sales, 1957 14,721, with a further leap to 25,268 despatched to American owners the following year. By 1960 the 30,000 mark per annum had been easily achieved with 31,337 Transporters sold. In the last full year of first generation Transporter production in 1966, sales amounted to 40,198 vehicles, second only to the total of 41,051 achieved in 1964.

Being somewhat partisan, a word or two concerning the British market cannot be omitted, despite its relatively insignificant position in the larger picture of Volkswagen exports. Volkswagen Motors of Great Britain made a loss in 1953, its first year of operation. Well short of 1,000 Beetles were sold. As for the Transporter, it was 1954 before it had any impact. 827 vehicles were imported, to be followed by 1,054 the following year. Only with the new decade was there a significant increase. From the 1,242 Transporters sold in 1959, 3,029 made their way onto British roads in 1960. A peak of 3,800 sales was achieved in 1964 before first generation figures ebbed to 2,999 in 1965 and 3,251 the following year, the last full 12 months of production.

▲ Lest we forget! Germany conquered Britain with the Beetle initially – but the Transporter wasn't far behind. *(BS)*

◀ A delightful period image showing how labour intensive the process of shipping and receiving delivery of a fleet of Volkswagens was. *(BS)*

▶ This cheery image depicts the Micro Bus De Luxe in Paris – or could that be Blackpool?

In 1950 exports were also made to Austria, Belgium, Brazil, Denmark, the Netherlands, Portugal, the Saar territory (at the time separated from Germany), Sweden, Switzerland and Uruguay, not forgetting the two Transporters delivered to the USA and one to Finland. By 1954 the number of countries invaded by German Volkswagens had reached 94 (a decade later that had increased again to the magical 136 already mentioned). The number of Transporters imported annually into Austria jumped from 22 in 1950 to 2,022 in 1954, in Belgium from 523 to 2,956, in Denmark from 25 to 1,806, in the Netherlands from 180 to 2,919, in Portugal from 94 to a surprisingly low 302, in the Saar territory from 10 to 25, in Sweden from 142 to 2,318, in Switzerland from 237 to 1,380 and in Uruguay from 5 to 26.

Volkswagen do Brasil SA

Amongst the early recipients of Transporters, Brazil deserves a special mention, for this was one of the first operations to be involved with both CKD (completely knocked down) assembly and, a few years later, full manufacture.

In 1949, José Thompson, Head of Brasmotor, the Chrysler Importer based in Rio de Janeiro, made an approach to Wolfsburg to sell the Beetle. Nordhoff duly visited Brazil accompanied by Dr Friedrich Schultz-Wenck. Such was the latter's enthusiasm for the country and the product that years later he would become a Brazilian citizen. Thompson was given the go-ahead by Nordhoff, ever open to an additional opportunity to expand the Volkswagen empire. Possibly the Director General was somewhat disappointed by the initial uptake for his products, as imports of the Transporter were hardly earth shattering in their volume. From the initial 302 vehicles which found their way to Brazil in 1950, the figure plummeted to just 97 the following year, though 1952 saw the tables turned with 495 imports.

1953 was an important year, not for the measly number of Transporters that were imported (a mere 42), but because of the establishment of Volkswagen do Brasil SA, a body with a 20 per cent Brazilian shareholding, the other 80 per cent being held by Wolfsburg. With effect from 23 March 1953, and working from a rented industrial unit – or perhaps more accurately a shed – in Ipiranga, a suburb of São Paulo, the Brazilian operation started assembly of CKD Transporters and Beetles. Although numbers were hardly significant, with just 552 Transporters being completed in the years up to and including the early part of 1957, it was nevertheless a timely stepping stone on the road to full manufacture.

In 1956 work started on a new factory of some 10,000m² approximately 14 miles distant from São Paulo on the Via Anchieta, a highway linking the city with the sea and the port of Santos. Here Transporter production, consisting of 50 per cent Brazilian components, officially commenced on 2 September 1957, a full 16 months before Beetle manufacture started. As the chart opposite indicates, once operational there appeared to be no holding the Transporter. In addition to spiralling demand resulting in a daily output of some 70 vehicles by the end of the decade, local content had increased from the aforementioned 50 per cent to an astonishing 95 per cent. Perhaps inevitably, divergences in the specification of the German-built original and the officially sanctioned usurper began to emerge; a pattern that would continue, and on some occasions in dramatically radical ways, throughout subsequent decades right up to the present day.

Nordhoff's backing for the Brazilian adventure had been justified. Dealerships blossomed, and one day Volkswagen would hold the enviable position of providing close to 50 per cent of Brazil's total motor production.

The new decade saw Transporter production break the 10,000 barrier for the first time as 11,299 vehicles left the assembly line during the course of the year. More significantly still, on 28 December 1960 the 500,000th Transporter to have been assembled in Brazil made its appearance. Manufacture continued apace at a rate of around 200 units per day, at least to the point when German production of the first generation Transporter came to an end. From a peak of 16,315 units in 1961 annual numbers hovered in the low teens of thousands before suddenly spiralling upwards in 1967 to previously unprecedented levels.

Production of the Kombi 1957–66	
1957	371
1958	4,819
1959	8,383
1960	11,299
1961	16,315
1962	14,563
1963	14,428
1964	12,378
1965	13,114
1966	15,138

In 1967 the Brazilian version of the Transporter finally received the 1500 engine. However, no attempt was made in the summer of that year to follow Hanover's lead, and the rather quirky first generation Kombi stayed in production for a further eight years, finally being replaced in October 1975 by a model best described as a hybrid between the German first and second generation models. This model is assessed in Chapter 3.

Brazilian Transporter production modelled on the first generation vehicle was substantial, as the table on the next page serves to substantiate. Additionally, with effect from 1971 Brazil started to supply CKD kits to other countries, primarily, but not exclusively, in Latin America. One Volkswagen stronghold more than any other would in later years surprise enthusiasts wishing to purchase a sound example of a first generation Transporter, and for British fans a right-hand-drive model too. All will be revealed shortly!

Production of the Kombi 1967–75

Year and notes	Production	Additional CKD kits
1967 – includes months when German production would have been of first generation	21,172	–
1968	26,883	–
1969	28,253	–
1970	30,205	–
1971	28,316	444
1972	34,898	720
1973	44,083	1,536
1974	48,803	3,540
1975 – includes months after October when production had changed to new model	53,335	6,060

▼ CKD Transporter of pre-March 1955 vintage at work in Brazil.

Unlike the generally rigid pattern of important changes occurring at the end and beginning of old and new model years, the Brazilian operation seemed to be content with a nonchalant approach to year specifications, gaily interchanging parts from a number of different years. Aided in such tactics by the parent operation in Germany shipping out old presses and dies, a Brazilian Kombi (the name used for each and every Brazilian Transporter) dating from the 1960s would feature the loading doors associated with the earliest of German models, while the original style of bumper matched to American specification overriders was commonplace until 1962. The much coveted 1500 engine didn't arrive in Brazil until 1966, while the 23 windows associated with the top-of-the-range Micro Bus De Luxe in Germany (until a larger tailgate robbed it of such a distinction) persisted to the end of production of the Brazilian first generation model in 1975.

Volkswagen of South Africa

Although it was 1955 before the first Transporter was assembled in South Africa, the origins of Wolfsburg's relationship with South African Motor Assemblers and Distributors Limited, invariably known as SAMAD, dates back to 1951 when Dr Nordhoff, accompanied by the man who would lead the South African operation in future years, Baron Klaus von Oertzen, met with SAMAD's Mel Brooks, who was eager to expand his portfolio from Studebakers and Austins. Brooks got the deal he wanted and on 31 August 1951 the first Beetle rolled off the Uitenhage assembly line. Beetle assembly was accompanied by the import of complete cars, and in 1952 24 Transporters were similarly imported, to be followed by six in 1953 and a further 38 in 1954.

In 1956 Volkswagen assumed a controlling interest in SAMAD and immediately set about a one million rand expansion programme, resulting in rapid growth in the assembly of vehicles. During the course of 1963 the 100,000th Volkswagen rolled off the Uitenhage line and while the majority of the vehicles produced were Beetles, the Transporter nevertheless made an important contribution to the total. Such was the demand that an additional investment of eight million rand led to the development of both press and engine machine shops. Gradually the change from simple assembly to full manufacture was taking place, although assembly would never disappear entirely. In 1966 the company name was changed to Volkswagen of South Africa and further investment resulted.

A typical Transporter of South African origin differed somewhat to one of pure German extraction, as local components were used in ever increasing numbers. Additionally, some CKD kits were obtained from Brazil. Although the disparity in specification was not as pronounced as with Brazilian Transporters, South African models can usually be identified by features such as reflectors front and rear and a flat bulkhead.

As far as the first generation Transporter goes, or at least a Brazilian interpretation of the design, the fascinating part of the South African story came after the all-important date of July 1967, when production ceased in Germany. For in addition to the new second generation Transporter, the Uitenhage factory assembled Brazilian first generation models to be sold at what might best be described as a budget price, branded as the Fleetline. In addition to a Delivery Van and Pick-up, a Kombi with the 23 windows of a Micro Bus De Luxe was offered. Although the numbers involved weren't massive, one source suggesting a total of no more than 789, these vehicles in Kombi style have nevertheless made their mark. To some enthusiasts, however, a product originating from Volkswagen's Brazilian operation carried some sort of stigma, and to a lesser extent this view has perpetuated to today's models. The baby model of the current range, The Fox, might be cheap, so the argument goes, but there is a price to pay for this in terms of quality or the lack of it, an aspect intrinsically linked with Brazil. Volkswagen of South Africa, however, was completely open about the origins of the Fleetline, as the following extracts from a brochure dating to 1975 serve to indicate:

'Do a lot for a little in a VW Fleetline Kombi.
'If you want a vehicle that will do about everything under the sun, and do it for ten people all at once, then the VW Fleetline Kombi's for you. And because it's a member of the VW Fleetline, it comes at an incredibly low price – a price that you'll probably decide is nicely old fashioned …

'How can we afford to give you such a low, low price on our Volkswagen Fleetline vehicles? Well first we import VW Transporter bodies from Brazil. Then we fit the latest rugged 1.6 litre engines that never quit. Once fully assembled, we're able to pass the saving to you…

▶ These are no ordinary first generation Transporters! Instead, these South African-assembled models are of Brazilian origin, available at highly competitive prices. As the copywriter boasts, owners could 'do a lot for a little in a VW Fleetline Kombi'. (bottom BS)

'...Inflation hasn't caught up with the Fleetline. And that means a lot of extra profit for you whether you're bussing people, or carrying merchandise.'

According to at least one source the Fleetline models were regarded as a poor second to the fully-fledged vehicles. Whether or not they were 'cheap and nasty' and susceptible to premature rusting remains as a matter of debate to this day.

The magazine *Car South Africa* had no doubts when it reviewed the VW Kombi Fleetline 1600 in October 1975. After informing its readership that VW do Brasil had little option but to develop 'a rigid local manufacture programme', and had therefore 'adopted a policy of freezing vehicle models at the beginning of the last decade', the author stressed that the Fleetline was 'not just an obsolete car resuscitated in modern manufacture', for it had 'some very up-to-date features'. For example, 'VW South Africa wisely decided not to use the old, low-performance Brazilian engine, and instead, fits the modern 1600 unit from Germany, complete with oil cooler and electronic diagnosis plug-in point'. In concluding,

Car South Africa uttered a word or two of caution before launching into a paragraph that must have been music to Volkswagen of South Africa's bank balance:

'In deference to the simple swing-axle layout, it needs to be driven more sedately than the dual-joint axle models, and firm tyre pressures are needed to aid directional stability.

'The fact that this is our third VW Kombi test this year is an indication of how the demand for this class of vehicle has grown. The Fleetline models were originally intended for the fleet owner as economy models, but the Kombi in particular, has been "adopted" as a good-value family car by hundreds of motorists. Priced about R800 lower than the 10-seater model, it is notable value'.

To put the Fleetline into the context of today's enthusiast marketplace, these vehicles do appear on the market quite often, but as a general rule, although reasonably valuable, they don't command the same kind of premium price applicable to a pristine example of a German model.

Transporters in Australia

Although perhaps inevitably the Beetle led Wolfsburg's invasion of Australia, with the first official import arriving in Melbourne on 11 October 1953, soon to be followed by a further 30 examples, the Transporter wasn't all that far behind.

Baron Klaus von Oertzen, already encountered in relation to the South African Transporter story, had persuaded one of his Australian acquaintances, Lionel Spencer, owner of Regent Motor Holdings in Melbourne, not only to import Volkswagens but also, with Nordhoff's blessing, to organise a dealer network down-under. Cannily the whole package was confirmed without any form of capital investment from the *Volkswagenwerke*.

The first four Transporters to travel on Australian soil officially arrived in the last months of 1953. Although registrations show that only 299 Transporters – a mixture of fully assembled vehicles imported from Wolfsburg and a small number of vans built up from CKD kits – found their way to enthusiastic owners during the course of 1954, in themselves equating to a tiny 0.5 per cent of the market, the future nevertheless appeared bright. CKD assembly, if not a prime objective as far as Nordhoff and his fellow board members were concerned, was unquestionably on the Australian agenda from the start. In May–June 1954, and on the

recommendation of Regent Motors, coachbuilders Martin and King of Clayton, a suburb of Melbourne, began assembly work, albeit initially restricted to the Beetle.

In 1955, the year in which the first CKD Transporter was assembled, 546 Transporters were completed, but this figure was dwarfed by the 2,989 vehicles produced in 1956. With the transfer of German production from Wolfsburg to Hanover in the same year, additional capacity and a greater number of variations on the theme became available. Such was the Transporter's appeal that Australian Government departments took the first generation model to their collective hearts. From the office of the Post Master General (1,200 vehicles ordered), to the army, air force and other fleet owners, the Transporter, known generically as the Kombi, was soon in such demand that the order books outstripped available supplies, and lengthy waiting lists increased by the week.

An atmosphere of seemingly insatiable demand, both for the Beetle and the Transporter, led hand-in-hand to the creation of a new company with the *Volkswagenwerke's* direct involvement and to the construction of a £12 million manufacturing plant. Martin and King's site was duly acquired by the new company, Volkswagen (Australasia) Pty Ltd, in which Volkswagen of Germany had a 51 per cent holding. In 1958, 2,895 Transporters were registered, followed by 3,255 the following year and 3,944 in 1960. In ever-increasing numbers the Australian operation despatched vehicles to other countries in the area, the most important being New Zealand. Additionally, full manufacture was now on the horizon, its first steps coming in the form of a press shop to supplement the panel pressings relating to the relatively complex, and certainly multitudinous in nature, front section of the Transporter. Quick to follow were an engine manufacturing plant, a foundry and suitably upgraded paint shop facilities. During this period local content of the Australian market Transporter was increased slowly but surely to an honest 40 per cent, while derivatives, very much in the style of Hanover, were openly promoted.

Although not in the same league as Brazil for deviation from the German specification, but probably on a par with the South African operation, Australian Transporters came to incorporate features unique to their market. For example, with effect from 1963 the engine air intake vents were relocated to the upper part of the body above the vehicle's waistline rather than being in their traditional position below it. The vents were considerably longer than anything seen previously too. This modification, prompted by the arid and dusty climate, was pertinent to all models but the Pick-up, which was instead fitted with vents in the peak above the cab, previously exclusive to the first stage of air circulation management. To duct the essential cooling air from the front of the vehicle all the way to the Pick-up's rear-mounted engine it was necessary to redesign the cab roof by creating a double panel cavity, which externally gave it a more domed appearance. Duct work at the rear of the cab ensured the air travelled under the loading platform bed and hence to the engine compartment at the rear.

In addition to such functional deviations from the original design, Australia produced its own unique variation on the Transporter theme. At first sight similar to Hanover's High Roofed Delivery Van, the Container Van was a bespoke offering demanding the creation of a Special Body Department, which also catered for the demands of fleet buyers and anyone else requiring a non-standard arrangement. Developed in 1962 for the '63 model year, the Container Van – a slab-sided vehicle with side doors of 63½in height and 42in width, and near comparable double doors at its rear – was, according to Volkswagen's marketing material, ideal for furniture and office equipment salesmen amongst others.

A second and even larger expansion programme of some £20 million began in 1964, while the name changed once more to Volkswagen Australasia Ltd, a public company wholly owned by Wolfsburg. A local content pledge of 80 per cent or more for the Beetle and 40 per cent for the Transporter further illustrated the ever-increasing change from assembly to manufacture.

Sadly, production and demand for the first generation Transporter hit the doldrums in the latter part of the mid-1960s, dwindling to as few as 1,568 vehicles manufactured in 1966, despite the relatively recent introduction of the 1500 engine in February 1964. External influences were the root cause and the Beetle was equally adversely affected. The longer term consequences were a return to assembly rather than full manufacture. However, this backwards step coincided with the introduction of the second generation Transporter and as such has no real place in the current story.

A concluding comment

With the possible exception of the Brazilian operation it is worth noting that the significance of the satellite operations shouldn't be overemphasised. Although, to the enthusiast, the curiosities of Transporters built outside Germany are of immense interest, in the bigger picture the total worldwide production per annum compared to that of the Hanover factory (and in later years of other factories on German soil) was relatively insignificant. Without labouring the point too far, in 1964 – the production peak for the first generation model in Germany – 187,947 vehicles were produced in the Fatherland, while total world production amounted to 200,325 Transporters, a difference of just 12,378, or in percentage terms a little over 6.5 per cent. Delving into the era of the second generation Transporter, and again to the highest production figure in a 12-month period, 1972 saw 259,101 vehicles emerge from the Hanover and Emden factories, while worldwide production amounted to 294,932, meaning that just 35,831 vehicles were built outside Germany, a point or two short of 14 per cent.

If the first generation Transporter-based Fleetline arouses the inquisitiveness of many enthusiasts today, then the enduring popularity of the second generation Transporter overseas has the same effect. An assessment of this model after its demise in Germany can be found on pages 220–229.

1967-79

PART III

Production peaks

Company background and production figures

The man that gave the go-ahead for a new commercial Volkswagen, the latest Station Wagon or Micro Bus, the innovative second generation Transporter, was none other than Heinz Nordhoff. His apparent obstinacy to change models with reference to the Beetle has already been touched on, and the appreciable logic behind his decision to abandon the first generation Transporter has been discussed. His presence and the speech he made when the two-millionth Transporter rolled off the assembly line at Hanover on 5 February 1968, more than six months into second generation production, is of sufficient importance for the prelude to the main text of this volume to be dedicated to it.

▶ As was befitting, following Nordhoff's death his body was carried to its final resting place in a specially assembled second generation Transporter hearse. Based on the Pick-up, but lacking a cab roof, the entire vehicle, including both the front and rear bumpers, was painted in Ebony Black. Features normally associated with the Clipper L, or the top model in the range, were also incorporated, including rubber mouldings on both bumpers; bright trim around the front grille and along the doors; a large chrome VW roundel at the front; and the optional extra of whitewall tyres. As the VW archive photograph illustrates, the streets of Wolfsburg thronged with people wishing to pay their last respects to the man who had made Volkswagen great over the previous 20 years.

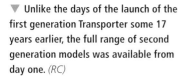

▼ Unlike the days of the launch of the first generation Transporter some 17 years earlier, the full range of second generation models was available from day one. (RC)

◀ **Hanover in the late 1960s – note how some of the vehicles pictured were destined for the US, indicated by the side marker reflectors standard to this market.**

Yet to many the era of the second generation Transporter, known to many of its admiring fans as the Bay, is post-Nordhoff, and a period of problems for the car giant. After Nordhoff's death in April 1968, although Beetle sales initially continued to blossom, his successor, Kurt Lotz, had only one goal in mind: to rid the company of the car. Poor policy decisions – witness as an example the debut of the NSU-designed K70, Volkswagen's first dabble with water-cooled technology – led to tumbling profits. Fortunately for Volkswagen, Lotz's contract wasn't renewed after his initial four-year stint at the helm. His successor, Rudolph Leiding, a Volkswagen man through and through, was the real creator of the Golf, the Passat and the Polo, but only at enormous expense to a company struggling with the after-effects of four years wasted, a Beetle bloodied and bruised if not actually down and out, and, to top it all, recurrent oil crises and economic turmoil throughout Europe. Leiding's Volkswagen was so far in the red that some wondered if the giant would tumble. Throughout, however, Nordhoff's new Transporter was a rock on which the company could depend.

In 1968, the first full year of the second generation Transporter, and looking at German production alone, 228,290 vehicles rolled off the assembly lines at Hanover and Emden, some 40,000 more vehicles than the best year for its predecessor. Furthermore, this pattern was set to continue at least until the above-mentioned oil crises took hold of both Europe and, particularly, America. It had

taken Nordhoff's Volkswagen 12 years to generate one million Transporters, but it took only five and a third years to achieve another million. It would only take around a further three and a half years for the three millionth Transporter to be produced, on 3 September 1971, and only a month short of four years, despite what was happening in the world, for the four millionth to be produced, on 10 July 1975. 1970 bore witness to the highest number of exports to the most important market of all, the United States. 72,515 Transporters made their way across the Atlantic that year, a figure that hadn't been achieved before and, more significantly, hasn't been matched since. In 1972, 259,101 Transporters were manufactured at Hanover and Emden, another record that hasn't been equalled in more than 35 years, just as the 234,788 vehicles produced at Hanover in 1973 still stands as an all-time record. Compared to the highly successful first generation Transporter with 1,833,000 examples to its name, 2,465,000 Bay-window models emerged from Hanover and Emden, and primarily the former.

The second generation Transporter seems likely to retain the accolade of the zenith of production ad infinitum, and might also hold the trophy in perpetuity as the model to be produced longer than any other of its ilk. Over 40 years after its introduction in 1968, an admittedly modified but instantly recognisable second generation Transporter remains in production in Brazil to this day, and shows no sign of being replaced in the foreseeable future.

The figures below were supplied by Volkswagen, but are certainly not the only set of sometimes varying numbers in existence. A different set of totals is presented in the next chapter, and those too are taken from an official Volkswagen source!

Year	Total	Delivery Van	Kombi	Micro Bus	Pick-up	Double Cab Pick-up	Ambulance
1967	73,500	–	–	–	–	–	–
1968	228,290	50,880	68,597	64,411	31,070	12,091	1,241
1969	244,945	54,929	77,956	64,326	31,296	15,152	1,270
1970	257,873	53,759	87,391	71,719	28,340	15,393	1,242
1971	250,802	47,913	87,136	74,850	24,639	14,896	1,357
1972	259,101	56,119	90,712	66,400	27,175	16,829	1,860
1973	246,177	56,866	87,849	58,442	25,490	15,506	2,023
1974	174,121	39,822	64,027	38,700	17,715	12,082	1,762
1975	159,752	39,392	63,928	29,062	14,808	11,043	1,699
1976	169,494	45,263	65,799	31,390	14,014	11,807	1,221
1977	160,986	40,008	55,245	38,068	14,139	12,115	1,411
1978	154,436	40,454	52,251	34,331	12,694	13,396	1,310
1979	85,632	28,569	31,732	13,566	5,667	5,475	623

The road to the launch

As with the Beetle, Nordhoff didn't discount the option of discarding the first generation Transporter in favour of a new model many years before such a notion became reality. However, for a number of years, and again paralleling Volkswagen's saloon, what the design department presented was rejected on the grounds that it was either no better than the first generation Transporter, or possibly more likely would be seen by potential purchasers as a retrograde step. The first of the potential replacements emerged in prototype form under the code name EA 114 as long ago as 1960, a number of years before production of the first generation Transporter peaked. Although its rejection was swift, such a decisive rebuff didn't mean that any further proposals were smothered by the higher echelons of VW's management.

In 1964 Nordhoff and his fellow board members directed Gustav Mayer, then head of the design and development department for commercial vehicles, to set about a thorough reworking of the first generation Transporter. Typically, Nordhoff set a series of tight deadlines, anticipating that the new all-singing, all-dancing second generation Transporter would be on sale in showrooms around the world within a three-year period. As might be anticipated when working under such pressure, ways were found to expedite progress along the road to production, while at the same time ensuring that no corners were cut in the process – which would have been anathema to a company whose reputation was based on quality and perfection. As an example of the necessary steps that had to be taken to meet Nordhoff's deadlines, in the latter stages of the development process testing under the so-called 'time lapse' method was employed. This involved the representation of each kilometre driven as five under more regular circumstances. However, that is not to say that Nordhoff's team were anything other than thorough. In 1966, prototype second generation Transporters were summarily despatched to the northernmost reaches of Sweden to assess the model's capabilities under the harshest of snowy and icy conditions, while South Africa played host to the models arranged to undergo a spot of heat treatment.

However odd it may sound, perhaps conveniently, during the course of testing it became apparent that the new model wasn't entirely fit for purpose. Succinctly, the essentially robust, or rigid, nature of the first generation Transporter wasn't demonstrating itself fully in the new design. As a result the bodywork had to be totally reworked, creating in the process a fully self-supportive arrangement. An inner skin of metalwork, in effect resulting in a double-walled construction, not only resolved the issues relating to strength, but also allowed the designers to take away the characteristic braces between each side window of the original Transporter, with the result that it was possible to modernise the vehicle's appearance through the use of larger windows.

▶ Visually identical to the production model Double Cab Pick-up, Volkswagen advise that this is an official prototype image.

Coupled to the panoramic single-pane windscreen, the new vehicle not only appeared lighter and airier but considerably larger as well, despite a wheelbase that was no greater than that of the first generation Transporter. Better still, the revised new body was actually more rigid than that of the original Transporter, a conclusion confirmed by further extensive testing.

Coupled to the other rudiments of the new design, including the overall increase in size in terms of both length and available carrying capacity, and for Volkswagen at least the revolutionary one-piece front screen, there was also a sliding side door as standard, a bigger and allegedly better engine and a double-jointed rear axle to replace the relatively archaic swing axle of old, all in all the second generation Transporter was a much better vehicle. More minor changes, such as the replacement of the old cloth fold-back sunroof of the Micro Bus De Luxe with one of all-steel construction for the new top-of-the-range model, and the debut of safety-conscious, flat-topped, rubber-edged control switches, all seemed to demand a roof-top assertion that here was a brand new design of Transporter.

However, for reasons best known only to those who set the rules, when the copywriters got to work with literature to promote the second generation Transporter, Volkswagen did little to stress the debut of a completely new model, instead apparently carrying forward the message from the design brief of 1964 of a reworking rather than a new model. Considering that the revamped Beetle – launched, like the second generation Transporter, at the start of the '68 model year – consisted of nothing more essential than new wings, valances, vertically set headlamps, redesigned taillights and new box-shaped bumpers, and yet could be branded as '*Die neuen Käfer*', the New Beetle, this seemed particularly odd.

Take, for example, a brochure designed for the British market. Despite being entitled 'The new VW Commercial', the first heading concedes little more than a revamp. 'The new VW Commercial has had a face lift. Its looks have been improved.' A bigger, more colourful brochure of slightly later vintage, simply headed up as 'The new one', offered the same message, albeit in a more catchy way. 'It's been given a face lift. To improve its looks.' For the important US market, in the normally more than competent hands of the DDB agency, the virtual dismissal of such a significant selling point is even more sensational. Take this extract from a 1967 brochure: 'The Volkswagen family of trucks – Come on inside and meet them. You might want to take one into your business.' With not the slightest reference to a new model or even a face-lift, the individual selling point subheadings – 'They're pinchpennies', 'They're getting soft', 'They drive in nearly undrivable places' – reveal little more. Only

at the level of detailed text does the new Transporter emerge chrysalis-like rather than as the butterfly that might have been expected. Once there, the text is clever, as might be expected of DDB, hence this reasonably lengthy extract on the subject of the cab:

'They're getting soft.

'This year, for instance, we completely redesigned the cab. (It's the first time anything that drastic has happened since 1949, when the first Volkswagen Truck was made.)

'The dashboard is all new. We recessed the dials to make them easier to read. Replaced our open under-dash parcel shelf with a huge glove compartment (with a door). Then padded the entire panel and covered it with black vinyl. We tilted the steering wheel toward the driver, moved the gear shift lever closer and added a pistol-grip to the parking brake. We made the driver's seat slide back and forth to 9 positions – and added a rotary knob that adjusts the seatback to an infinite number of angles within a 14° arc.

'And to keep driver and passengers cool, we designed a completely new fresh air ventilating system with control levers and round, louvered vents, and demister outlets below the windshield. And just in case that still wouldn't be enough, we added one more (new for us) innovation: roll-down windows in the doors.

'It's even easier to see out of a VW Truck. We removed the centerpost and made the windshield bigger. 27% bigger. Then we lengthened the wipers and improved the pneumatic washer system, adding a pushbutton in the center of the 2-speed wiper knob (as in our sedan).

'We widened the front doors and built a rubber-matted step onto both sides of our new wrap-around bumper. So if you're ready to step into something new in a Volkswagen Truck, you'll find we made even that easier.'

Clearly this extract demonstrates just *how* new the new second generation Transporter was. So why it was played down remains a mystery. Incredibly, though, the 'facelift' myth has even extended to some of those who have written about the Transporter in more recent times. Witness as the most obvious example the words of Joachim Kuch, author of *Volkswagen Model History* (1999), whose section on the second generation Transporter opens with the statement that the commercial vehicle 'got a facelift after the factory vacation in 1967…'. Fortunately, at least for the sanity of Transporter enthusiasts, at around the same time leading writer Laurence Meredith presented the facts in an altogether more satisfactory manner. In his *Original VW Bus* (1997) he refers to 'a wholly new model', a Transporter that 'differed from its predecessor in nearly all respects.'

▲ ◀ The face and profile of the second generation Delivery Van as it was launched. The practice of signwriting vehicles continued apace as might have been expected.

All models at once

As might be anticipated, when the new Transporter made its debut Nordhoff expected all variations on the theme to be available instantly, which to the eternal credit of everyone involved proved to be the case. As a result there was the Delivery Van and Kombi, single and double cab Pick-ups and, worthy of a separate sentence or two, a High Roofed Delivery Van. Unlike its all-metal predecessor, this featured a fibreglass extended roof section, presumably designed to keep the vehicle's overall weight down – previously, like most other manufacturers of the time, Volkswagen had avoided the use of materials where both longevity and durability might have been called into question. While the first generation High Roofed model might hardly be described as the most elegant of vehicles, at least the contours of its extended design blended into its overall structure with some semblance of thought; this could not be said of the new second generation model.

▶ A carefully composed picture of the Delivery Van being loaded with boxes. Note the axle load and maximum weight lettering – a compulsory feature for some European markets. *(BS)*

◀ These traightforward images of an early second generation Pick-up undoubtedly sold the vehicle without any frills, today the contemporary action image holds greater fascination. *(BS)*

▶ What better way could there be to promote the Kombi's attributes than by this posed action shot? However, it is worth noting how basic the vehicle still was at the end of the 1960s, as demonstrated by the abundance of bare metal in evidence. *(BS)*

◀ ▼ ▶ Over 30 years after the second generation Double Cab Pick-up's launch, the wealth of images officially available is remarkable, and is perhaps indicative of the current interest in people-carrying vehicles also capable of delivering large items. *(p181 BS)*

▲ Until circumstances dictated otherwise the second generation Micro Bus was branded as the Clipper. Volkswagen's Press and Public Relations Office dubbed it the 'estate car' and placed considerable emphasis on its car-like attributes in all respects. *(RC)*

Bearing an uncanny resemblance to an upturned bath, and coming complete with the necessary undulations in the material to retain rigidity, the aesthetics of the High Roofed Delivery Van were appalling, but since it was a workhorse, few purchasers, if any, were concerned. Indeed, some considered Volkswagen's planned use of lighter materials, with the consequent saving in weight and hence fuel, far more important.

However, in respect of the two remaining models in the standard range of second generation Transporters there was more than a suggestion of concern; Volkswagen found themselves in very hot water – with legal wrangles pending.

An extract from a brochure dating from 1972 serves to indicate how Volkswagen perceived its usefulness and how they could adapt the vehicle to an individual customer's needs:

'219 cu.ft. load capacity – Practical load compartment doors – Direct access from the cab.

The roof of the VW High Roofed Delivery Van is made of fibreglass reinforced polyester – light, *durable and insulating. The load compartment can be fitted with special equipment to meet your special requirements. With rods to take coat-hangers, for example. With shelves, so you can see what's what and where. With folding or sliding racks. The walls can be insulated. Or padded all round. Or fitted with padded strips.*

The first step towards economical transportation is rapid loading. Take a good look at the doors of the VW High Roofed Delivery Van. First of all there's a sliding door on the pavement side. Saves space, work, time and it's safe into the bargain. It doesn't get in the way. It can't blow open too. It can't slam of its own accord when you have to load on a slope. When you open it, it locks open automatically. And then there's a second door at the back which opens upwards. … The VW High Roofed Delivery Van has direct access from the cab through to the load compartment. Practical and safe. You don't have to get out and risk life and limb in the traffic every time you want to unload some small item. You simply take a couple of steps back into the load compartment and you can load or unload in complete safety.'

▲ ▲ ▶ The first generation High
Roof Delivery Van could hardly be
described as particularly elegant,
but when compared to the model
depicted it certainly appeared more
graceful. Clearly a case of practicality
versus aesthetic attributes, as the
new model featured a lightweight
fibreglass roof. *(top RC)*

Exactly why both the Micro Bus and its De Luxe counterpart were given a new name to coincide with the second generation Transporter's launch is unclear. Instead of the familiar designations of Micro Bus and the Micro Bus De Luxe for the passenger carrying vehicles (any notion of Volkswagen officially calling the first generation version of the latter the Samba should be summarily dismissed), they were now allocated the names of Clipper and Clipper L. All might have been well, particularly as the Station Wagon appendage persisted in the United States, if it hadn't been for the Airline Company BOAC, who had been running a Clipper Class of flights to the United States for a number of years. Not unreasonably, BOAC objected to Volkswagen's innovation and took appropriate action to clip the wings of the car giant. Fated to lose, Volkswagen beat a hasty retreat after the first few skirmishes in what could have turned into a particularly hostile affair and henceforth the name Micro Bus was reinstated.

Compared to its successor, the wedge-shaped, slab-sided third generation Transporter, the new model of August 1967 vintage should have been awarded

a catalogue of medals for aesthetical appeal, which on the whole it was, with one exception – the now strikingly underplayed appearance of the flagship model, the aforementioned Clipper L. Consider for a moment what made the first generation model of this ilk stand out from the crowd: a mass of windows, including skylights in profusion; striking and prominent two-tone paint combinations; an abundance of chrome or general brightwork; and the luxury of a full-length, fold-back sunroof. While the interior trim level of the new model was undoubtedly more luxurious by the standards of the day compared to that of its siblings, the vibrancy of the old model was lost.

There was nothing to distinguish the Clipper L from the lowly Kombi in terms of the number of windows – skylights, for example, being a thing of the past. Two-tone paint persisted but only in the form of a Cloud White roof panel to contrast the main body colour, with the emphasis firmly on a break at the point where the rain gutters divided the top of the vehicle from the rest. Brightwork admittedly surrounded the Clipper L's windows, its

▲ This press photo of the second generation Micro Bus L illustrates amply all the vehicle's exterior assets traditionally associated with the model at launch, which included brightwork trim around each window, chromed quarter-lights, a trim strip under the window line, brightwork surrounding the frontal grille, a chromed VW logo and rubber trim on the front bumper. (RC)

▶ Compare this image with the others on this page and it soon becomes noticeable that the specification of the Micro Bus L, or Clipper L, appears to vary. Certainly the top-of-the-range model could be specified without a steel sliding sunroof, for example, but note how the 'jail bars' are missing in one of the other official pictures. (BS)

▶ Loading Transporters onto Volkswagen's fleet of boats in preparation for export to destinations across the world. The vehicle dominating the foreground is a Micro Bus L.

frontal air intake grille and the swage line below the side windows, while the prominent roundel on the new model's front was chromed rather than painted white as with the rest of the range. Even the bumpers were adorned with rubber strips, while jail bars protected the glass from damage by luggage in the load area – but the result was muted, understated, or plain dull. The new and perhaps questionably more serviceable metal wind-back sunroof was small, much smaller, than of old. Nevertheless, the model made its contribution to the overall success of the second generation Transporter, the reason being that the new Transporter itself was a big improvement on the old.

Specification of the second generation Transporter

Although the respective wheelbases of the first and second generation Transporters were identical at 2,400mm, the track varied from the first generation's 1,375mm front and 1,360mm rear to the second's 1,384mm and 1,425mm respectively. Significantly, though, the new model was longer, wider and taller – a bigger, roomier animal in all respects (first generation: length 4,280mm, width 1,750mm, height 1,925mm; second generation: length 4,420mm, width 1,765mm, height 1,956mm; the payload of the two vehicles was identical at 1,000kg). This resulted in the volume of the load compartment increasing from 4.8m^3 to 5m^3, a useful improvement for those carrying cumbersome parcels, but also beneficial in terms of space to enjoy a journey in the passenger-carrying options. Knock-on effects were cab doors that were wider by some 625mm, and a sliding side-door – only ever an extra-cost option on the first generation model – that was both more practical and bigger than the double pull-out doors of old (1,196mm compared to 1,170mm).

Although constructed on the same basic principles as the first generation Transporter of a unitary body and chassis, the use of double-walled (to use Volkswagen's term) or double-skinned metal sheets not only improved the overall rigidity of the structure, but also made it possible to abandon the first generation's use of small square windows – partly dictated by the location of necessary body strengthening bows – in favour of modern and airy rectangular windows. Although from the rear a late

first generation model and the new Transporter might be mistaken for each other, there was no danger of such confusion at the front. Out went the antiquated and once upon a time cost-saving device of two flat panes of glass held in place, but divided from each other, by intrusive metalwork, and in came a single panoramic wraparound windscreen, 27 per cent larger in total. More than any other improvement this new screen epitomised the transformation, its appearance even giving this model its nickname of the Bay, an endearment by which the second generation Transporter quickly came to be known in many countries.

Gone was the need to create a complicated peaked roof, as interior ventilation was incorporated into the design of the front panel, positioned neatly below the windscreen. Other tidying or modernisation details came in the form of wind-down rather than the cheaper sliding cab-door windows, and cleverly designed crescent-shaped air intake louvres neatly positioned on the upper rear quarter panels on all but the Pick-up models. The front indicators, which were now rectangular, were positioned lower down and much closer to the bumper than previously, while retention of a large VW roundel on the front helped to remind all road users of the vehicle's identity. In a particularly well thought-out move, rubber-lined cab step-ups were created out of the ends of the front bumper. Inside, a modern, if by 21st-century terms spartan, dashboard was partially trimmed with protective and reflection-free padded plastic, while

the flat and rubber-edged safety controls introduced in the final years of first generation production were retained. The more upmarket passenger-carrying vehicles also benefited from a series of box-shaped tubes which connected with the heater outlets in the cab and conveyed warm air to passengers in the rear of the vehicle when required.

Although the second generation Transporter was a heavier beast than its predecessor, with an unladen weight of 1,175kg in Delivery Van guise compared to the first generation's 1,070kg, there was more than adequate compensation in the form of a new, and more powerful, engine. While the first generation's delightfully smooth gearbox action and famous independent torsion bar suspension system were retained as might be expected, the introduction of a double-jointed rear axle, replacing the on occasion somewhat wayward swing axle of the old model, led to almost car-like handling, the aforementioned increase in track being a further contributory factor.

Although, to someone not versed in the model range or the workings of Volkswagen's management, the specification increase implied by the introduction of a 1600 engine in place of the first generation's 1500 might appear unnecessarily generous, this was not the case. The reality of the situation was that Volkswagen's larger family saloon, the Type 3, or VW 1500, had been granted a new 1600 engine (and, accordingly, a new name at the same time), and it was this unit that was dropped into the second generation Transporter. Bore and stroke stood at 85.5mm x 69mm, compared to an 83mm bore for the 1500, while compression was raised from the 7.5:1 of the outgoing engine to 7.7:1. The result was an increase of 3PS over the 1500, the maximum of 47PS being achieved at 4,000rpm. A maximum speed of 65mph was still quoted, just as it had been for the 1500, which had been burdened by a throttle governor. This apparent discrepancy was to be explained by the new vehicle's increase in weight, but at least when it came to fuel economy owners didn't suffer, as a reasonably healthy average of between 23 and 25mpg was achievable.

▼ Reliability was stressed by publicity shots of the second generation Transporter in remote locations.

Promoting the new Transporter

The VW Kombi

It has a 177 cu. ft. load compartment or seats for 2 to 8 people.

Despite playing down the fact that the Volkswagen Transporter available from August 1967 was an entirely new model, as has already been seen most of the 'improvements' were catalogued in the more detailed text of the various brochures designed to promote the latest model year.

An extract from a DDB-created brochure prepared for the 1968 model year covers the heart of the mechanical changes in a style only too familiar to aficionados of the agency:

This year's engine is stronger. A little more horsepower and a lot more torque. (Not to make the truck go faster. But just so it doesn't have to work so hard.) And we redesigned the entire rear-end suspension system to make the rear wheels (the driving wheels) hug the road better.'

(The torque issue is one rarely mentioned in relation to the Transporter, despite its relevance to the vehicle's performance. In US parlance, noting the SAE horsepower rating of 57 at 4,400rpm, torque increased from 78.1lb ft at 2,600rpm with the 1500 engine of the first generation Transporter, to 81.7lb ft at 3,000rpm with the 1600. While some might argue that such an increase was little more than marginal, Volkswagen's copywriters clearly thought otherwise!)

A similar message was forthcoming from another brochure for the US market. Again, a section relating to 'changes that you won't be able to see' has been selected:

The '68 is the best handling Wagon we've ever made. We modified the front end to improve steering. So swinging your Wagon into a parking space that's too small for big conventional wagons will be more of a snap than ever. In the rear, we put in a new axle. Each side of it has two joints and extra stabilizing devices. This helps the rear wheels (the drive wheels) hug the road securely when you're taking a sharp

LEFT, OPPOSITE AND OVERLEAF Dating from 1970, this attractive set of carefully posed images taken for brochure usage illustrates the kind of role each model variation might be likely to fulfil. (RC)

turn. … We made our engine larger (1600cc) and a little more powerful. But we didn't do it to make the car go faster. We did it so the engine could turn slower and last longer.'

As a final insight into the promotion of the new generation Transporter through brochures, there's a cab-dominated paragraph or two, taken from an English language brochure printed in Germany:

'The new cab has new doors. Large doors. To make it easier to get in and out of. And these large doors have large, new windows. Not sliding windows – winding windows. A really new feature. Just below the windows you'll find another interesting new idea. The safety door lock. And a little further to the right there's another one. Safety window winders. And while we were about it, we thought we'd add the final touch to the door. From a safety point of view that is. By bringing the hinges inside. And tucking them out of harm's way.

'It has a new cab. To add a touch of luxury to your workaday life. When we developed the new Commercial we weren't only thinking of the person who was going to pay for it. We were thinking of the person who was going to drive it, too. (If owner and driver happen to be one and the same person, so much the better.) And the cab is the best proof of

our good intentions on this point. It's larger. To give you more room to move. And we made it safer as well. By including a new safety-type dished steering wheel. Non-reflecting instrument panel padding. Padded sun visors. And anchorage points for safety belts. For worry-free driving. The cab's been made more attractive, too. With leatherette trim panels on the doors. And with plastic headlining. Just like a passenger car. To help keep your mind off your work. Even when it's on it. And it's more comfortable as well.'

The general reaction to the new Transporter was on the whole favourable. *Motor*, for example, approved of the second generation model's 'comfortable' seats, 'light' foot controls, and well laid-out dashboard. Although the journalist involved thought the vehicle to be 'reasonably quick', he wasn't impressed with the 'resonant beat' of the engine above 60mph in top and 40mph in third. Redemption came in the form a feeling of stability on wet journeys, while 'rough roads are taken in a restrained flat and pitch is damped out quickly'. All-round vision was considered to be 'good', whilst 'even without the external rear-view mirrors there are no notable blind spots'.

The American magazine *Popular Imported Cars* concluded its lengthy review with the optimistic opinion that 'all in all, the VW "boxes" have been

The VW Delivery Van

The load compartment has a volume of 177 cu. ft., a surface area of 44.1 sq. ft. and a payload of up to 2205 lbs.

The VW High Roofed Delivery Van

It has a 219 cu. ft. load compartment, a 44.1 sq. ft. load surface and a payload of up to 2039 lbs.

considerably improved in all the important areas'. This verdict arose out of observations such as 'higher, stronger, larger, one piece bumpers'; 'better light output'; 'excellent driver visibility'; an interior which 'now has what can be called décor'; 'all new heating and ventilating systems' which were 'an interesting surprise' and seemed 'to perform more than adequately'; and the importance of 'negative rear wheel camber achieved regardless of vehicle loading or body lean, and the minimised track, toe-in and camber changes during the full range of vehicle loading and body lean'. Perhaps best of all, though, was the additional comment in the reviewer's conclusion which simply said 'they have got to be driven to be believed'.

From *Lasauto*, in its December 1967 omnibus edition, there was nothing but praise:

'Compared with before, handling and suspension, road holding, ride comfort and cab space of the new VW Transporter have changed beyond recognition … A solidly built thoroughly sturdy 1-tonne panel van with car-like handling – an economical load carrier with high value and resale value. … You can buy a VW Transporter like an off-the-peg suit. There is a complete collection offering a wide range of options. There are standard models and intermediate

sizes. Like the raised roof panel vans, for example, and there is almost no limit to the range of different interiors to suit the needs of individual customers.'

Reviews tended to stay in the same vein throughout the lifespan of the second generation Transporter, as the following selection of extracts, dating from its later years of production, confirm:

'Vision on the Volks was excellent, with the big curved screen, and lots of glass in the sides and rear…' – Truck, *December 1974.*

'The vehicle's heating and ventilating system is amongst the best I have encountered in this category. Starting from cold, warm air was available for cab heating within seconds – one of the advantages of an air-cooled engine … On the high speed motorway run the overdrive top gear came into its own to return a respectable 27.6mpg.' – Commercial Motor, *August 1974.*

'The ride both laden and unladen was very good. There was no pitching and rough side streets were no problem to the bus … The brakes were excellent being positive and progressive. In dry wet and greasy conditions the vehicle pulled up straight every time

The VW Pick-Up

It has a payload of up to 2205 lbs. and a 46.3 sq. ft. load surface.

The VW Pick-Up with enlarged platform

It has a 56.2 sq. ft. load surface and a payload of up to 2028 lbs.

... There is no doubt that for any company needing a personnel carrier this vehicle would prove very suitable in the seven seater range.' – Motor Transport, *August 1974.*

'How pleasant to find a van that's coach built – the Volkswagen ... The doors close with a coach built clunk, reminiscent of the days when vehicles were built in dozens not millions ... The cab floor has a wall to wall rubber carpet, which is very practical ... We were particularly conscious of the fact that nothing rattled. Every part seemed to have been so well put together that the usual squeaks and vibrations that come and go so mysteriously were absent ... and the door handles – Ah! Those handles. Forgive us if we enthuse a little! ... The sliding door is an example of the high standards of engineering skill which seems to abound in the van's many unusual features ... There is good access between the front seats which is a great time saver on small stopstart deliveries ... The VW would make an excellent dual purpose vehicle for the owner/driver who requires something a little more comfortable than the van.' – Hardware Trade Journal, *August 1974.*

Finally, well-known commentator on all things Volkswagen, Peter Noad, writing in *Safer VW*

Motoring in the summer of 1979, when the third generation model was almost upon dealers and customers alike, still found much to praise in the last of the second generation Transporters. Specific to the 2.0-litre engine, the most powerful air-cooled engine fitted to the Transporter – or for that matter any standard Volkswagen – praise couldn't come any higher than this:

'On the road the 2-litre ... is ... impressive. The twin carb Type 4 engine delivers 70bhp, offering performance which makes it much more enjoyable to drive than the 1600cc version. It will out accelerate many cars and easily cruise at the legal limit on motorways, regardless of headwinds or hills. The 0–60 mph time is 21 seconds, top speed is about 80mph, and the 30–50 mph acceleration in top gear takes only 13.2 seconds ... Overtaking presents no problems and I found it just as easy to drive as a car, and capable of averaging the same speeds on a typical journey. I have always found the 1600cc Type 2 a little more tiring on long journeys because you have to think about headwind and gradient before overtaking. With 40% more power the 2-litre has a much greater reserve to deal with such situations and you can make quite rapid progress without having to keep your foot hard on the floor.'

The VW Double Cab Pick-Up

With a 31.2 sq. ft. load surface, a payload of up to 2094 lbs. and six seats.

The VW Microbus L

With 212 cu. ft. inside.
35 cu. ft. of which is luggage space.

Continuing the tradition of optional equipment and special models

Although nearly two and a half million second generation Transporters were built in Germany in 12 years, compared to a little over 1.8 million first generation models in 17 years – an increase of over 34 per cent in a much shorter time – it requires proportionately fewer words to describe all the principal variants of the new model. If Nordhoff's intention had been to preach continuity, Volkswagen's was unquestionably to continue to develop options that would generate additional income. Many were added to the M-code list during the second generation Transporter's run, and some of these are now, many years later, highly sought-after. Of particular interest, or perhaps curiosity value, are the following:

M010	Additional dust exclusion equipment for the engine compartment (1968–73).
M027	Plate indicating emissions, to comply with California exhaust emission standards (1973–4).
M047	Two reversing lights (1968–71).
M060	Eberspächer BA6 petrol heater (fitted under load compartment floor) (1974–9).
M127	Tailgate without window (1968–79).
M130	Micro Bus De Luxe without sliding steel roof (1968–73).
M161	Rubber strips for later girder-style bumper (1973–9).
M288	Headlight washer kit (1974–9).
M517	Prepared by the factory for Campmobile interior (1968–79).

▼ **Transporter prepared for Red Cross usage as a baby emergency vehicle.**

▶ The rather odd-looking overriders on the Double Cab Pick-up are in reality M288 headlight washers.

▼ Pick-up with hydraulic tipper.

M518   Reinforced roof opening for Westfalia pop-up roof (1968–79).

M520   Sliding doors on both sides of the load compartment (1968–79).

M530   Automatic step fitted in conjunction with sliding door on passenger side (1968–79).

M571   Rear fog-lamp (1973–9).

M659   Two bumper-mounted rectangular halogen fog-lamps (1973–9).

Many of the special models (as indicated by an SO code) developed during the lifetime of the first generation Transporter were simply carried forward to the new model. Hence there was both a first and second generation Mobile Shop (SO1), just as there was a Refrigerated Delivery Van complete with 140mm insulating board in both guises (SO5).

As previously, some specials were manufactured by Volkswagen within the confines of the Hanover factory, while many others were converted by approved specialist companies. For example, Westfalia's main

◀ The High Roof Delivery Van factory-fitted with a wooden partition to prevent parcels falling out was developed specifically for the *Deutsche Bundespost*.

▼ The two Delivery Vans depicted are only of interest when it comes to distinguishing their respective roles. The yellow vehicle (rear) was a straightforward mail van, while the green one (front) was for the *Deutsche Bundespost* telecommunication department.

▲ The Ambulance as illustrated in a brochure produced by Pon's Automobielhandel BV. *(RC)*

▶ Loading platform to assist with manoeuvring particularly heavy goods. *(RC)*

business of producing Campers has already been covered in some detail; few people, however, realise that they were also involved in the conversion of Transporters to taxis, mobile offices, police road-traffic accident emergency vehicles, shops, low-loaders, and Pick-ups with an enlarged wooden platform. The famous Dutch importers Pon's Automobielhandel BV were responsible for a considerable collection of specials, while another Dutch firm, Kemperink, produced long-wheelbase second generation Transporters, surviving examples of which have a certain appeal to modern-day enthusiasts. Other less well-known but equally skilled names produced a variety of special models, ranging from a Pick-up with turntable ladder to another vehicle of the same ilk adapted to carry long poles or even pipes.

A skim through a specialist brochure issued by Pon's Automobielhandel in 1976 illustrates the second generation Transporter as a taxi, police vehicle,

▲ Tipmaster dust-cart. *(RC)*

◄ Pick-up road sweeper/dust cart. *(RC)*

▶ More special models! 'The Volkswagen's renowned versatility enables it to be modified to cope with almost any task', wrote one confident copywriter. *(RC)*

ambulance, insulated cargo area Delivery Van, snack bar on an extended Pick-up base, delivery van on an extended pick-up base, Delivery Van with an hydraulic ramp to manoeuvre heavy goods through the side loading door, Delivery Van with a 220-volt generator, Double Cab Pick-up with an extended wheelbase, Pick-up with an hydraulic lifting platform, Kombi ladder-truck complete with roof rack and ladders capable of extending to a height of 10m, Pick-up with special steel and wood side panels designed to carry large sheets of glass, Pick-up 'Tipmaster' dust-cart,

Pick-up fitted with a device at the front to act as either a road sweeper or snowplough, and Pick-up with hydraulically-operated tipping platform.

Taking the opportunity to illustrate a selection of vehicles, mention should also be made of the *VW-Groentewagen*, or vegetable carrier, again based on the Pick-up, and the *VW-Isolatie* container, a variation on the refrigerated vehicle theme, this time taking the form of a large container perched on the back of a Pick-up.

Volkswagen GB Ltd's 1977 folder entitled 'Fact analysis' – something of a specialist affair directed at the trade rather than casual observer – included a loose-leaf insert headed 'Special Conversions', the following text and four black and white illustrations:

'The Volkswagen commercial range consists of 11 basic models all derived from the 1 Ton Van. Of course, that's not the end of it. The Volkswagen's renowned versatility enables it to be modified to cope with almost any task. It's worth taking a closer look at our range now, it offers far more than you think.

'Versatility – Not everyone's requirements are satisfied by the basic range. The Volkswagen's extreme versatility however makes it the ideal basis for conversion to suit your needs …

Branbridge VW Fire Appliance
VW–PCS Tipmaster Electro Hydraulic Tipper
VW–Osborne Rhineland Milk Float
VW–Sloans Freezawagen.'

Unquestionably one of the most touching specials was the hearse manufactured by Volkswagen to transport the body of their late Director General, Heinz Nordhoff, through the packed streets of Wolfsburg to his funeral service on 15 May 1968, and then to the great man's final resting place. Based on a single cab Pick-up, but without a roof, the Transporter was painted in its entirety, including items such as the bumpers, in rich, glossy Ebony Black. As befitted a vehicle built for such a special purpose, rubber bumper strips, brightwork door mouldings and air intake surround, plus a chrome VW roundel, all of which were standard on the Micro Bus De Luxe of the day, were fitted, as were whitewall tyres (see page 171 for an illustration of this vehicle).

By way of both a diversion and conclusion to this section covering special models, let us take the opportunity to delve into the history of the Dutch firm Kemperink, an operation with origins dating as far back as the 1890s. In 1931, having been involved in a number of activities, one of which was coach trimming, Kemperink settled on becoming coachbuilders, their work extending as far as the conversion and building of heavy goods vehicles.

If you're in business, we're in the business you're in.

RANGE 3
SPECIAL CONVERSIONS

The Volkswagen commercial range consists of 11 basic models all derived from the famous 1 Ton Van. Of course, that's not the end of it. The Volkswagen's renowned versatility enables it to be modified to cope with almost any task. It's worth taking a closer look at our range now, it offers far more than you think.

Versatility
Not everyone's requirements are satisfied by the basic range. The Volkswagen's extreme versatility however makes it the ideal basis for conversion to suit your needs.
Illustrated : Branbridge VW Fire Appliance.
VW – PCS Tipmaster Electro Hydraulic Tipper.
VW – Osborne Rhineland Milk Float.
VW – Sloans Freezawagen

▶ Ladder truck. (RC)

▲ Refrigerated vehicle based on the Pick-up. (RC)

▼ Pick-up with hydraulic tipper. (RC)

▲ Vegetable carrier based on the Pick-up. (RC)

▼ Glass transporter. (RC)

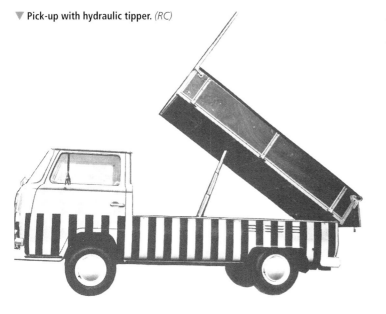

In 1954 they created their first long-wheelbase Volkswagen Transporter, designed for a mattress manufacturer based in Rotterdam. To produce it, Kemperink took a normal VW Pick-up, cut through the platform area and inserted a 900mm extension, changing the wheelbase in the process from the standard 2,400mm to 3,300mm. On this new longer body they fitted a box-like structure, which at first sight suggested a straightforward longer version of the Delivery Van. The result was an almost inconceivable 10m^3 of space compared to the standard 4.8m^3 of the first generation Delivery Van. The storage area consisted of a square-section tubular steel frame clad with steel sides. The roof was made out of fibreglass, no doubt partly to reduce weight, while the central section utilised clear materials allowing natural light to pervade the cavernous, and by implication dark, interior. From the early days of a flat roof with

rounded edges, Kemperink progressed to a much more bowed profile, affording additional headroom inside. While the cab logically always remained separate, the conversion being based on a Pick-up, most vehicles featured a side door, or possibly doors, later versions of which were of a sliding nature just like those of the standard second generation Transporter, as well as a large rear door fitted with gas struts.

From the first conversion, Kemperink moved on to supply the biscuit manufacturer Bolletje with several examples of what was the ideal vehicle for such a firm. Orders then followed from the clothing company C&A and the Dutch Army. Amazingly, thanks initially to the efforts of the VW dealers

▼ The Kemperink long-wheelbase Delivery Van based on the Pick-up. *(RC)*

▲ The Kemperink Double-cab Pick-up. *(RC)*

Dovercourt of St John's Wood, ten such vehicles were sold officially in Britain. Sadly, though, the undertaking was relatively short-lived, as owners overloaded the spacious vehicles with heavy goods, causing bodywork defects, usually in the vicinity of the section below the side doors. There were also cases recorded of broken or damaged front axles. Nevertheless, as late as 1977 Volkswagen GB Ltd listed a 'Long Wheelbase Van' amongst its range of available 'vans and buses'. Described as being 'designed to meet the requirements for transporting high volume/low density goods', the summary specification made interesting reading, particularly when compared with the '1.0 or 1.2 Ton Payload Van'. Similarly, a 'Long Wheelbase Pick Up' was also listed, together with the following details:

'The unusually long 12.1ft. platform length is just the job for those long lightweight loads. With an overall length of 217ins. the pick up retains the unique underfloor locker which is twice the size of the locker on the standard pick up. Also available with the double cab.'

	Long wheelbase	*1.0 or 1.2 Payload Van*
Internal usable volume	*353 cu. ft.*	*177 cu. ft.*
Payload capacity including an allowance for a driver	*1870 lbs.*	*1600cc 2205 lbs. or 2647 lbs. 1800cc 2160 lbs. or 2660 lbs.*
Maximum internal length and height	*147.1" x 74.5"*	
Load area		*44.1 sq. ft.*
Side door height and width	*62.2" x 48.0"*	*48.4" x 41.7"*

A figure in excess of 2,000 Kemperinks were built, their demise finally coming at the hands of Volkswagen with the introduction of the long-wheelbase LT. Records indicate that the last Kemperink was built in 1979, shortly after the introduction of the third generation Transporter.

▶ Inevitably a whole crop of emergency service vehicles was produced. These two images – from the VW Archive at Wolfsburg – illustrate a Police Kombi and a Fire Kombi.

Second generation Transporter chronology

▼ The revamped Transporter made its debut at the start of the '73 model year. All models featured new, stronger euro-bumpers; a smaller VW roundel on the front of the vehicle; front indicators located much higher up on the frontal elevation; and in the case of the Micro Bus L, a full-width rubber bumper insert. All vehicles lacked the cab step-up ends. *(RC)*

1967

August

Production of the second generation Transporter began at Hanover, to be followed in December by the start of assembly work at Emden, for the US market, of models requiring the most work, particularly the two variations on the Station Wagon theme.

1968

February

5 February saw the two-millionth Transporter, a Titian Red Clipper L with a Cloud White roof panel, roll off the assembly line. Heinz Nordhoff was in attendance and made his customary speech to mark such occasions. The vehicle was donated to the German charity Aktion Sorgenkind.

1969

August

For the 1970 model year the US-spec side reflectors changed from circular to square. Although such a detail might appear insignificant, as many Campers from California find their way to Europe this is one way for passing enthusiasts to date the model!

▶ This image taken on the assembly line highlights to perfection the location of the indicators on early second generation Transporters.

Another apparent triviality was the banishment of colour-coded painted sections from the dashboards of all Transporter specifications. These now comprised a combination of black paint and black padding.

Of considerably more significance were the measures taken to improve passenger safety, albeit that it was the arrival of legal requirements to this effect in the United States that prompted the move. The Transporter's doors were fitted with stronger frames affording better protection in the case of an accident involving impact from the side. Equally sensible was the stiffening of the four hoops that rose from the vehicle's 'chassis' to create the basis of the structure on which the side panels were lodged, and by which the roof was reinforced.

1970

72,515 second generation Transporters were exported to America – a record then, and now.

August
Amongst the trivia of annual changes for the 1971 model year there were two significant developments. In what would be regarded as the first of a series of engine upgrades, the 1600 engine benefited from modified cylinder heads with twin inlet ports rather than one. As a result, the engine could breathe more easily and power increased from 47PS to a maximum of 50PS at 4,000rpm.

Whether this modest increase in power prompted Volkswagen to fit its Transporter with 278.2mm ATE front disc brakes is questionable, but to the delight of many they were a part of the specification for all Transporters built after the end of July 1970. For those not entirely au fait with the development of the Beetle, the 1,500cc model (introduced in August 1966) was the first such car to be fitted with discs, provided it wasn't destined for export to America, where drums remained in use throughout. Perhaps inevitably, one or two eyebrows were raised regarding the four-year wait for purchasers of the Transporter.

The five-stud wheels of the Transporter were also altered, the latest models losing the charming domed hubcaps of earlier years in favour of the flat type offered on the Beetle and other members of the Volkswagen family. Similarly, instead of the traditional four elongated ventilation slots between the rim and the centre of the wheel there was now a series of round holes punched through the steel. Finally, an increase in size also occurred, from the by now traditional 5J x 14in to 5½J x 14in.

1971

August
For the 1972 model year, although the 1600 engine remained an option – as it would until the end of German production of the second generation Transporter some eight years hence – a new and

inevitably more powerful engine was added to the line-up. Although fresh to the Transporter, the engine wasn't new to Volkswagen, having been purloined from the VW 411, the latest, last and largest of Volkswagen's air-cooled saloon cars. Although unquestionably the same in general principle as all the engines that had previously graced the Transporter, the 1700 was the first 'suitcase' engine, as they are known in Volkslore, a redesigned and altogether stronger unit. By definition this was a compact unit – it needed to be to be squeezed beneath a decent-sized boot at the rear of the 411 saloon, or under the load area in the corresponding estate. The 1700 featured a cooling fan moved from its traditional position at the top of the engine to the nose of the crankshaft at the rear. The fan was contained within a different style of housing which conducted air over the engine through cleverly channelled ducts, leading to a more efficient method of cooling.

The 1,679cc engine's bore and stroke stood at 90mm x 66mm and developed a maximum of 66PS at 4,800rpm. Those reviewing the Transporter with a 1700 engine and recalling the era of Nordhoff's supremacy would have been genuinely shocked to find not one, but two Solex 34 PDSIT carburettors, a feature the old master thought out of place and unnecessary for a commercial vehicle. One point, though, had to be conceded even by those of the old school – the age of icing in cold weather was gone forever.

Of all the magazines to test the Transporter with the new 1700 engine, *Car South Africa* was perhaps the one that told its readers of what they really wanted to know. Starting from the premise of 'much-improved power and performance', *Car* explained that the engine was 'a slightly detuned version of the 1700 used in the VW 411 models', the defining factor being that 'compression dropped from 7.8 down to 7.3 to 1 to take regular grade fuel. In this form, it develops 55kW, which is 74bhp: 23 per cent more power than the uprated 1600 engine. It transforms the vehicle's performance, giving it real punch through the gears, a quite respectable top speed, and sound cruising ability.' More followed:

'This big-bodied vehicle is streets ahead of the earlier 1500/1600 models in performance. To give some idea, a brief comparison with the 1968 test (in imperial measures):

	1600	1700
0–60	*–*	*23.4*
¼ Mile	*25.5*	*21.4*
Speed	*61.8*	*76.0*

'In addition, gradient ability is substantially improved: the new model will take a 1 in 16 gradient in top, compared to the old model's best of 1 in 22. Surprisingly, with the twin carburettor 1700 engine there is also a noticeable improvement in economy…'

▲ The accompanying press release stated that 'the only visible external changes to the 1971 model' were 'perforated road wheels (for better brake cooling) and flared wheel arches above the rear wheels to accommodate the wider road track.' *(RC)*

Volkswagen's copywriters charged with telling the world about the new 1700 engine also did a particularly good job, for not only did they cover the attributes of the power plant but they also cleverly linked their story to technical aspects of the Transporter's development that could well have been overlooked. Take this example dating to August 1971:

'Drive the VW Commercial – now even faster.

'Some VW Commercials are available with a 1700cc, 74bhp (SAE) engine (at extra charge). It can take the Commercial from 0–50mph in just about 18 seconds. Not that we wanted to transform it into a sports car. Merely into the most reliable Commercial ever. A big engine runs with less effort than a smaller one. And lasts longer too. A considerable number of technical improvements were made to the VW Commercials in the past year. Longer-lasting brakes. Strengthened floor assembly and rear end, which further improves the durability and service life of the chassis. Eleven basic changes alone guarantee distortion resistance even under extreme stress. The VW Commercial thus has no trouble in taking the strain of the more powerful 74bhp engine. Plus various improvements to carburettor and ignition. Which makes for cleaner air. You may claim to have driven a lot of commercials. But you've never driven one like this.'

▲ The 1972 model year vehicles can be identified by the larger outward-facing cooling vents in the upper rear quarter panels and much bigger rear lights, unfortunately not visible in this picture of a Station Wagon. Significant changes would occur the following year, making the identification of the 'crossover' Transporter an easy task. *(RC)*

▼ Posed press shots were less common than static vehicle images in the days of the second generation Transporter. The eagle-eyed will spot that this Microbus L dates from the 1972 model year when perforated wheels and chunkier rear light clusters were fitted. *(RC)*

A specific point to glean from the above relates to the 'strengthened ... rear end'. To accommodate the compact, but nevertheless wider, 1700, the engine compartment was changed considerably. The rear beam under the engine lid was now welded into position, rather than being held in place by bolts which could be undone when the engine needed to come out.

Many enthusiasts will know that any Beetle produced from October 1952 through to March 1953 is likely to be given the nickname of '*Zwitter*', a German word meaning crossover. The Beetle had been extensively updated in October 1952, with a new style of dash, extra bright trim and bigger, sturdier bumpers to name but three improvements. However, the single act of removing the metalwork between the split panes of glass forming the rear window – something which occurred in March 1953 – did far more to identify the new car from the old. Come August 1971 and the start of the 1972 model year a similar crossover look was achieved for the Transporter, before it was given a serious revamp the following year. To accommodate the extra needs of the new 1700 engine the once unobtrusive cooling vents tucked high up on the rear quarter panels were both increased in size and made to stand proud of the adjoining metalwork.

▲ ▶ These two images of the 1972 model year Delivery Van illustrate the changes in specification to perfection: bigger vents and larger tail-lights – both set against an as yet unaltered front end. *(BS)*

◀ Compare this assembly line image with the one reproduced on page 172. The Transporters shown here date from a point after the makeover of August 1972.

▼ Although not commonplace, some of Volkswagen's press photos were produced in colour by the 1970s. Compare this with the black and white image on page 202.

Meanwhile at the rear new tail lamps were considerably larger, demanding a slight reworking of the adjoining metalwork, while there was also a facility (in the shape of a clear section at the base of the unit) to include integral reversing-lamps where these were included in the specification. Both features would be incorporated into the new-look Transporter of the following year.

September
On 3 September the three millionth Transporter rolled off the Hanover assembly line, just three and a half years after the two millionth.

1972

August
Hot on the heels of the 1700 engine, the second generation Transporter received the only major makeover of its 12-year run for the '73 model year. The great divide in appearance has led some to christen the older Transporters as type 2a and the new models as type 2b. Invariably, in the hype surrounding the two distinctive looks of the second generation Transporter one of the most important new aspects has been overlooked, this

being a redesign of the cab floor to create a 'crumple zone' that would buckle concertina-style should a Transporter be unfortunate enough to be involved in a head-on collision. Volkswagen's copywriters, like the rest, had other things on their minds: 'This year we've strengthened the bumpers, raised the indicators, so that people can see where they are going. And put the cab steps inside the doors. That VW symbol isn't just for looks. It means something. Craftsmanship, reliability, economy and quality.'

Emulating the type fitted to all but 1200 Beetles from the '68 model year on, the Transporter now featured sectional girder bumpers both front and rear. The front indicators sat at either end of the cab ventilation grille and were both squarer and larger than their predecessors. Volkswagen's claim that they were more visible might be considered a little misplaced, however, as the general trend within the company was to site indicators lower rather than higher on a vehicle, even the Beetle following this trend with bumper indicators being the order of the day with effect from the '75 model year. Why Volkswagen chose to shrink the size of the VW roundel on the Transporter's front is also something of a mystery.

◀ The revised Transporter in Delivery Van guise: Volkswagen's publicity shots amply illustrate all the important features of the 'new' model.

▶ The VW Pick-up in revamped guise. Volkswagen described the vehicle as having 'improved safety'. (RC)

▼ This attractive posed image dates from a little later than the launch of the revamped Transporter, but it highlights all the most significant features in a single photograph. (BS)

After owners had struggled for 12 months to access the 1700 suitcase engine, Volkswagen thought it wise to cut a hole in the Transporter's luggage compartment, creating in the process an arrangement very similar to the hatch offered on the 411 and later the 412.

Inevitably geared towards the American market, Volkswagen introduced the Transporter with a three-speed auto box at the same time. What had been a sluggish vehicle had just become a whole lot slower still.

1973

April
Production of the second generation Transporter came to an end at Emden.

August
For the 1974 model year, Volkswagen upgraded the larger of the two engines offered on the Transporter for a second time in as many years. That they were either wise or were forced to do so demonstrates just how many other manufacturers were attempting to snap at the heels of the pack leader. Like the 1700, the new offering, a 1,796cc or 1800 suitcase engine, was appropriated from the upgraded version of the VW 411, now known as the 412. For the questionable benefits of a measly 2PS increase in overall power to 68PS, achieved by widening the

cylinder bore from 90mm to 93mm, it hardly seemed worthwhile. Volkswagen quoted a new top speed of 82mph, an increase of just 4mph, which again begs the question of why they had bothered. The answer came in the form of torque – and quite a bit more of it! From the 1700's 81lb at 3,200rpm, the 1800 pumped out a maximum of 92.4lb at 3,000rpm.

Car South Africa offered a fair summary of the 1800 model, suggesting that the 1800 had 'more steam for general driving ability, without detracting from fuel economy', while although 'in actual acceleration, the new Kombi is very much the same as the 1700 model … it pulls a better gradient in top, and has a much enhanced top speed potential, becoming the first Kombi to top a true 80mph'. Indeed, the 1800 was capable of romping 'to 80 in third, to have full climbing and overtaking ability'.

Initially to meet the demands of California state legislation, Transporters exported there were fitted with Bosch L-Jetronic fuel injection, although inevitably by August 1974 and the 1975 model year this practice encompassed all production destined for North America.

Although considerable time and effort went into making the revised second generation Transporter a much safer vehicle for its occupants, publicity material covering this aspect was somewhat thin on the ground. For example, although a brochure produced in August 1972 included the heading 'With

more safety and more speed', the accompanying text made no more than a vague reference to the crumple zone: 'More safety because of our new stronger bumpers, with a deformable impact absorbing section at the front. Plus all our old safety features, like a safety steering column.' Dealers, however, were made aware of what had happened in their own folder of preview brochures, which came bound with key points for the new model year and a more detailed text on the inside back cover:

'...driver and passenger safety has been increased by fitting new bumpers at the front and rear at the recommended International height. They have a new deformation element which brings substantial improvement to the passive safety. Behind the front bumper there is an energy absorbing box profile which together with the frame reinforcement in the doors, form an effective front end crumple zone...'

Much more explicit and readily available for all to read was the following – taken from *Fact Analysis*, a detailed guide for commercial vehicle buyers produced by Volkswagen GB Ltd's Marketing Service Department, and published in 1977:

'The Volkswagenwerk in Germany ... has conducted years of intensive research into safety ... The outcome has been a special safety steering and improvements in the front end design with the particular aim of protection in collisions. The VW Commercial was one of the first mass produced vehicles to have safety literally built in and complies with current regulations regarding vehicle safety. At the front, right across the front of the vehicle behind the bumper there is a deformation element which, when an impact takes place, is distorted thereby absorbing quite a proportion of the collision forces before the V shaped box members of the front frame buckle thereby damping further forces. This progressive absorption means that initial forces are reduced. Forces beyond this being transferred to the middle of the vehicle and thus the floor of the cab is preserved.

The vehicle has safety steering equipment. If the driver is thrown forward against the steering column it tips over so that the relatively large area of the wheel pad is against the upper torso. A flat bar between the front panel of the cab and the top of the steering column yields at a predetermined point so that the whole column can pivot forwards. ... Burst proof locks and stout hinges prevent doors from flying open in an accident. The doors are also stiffened by profiles so that they act as anti buckle panels between the door pillars and transfer the energy of an impact again to the middle of the vehicle. The ventilation ducts welded onto the forward panel provide the front of the cab with full width stability.'

▲ The Press Office text attached to this promotional photo of 1973 reads: 'The Micro Bus is a large passenger car. And it drives like one too. It is extremely comfortable for passengers and driver alike. Its highly effective heating and ventilation systems keep the atmosphere pleasant, both these features have been improved. It is now also available with automatic transmission which makes it the complete passenger car.' (RC)

◄ People-carrying Transporters of the early 1970s are pictured in abundance. That Volkswagen's demarcation zone between upper and lower colours (where these were applied) changed in the early years, from roof gutter to central swage line, is amply illustrated with the somewhat unusual combination of black upper panels and Sierra Yellow lower ones in this rare brochure shot. (Black proved decidedly unpopular!) *(RC)*

▼ Compare this image with the one opposite, and note that in August 1974 the side trim on the Micro Bus L was relocated to line up with the vehicle's door handles. *(RC)*

1974

August

The once individualistic Micro Bus De Luxe was revamped a little. From the hard-to-distinguish model of '68, where only the roof panel was painted in the contrasting shade of Cloud White, a change had been made for the '71 model year whereby the divide came at the under-window swage line, while the roof shade changed to Pastel White. During the course of the '71 model year Black also became an upper body colour option, at least for the home market, but was quickly deleted due to its lack of popularity. In August 1974, although the division between paintwork colours remained the same, the accompanying brightwork trim was lowered to align with the cab door handles, while a rubber insert was added and the notion of continuing trim across the rear of the vehicle was discontinued. For the final years of German second generation Micro Bus De Luxe production other options were added to the one-time single colour upper body.

1975

July

The arrival of the four-millionth Transporter was witnessed on 9 July. For those with an interest in statistics, the model breakdown consisted of 1,667,000 Delivery Vans and Pick-ups, 1,413,000 Kombis and 920,000 Micro Buses and Ambulances.

August

The last major upgrade of the second generation Transporter came in the form of a further hike in engine performance, this time to 2.0-litre specification. Unable to pilfer such an engine from the now defunct VW 412 range, Volkswagen had been inspired to borrow the largest of all their air-cooled engines from the joint project, mid-engined sports car the VW Porsche 914. The 1,970cc engine offered Transporter owners 70bhp at 4,200rpm, the bore and stroke having been increased to 94mm x 71mm, while a top speed of 90mph in the hands of an enthusiastically

▲ The Silver Fish, a special edition model based on the Micro Bus L and finished in silver metallic paint, with Marine Blue cloth upholstery. It featured a generous package of extras including trip meter and clock, lockable glove compartment, radio, heated rear window and a lockable fuel cap. Designed for the European market, it was launched in June 1978 and withdrawn in November.

◀ A post-August '74 Microbus L captured on camera by Volkswagen in rural Germany.

competent driver was realistic whatever Volkswagen's official figures.

Safer VW Motoring, once upon a time the organ of independent comment on all things Volkswagen in Britain, was suitably impressed with the last in the line of big engines, their appreciation of the vehicle already having been imparted. *Car South Africa*, however, no longer demonstrated quite the same enthusiasm as it had in the past: 'In pure performance tests – such as acceleration runs – the bigger engine did not feel all that much stronger than the 1800 … Even with two litres of engine and a good spread of torque, the big-bodied 10-seater is no performance vehicle…' However, consolation came for anxious VW executives in the

form of the following: 'Acceleration in the gears – and specially in top – is greatly enhanced in the new model, and gradient ability shows a marked improvement as well'.

1979

Although German production of the second generation Transporter has always been deemed to have occurred at the end of July, some vehicles were actually built after the factory holiday and into the new model year. The very last example, with the legend '*der lelzte Typ 2 der 2 Generation*' draped across its front, was paraded around Hanover in October.

Four-wheel drive would become an intrinsic part of the Transporter's make-up during the production run of the third generation. However, many enthusiasts will be aware not only that second generation Transporters with off-road capability were of great (if slightly unofficial) interest at Volkswagen, but also that more than one of the five prototypes created have survived to this day. A reasonable number of contemporary publicity shots have also been preserved for posterity.

After the demise of German production

Despite production in Germany having ended, even people without any deep knowledge of the Volkswagen marque will be aware that apparently newly registered second generation Transporters, particularly in Camper guise, are not infrequently seen on Britain's roads. However, catch one parked up somewhere and it soon becomes obvious that while such a vehicle might be fresh out of a showroom or workshop, none too subtle changes in the familiar specification will identify it as a vehicle built at one of Volkswagen's factories outside Germany. Inevitably suspicions will centre on either the Mexican or Brazilian operations, and in 2009 the latter hunch would be the correct one. A strange radiator-style grille melded onto the front panel will also suggest that over the years the model has changed in more ways than just the appearance of a few selected body

panels. In other words, buy either a Danbury Rio or Danbury Diamond camper interior (the Danbury name was purchased by the independent company that for a number of years had successfully sold the original Beetle manufactured in Mexico to a relatively small but passionate following) in conjunction with any of three trim levels – Picnicker, Classic or SE – and you'll find yourself running a second generation Transporter of Brazilian origins fitted with a 78bhp 1.4 fuel injected, water-cooled engine, purloined from the Polo. The engine, not unsurprisingly, is fitted with electronic ignition, while front servo assisted disc brakes and rear drum brakes are now also standard.

In Brazil the first generation Transporter soldiered on until 1975 and, as has already been described on pages 164–166, was supplied to Volkswagen of

▲ ▶ Brazilian second generation models almost inevitably bore a multitude of curious characteristics. Note the proliferation of first generation Micro Bus De Luxe-style windows, the odd side door arrangement, and the later European front matched to a semi-early front bumper – rounded, but lacking a step up. (RC)

◀ From 1997, the Brazilian-built Transporter looked much more like the old German models and included features adopted by the Mexican operation – such as a raised roof-line. This is one of the very last Transporters to be powered by an air-cooled engine. Acknowledging the end of an era, 200 Silver Line models were produced, all of which, as the name suggests, were painted in metallic silver. Green-tinted windows were additional to the standard package of the day. (RC)

South Africa in CKD form, where it was assembled and marketed as a budget model under the brand-name of Fleetline. During 1975 Brazil introduced what might best be described as a hybrid model, a vehicle that looked almost like a second generation Transporter from the front and more or less akin to an earlier model from the side and rear. To the amazement, perhaps, of anyone looking at such a vehicle from a European model perspective, these curiosities continued to lead the way in Brazil, as far as the commercial and people-carrying options were concerned, right through until 1997.

Glancing through VW family brochures dating from the early days of the alleged new model shows that the line-up consisted of both a Delivery Van and a Pick-up, plus a couple of people-carrying variations on the Kombi theme – the Kombi Standard and the Kombi De Luxe. A little later a re-branding exercise seems to have generated the use of the Micro Bus term for the more luxurious offering, while the Kombi name was retained for the vehicle in which it was quite obviously possible to remove the seats and the rear area lacked any form of trim. Around this time the Double Cab Pick-up was also added to the line-up.

From the front the Brazilian hybrid shared some of the characteristics of the later German models in that the indicators were placed adjacent to the ventilation grille. The small VW roundel featured on the front of the vehicle, but the grille itself was always finished in matt black while the roundel was formed out of an embossed section of the front panel rather than being a separate 'bolt-on' item. The bumper was of the rounded variety as seen on earlier German-produced models, but lacked the wraparound sections and integral steps. At the rear, the first generation-style panels incorporated the light clusters of post-August '71 vintage.

The Kombis and the later Micro Bus included the rear quarter panel wraparound window, abandoned on the German first generation Transporter when the larger window and tailgate was introduced in the relatively early 1960s. Glancing along the vehicle's sides, domed hubcaps were still part of the package initially, although these were subsequently replaced by the later flat type. The sliding side door was significant by its absence, but the German first generation's double outward-opening doors were present. The Kombi Standard and the later Micro Bus featured the four side windows associated with the German first generation Micro Bus De Luxe's four near-square windows, but the Kombi De Luxe appears to have been a law unto itself. This vehicle carried three side windows plus a blank metal rearward section, but its biggest peculiarity has to have been its two outward-opening doors divided by a substantial section of metal. At first glance

unquestionably strange, the logic of the arrangement becomes apparent when the interior passenger-carrying section of the vehicle, with full-length immovable bench seats, is taken into account.

An eccentricity of many Brazilian brochures is that a column of English text is included on each and every page. There follows what Volkswagen of Brazil found to say about the Kombi De Luxe, which, while being very brief, at least suggests that the door arrangement wasn't considered sufficiently unusual in its market that an explanation was required:

'Perfect for nine persons the Kombi De Luxe goes to the most distant places without discomfort to anyone. Besides it is equipped with all the items of comfort, safety and also is economical. It has a large panoramic windshield, bumpers fitted with a special anti-shock material, and a reverse light built into the rear lights. It has a glove compartment with a lid, a non dazzle rear view mirror. The Kombi De Luxe has also adjustable air outlets and internal heating. It is equipped with servo brakes, rear suspension with dual articulation and a 1600 engine.'

A snippet from a later brochure confirms that while the Micro Bus was added, the Kombi De Luxe wasn't abandoned totally – it merely became yet another option – and when the maths don't appear to add up, recall that the rear opening hatch is not included in the calculations: 'Now that you know the advantages [of the Transporter], choose the one that best suits your needs – VW Microbus 4 and 6 door, VW Kombi, VW Delivery Van or VW Pick-up.'

All Brazilian Transporters were powered by a 1600 engine with a specification similar if not necessarily identical to that of a second generation Transporter from Hanover. With a bore and stroke of 85.5mm x 69mm, and a compression ratio of 7.2:1, the 1,584cc unit developed a maximum of 48PS at 4,000rpm.

As for the so far overlooked Pick-up, this model also had a peculiarity, for the Brazilian market model featured what in European specification terms might best be described as an enlarged platform. Even then the specification wasn't straightforward, for every section of the load area, be it the platform or the drop-down sides or even the static sides, was clad with what the brochure-writers referred to as 'wooden ribs'. A nice touch, though, was the inclusion of a prominent VW roundel on the rearward-facing drop-down side.

In 1981 the Brazilian Transporter was revamped a little, with features like the steering wheel from the German third generation replacing the older version, and, more importantly, discs replacing drums on the front wheels, while a Double Cab Pick-up was added to the options. This vehicle came with what Europeans would regard as a standard load bed,

BE THRIFTY.

BUY A VW DIESEL VAN.

TODAY'S BEST CHOICE.

rather than the 'enlarged platform' of the single cab model. However, the biggest news of the year was the introduction of a water-cooled diesel engine.

Only available as an option with the Delivery Van and the Pick-up, the addition of a radiator resulted in the disfigurement of the front panel with what looked very much like a bolt-on box positioned between the headlamps, substantial enough to extend from just below the ventilation grille sufficiently far to virtually touch the bumper. Finished in black and bearing both a very small VW logo and the more prominent italic script word 'diesel', the design, or lack of it, did little for Transporter aesthetics. The 1,588cc inline engine produced a maximum output of 50PS at 4,500rpm and had a compression ratio of 23.5:1. Volkswagen quoted a top speed of 108kph (67mph). The diesel's existence was relatively short-lived, as both it and the Double Cab were deleted from the range in 1985 due to lack of demand.

During the course of 1997 the Brazilian Transporter was given more than a facelift, when, not far short of 20 years after German production of the second generation Transporter had ceased, the Latin American model finally began to bear a passing resemblance to it, the most notable difference being a slightly raised roof, borrowed from the Mexican model. By this time all models were referred to as Kombis despite six options being available initially, one of them, the Pick-up, being dropped in 2000. Apart from a Delivery Van, a school bus and ambulance, the two remaining options were what

▲ The Brazilian Diesel engine Transporter. Note the domed hubcaps on this 1982 model! *(RC)*

▶ Even though this steering wheel and dashboard image dates from 1997 and is linked with the photograph on page 220, few would fail to recognise this as belonging to a second generation Transporter.

Publicity shots of the Brazilian version of the second generation Transporter – to European eyes very strange in the case of the Kombi, and plain ugly in the case of the diesel Pick-up! *(this page RC)*

◀ ▼ ▶ Powered by a 78ps 1.4-litre fuel-injected water-cooled engine also fitted to Brazil's VW Fox (and available on certain Polo models), the latest Brazilian models still incorporate features associated with vehicles built over 40 years ago. The engine can be accessed via the traditional engine lid below the vehicle's tailgate, or through a hatch in the rear 'luggage' area.

most people would recognise as Kombis. One was the Kombi 12-seater, the other being the Kombi 'Standard'. Two engines were available, one of which ran on methanol. Curiously all Kombis were painted white for all but one day of each month, when the paint department switched to silver.

Turning full circle in this story of the Brazilian Transporter, the Danbury models currently available to UK residents feature the latest twist in the tale, with the replacement of the air-cooled engine by a water-cooled unit in November 2005 and the reappearance of the incredibly ugly, albeit slightly styled, radiator on the front of the vehicle.

Production numbers at the most singular of all Volkswagen's many factories throughout the period of the hybrid Transporter were steady verging on remarkable, albeit for very obvious reasons not in the same league as Hanover. Volkswagen has been in the enviable position of dominating the Brazilian market for many a year, extremely reasonable pricing being a contributory factor! From the 51,239 Transporters built in 1978, the annual figure subsequently fell away each year, reaching 35,437 in 1981 before rallying to a very healthy 45,339 in 1982. However, the revival was short-lived; 1983 saw just 21,845 Transporters built, and for the next ten years there was no great improvement. However, from the 35,168 examples built in 1993 production spiralled upwards, to peak at 55,481 in 1996. Curiously, once

the Brazilian Transporter looked much more like a second generation Transporter that the average European would instantly recognise, sales halved. By 2000 the annual figure stood at no more than 20,156 vehicles and over the next three years this fell to an all-time low of just 9,708. If this was a reaction by potential purchasers to such an antiquated design being revamped rather than replaced, Volkswagen didn't heed the warning, as we know. Many must wonder if, just like the Mexican Beetle, the only thing that will actually kill the model is circumstances beyond VW's control, such as government legislation.

Finally with reference to Brazil, following the demise of the Fleetline in South Africa the hybrid model also found its way there, being marketed as the Kombi 1600, 'by far the lowest priced 10-seater in the country'. Even its old-fashioned outward-opening doors were highlighted – 'Enter through the robust, wide swing-open side doors'!

The Mexican factory at Puebla was the other location where the life of the second generation Transporter was extended well beyond its European sell-by date. Although the first generation look was only axed on the last day of September 1971, at least the new model bore a remarkable resemblance to its German counterpart. Indeed, glancing through a Mexican-produced sales brochure even an enthusiast could be excused for assuming that the vehicles pictured were manufactured in Germany and exported either in fully made-up mode or in CKD format.

Until 1987, the Combi (note the unusual spelling) and Panel, to give Mexican models the names by which they were known across the country, were powered by the familiar 1600 air-cooled engine. Even without any knowledge of the country's language most people will be able to glean from the figures below that not only was the engine of the low compression variety designed to run on fuels not up to European and US standards, but also that it was not the upgraded twin-port version produced in Germany for the start of the 1971 model year:

Cilindrado	1,584cm³
Diámetro	85.5cm
Carrera	69mm
Compresión	6.6:1
Potencia	34kW a 4,000rpm (DIN)
	44 CP a 4,000rpm (SAE-neto)
	46 CP a 4,000rpm (DIN)
Par motor	100Nm a 2,200 rpm (DIN)
máximo	72.5lbs – pie/a 2,200rpm (SAE-neto)

In 1987 the Mexican Transporter was endowed with a 75PS engine borrowed from the Golf. Inevitably, design work was required and, just like the Brazilian Transporter already discussed, the result was an ugly radiator perched above the bumper, which, incidentally, was upgraded at the same time. In keeping with the trends of the day, the new and rather substantial bumpers were made of plastic and, perhaps surprisingly, suited the old-timer. Modern wheel trims, comparable in nature to those offered on German-built Passats and Golfs, similarly didn't look out of place on the more upmarket Caravelle. If anything was incongruous, it was perhaps the digital clock set within the original dashboard format.

From 1991 the Mexican-built Transporter incorporated the raised roof panel already described in relation to the Brazilian models, and in 1992 the engine was upgraded again, this time to a fuel-injected 1800, which developed an interesting 85PS, achieved at 5,400rpm. Bore and stroke stood at 81mm x 86.4mm respectively, with a compression ratio of 8.5:1.

Mexican production of the second generation Transporter finally ground to a halt in 1995, after 253,926 had been built. For a few more years Mexicans could obtain a second generation Transporter from their local VW dealer, providing they were happy to accept its Brazilian origins. Sadly, 30 years after the second generation Transporter first graced the roads of Mexico, the import of Brazilian models was also brought to a halt.

▶ As the years passed by, the Mexican operation slowly but surely modernised the looks of the Transporter. The two images reproduced here date from 1991 and a time when, amongst other things, the roof panel had been completely altered and the vehicles were powered by a water-cooled, rather than an air-cooled, engine – hence the disfiguring radiator grille on the front of the vehicle. The goods carrier is described simply as a 'Panel', while the people-carrier is a 'Caravelle'. The Combi was also still available.

▼ As might be anticipated, this Mexican Transporter – known as the Combi – bore a remarkable resemblance to second generation models produced in Hanover. (RC)

Travels with a Transporter

Since its earliest days the Transporter has appealed to many intrepid globetrotters as a means of independent long-distance travel. Amongst the first to recognise its potential were two members of the D'Ieteren family from Belgium, owners of an early Volkswagen franchise in Brussels called Anciens Etablissements D'Ieteren Freres. On 6 October 1950 Pierre D'Ieteren set out with three friends on a 25,000km trek from Brussels to the Belgian Congo in a Kombi, straight off the production line, and a split-window Beetle. Recorded in the book *Images du Souvenir*, their expedition took them across the Sahara, through Nigeria, Cameroon and Gabon and eventually to the Congo. Both vehicles bogged down regularly in sticky waterlogged clay, or in deep unstable sand, but the only breakdown was due to a broken torsion bar in Nigeria. They returned to Belgium in January 1951.

Next to take up the baton was Pierre's mother, redoubtable 65-year-old rally-driver Gabrielle D'Ieteren, who used another production-line Kombi, christened 'Charlotte', to undertake a 14,000km expedition down the east coast of Africa in the company of journalist Andre Villers. They departed from Brussels in February 1953, and in 74 days they had arrived at Stanleyville, in the Belgian Congo, having passed through many countries including Tunisia, Egypt, Ethiopia, Kenya and Uganda. They

▼ Erna Blenck demonstrates the carrying capacity of their VW Transporter before she and her husband Helmut set out on another of their off the beaten track tours of Southern Africa, in pursuit of their vocation as travel writers. *(BS)*

had numerous misadventures on the way, including a break-in to the bus, inadvertently giving a lift to a murder suspect, and getting stuck in deep mud, which forced them to unload the contents of the vehicle on to camels. Nevertheless, they considered their choice of vehicle 'excellent', although it seems to have been abandoned in Stanleyville at the end of their odyssey – it may still be languishing there, you never know … low mileage, one careful lady owner … The exploits of Gabrielle and Andre are described in the book *L'Afrique Mouvante*.

The D'Ieterens were no doubt the pioneers of long-distance Transporter travelling – indeed, they were quite literally the trailblazers, showing the way for the many travellers and explorers who followed in their cross-ply tyre-tracks. Soon after the D'Ieterens' travels were completed, the authors and photographers Erna and Helmut Blenck were using a VW Transporter for their long hauls around South Africa, researching various books including one called *South Africa Today – A Travel Book*, published in 1955. Their view of the VW was that 'we nomads of the twentieth century now have no need to give up our comforts – with a Transporter we can take them with us'.

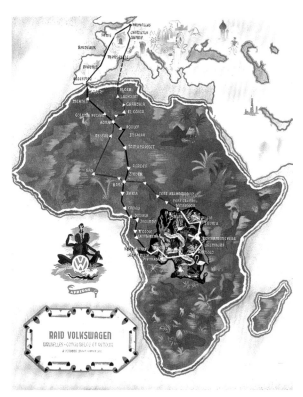

A map showing the route of Pierre D'Ieteren's epic journey to the Congo in 1950 in a factory-fresh VW Kombi, described in his book *Images du Souvenir*. *(D'Ieteren archive)*

▼ The VW Transporter 'was for me the key to the world', declared travel writer Dieter Kreuzkamp.

◀ The VW Kombi with sand ladders attached is loaded aboard ship at Algeciras with booms and rope slings, en route to Tangier. *(D'Ieteren archive)*

Before long, however, such seemingly monumental treks were shown to be mere sprints to the corner shop by comparison with a marathon overland expedition in a Kombi undertaken by a Swiss Family (no, not the Robinsons), Louis and Milly Mottiez and their young son Claude. Beginning in 1956 at the Volkswagen Factory in Wolfsburg, the Mottiez family eventually covered some 150, 000 miles in their VW through Europe, the Middle East, India, Australia, Africa, and the Americas. Young Claude was tutored by his mother throughout the trip, but must have learned even more from just being a part of this epic journey, which finished in San Francisco in February 1961.

By 1959 an Australian with the delightful name of Mr Thick was planning to set up an overland scheduled passenger service between Singapore and London. Needing a reliable vehicle for the type of terrain he would have to cover he chose a VW Samba, which he christened 'Waltzing Matilda'. The service was to run three times a year, with a journey time of 45 days. According to a contemporary issue of the in-house magazine *VW Information*, on the first trial run he called at the Volkswagen factory in Wolfsburg to 'express his satisfaction with our product'. How long this enterprising service lasted is not recorded.

A rather more sedate and relaxed journey was undertaken by Mr and Mrs J.R. Humphreys in about 1960, chronicled in the book *The Lost Towns and Roads of America*, published in 1961 and subtitled 'A Cross Country Tour in Search of America's Timeless Towns'. For their tour Mr and Mrs Humphreys chose a VW Camper, converted by Westfalia, because it would 'solve any problems we'd have of where to stay the night. It was also an insurance at mealtimes that we'd have a place to eat'. The idea of their journey from New Jersey to Monterey in California was to avoid the freeways and take the old roads through America, rediscovering towns and villages with names such as Eagle Nest, Cave-in-Rock and North English. J.R. was a collector of old maps and he and his wife covered 7,484 miles in 45 days in their Camper, following the roads that 'lead everywhere through the American past'.

William Stockdale was a man who must have been destined to do a marathon tour in a Volkswagen –

◀ Some of the local inhabitants help Pierre D'Ieteren and his crew through a particularly bad patch of road in Gabon, central Africa. *(D'Ieteren archive)*

for their honeymoon in 1949 he and his new bride crossed the United States on foot! By the early 1960s they had produced six children and were ready for another challenge. A 10,000-mile round trip from Connecticut to the Baja peninsula in California was just the ticket, but this time not on foot, but in a Station Wagon. As expected, the worst part of the trip was the road down the Baja peninsula, which Mr Stockdale called 'North America's longest bad road' although it was 'not all bad – only 800 of the 1,000 miles qualify as extreme torture'. However, despite lurching into potholes and rocks, bumping over dry riverbeds and inching along narrow cliff-top paths, they made it 'without so much as a flat tyre'. A professional lecturer, Mr Stockdale presented a film of his family's exploits at the New York Motor Show in 1963, which was called 'Baja – The Road of No Return' – unless, as he no doubt pointed out, you are driving a VW.

Another American family that completed an extensive journey in a Transporter were the Reverend and Mrs Van Helsema, from Michigan. Of Dutch origin, the Van Helsemas had relatives in Holland, and in 1962 decided to set out from that country on a 15,000-mile drive in a red and white Micro Bus christened 'Redbus'. Along with their five children they journeyed to the 'Bible Lands', reaching Damascus and Jerusalem, whilst Mrs Van Helsema recorded their wanderings, which were eventually publishing in 1967 in a book called *Safari for Seven*.

There's a change in continents for the next

marathon journey in a Transporter, for in 1966 Victor G.C. Norwood made an 8,000-mile partial circumnavigation of Australia in a second-hand split-screen Kombi, bought from a botanical researcher who had already partially converted the Kombi into a Camper by installing cooking and washing facilities, a bed and a 25-gallon water tank. Victor Norwood was a traveller and explorer, and, it seems, something of a chancer. A former heavyweight boxer and wrestling

▲ A bloodied but unbowed Kombi serves as an impromptu kitchen/diner for Pierre D'Ieteren (left) and his colleagues in the Sahara Desert on the return leg of their marathon trip. Note the roof cover which contained fibreglass, for heat insulation, and the Christmas tree attached above the windscreen – it was late December 1950. *(D'Ieteren archive)*

◄ Gabrielle D'Ieteren and her VW Kombi 'Charlotte' meet the locals in Southern Ethiopia during her trek down the eastern side of Africa to Stanleyville, as recorded in the book *L'Afrique Mouvante*. *(D'Ieteren archive)*

▶ The Swiss Family Mottiez pose for photographs in 1956 before setting out to cover 150,000 miles around the world, finishing their odyssey in San Francisco in 1961. (RC)

THE MODERN
SWISS FAMILY
MOTTIEZ
AND THEIR
VOLKSWAGEN
TRANSPORTER

AROUND
THE WORLD
IN 800 DAYS

VOLKSWAGEN

DEPENDABLE
All Over The World

▼ 'Singapore to London by Volkswagen' is the boast carried on the side of Mr Thick's VW Microbus De Luxe, called 'Waltzing Matilda'. Mr Thick, on the right of the photograph, is shown calling at Wolfsburg during his inaugural trip, with his first two passengers. How many more were 'transported' in this way is not known. (BS)

champion until he lost two fingers in a skirmish with Brazilian revolutionaries, his intentions in Australia were to mine for gold and agate, and to shoot the giant estuarine crocodile on a commercial basis and sell their skins. His escapades are related in the book *The Long Haul*, published in 1967, a delightfully non-PC tome in which Norwood hunts and shoots a good deal of Australian wildlife. He attests to a 'constant search for adventure in remote places', which is presumably why he lived in North Lincolnshire. The Kombi, incidentally, ended up buried beneath tons of rock in a landslide caused by Norwood crashing the much-abused vehicle into a cliff-face in Queensland.

Driving his Bay-window Devon Caravette with rather more care was 21-year-old Ron Watts from Greenwich, London, who in December 1969 drove ULM 771F all the way from the UK to Bombay (Mumbai) in India. No problem, you might think, but Ron took as his passenger his paralysed brother Leon, who had to sleep in an iron lung. Despite severe weather conditions, they arrived safely in Bombay in January 1970.

Perhaps the definitive handbook for long-distance overland travel in a Transporter was written by Theresa and Jonathan Hewat, from Corfe Castle in Dorset. Entitled *Overland and Beyond – Advice for Overland Travellers*, the book was published in 1977, and includes a description of the authors' precisely measured 88,607½-mile journey around the world in their Bay-window Camper OBY 761L. Starting from Archway Road, London, in January 1973, they motored on for three years and four months, through 56 countries in Europe, the Americas, Japan and Asia, before returning to London in May 1976. They crossed the Equator four times, and endured temperatures as low as −23°C in Canada. But the majority of the book comprises very helpful and detailed advice on all aspects of such an overland journey, covering everything that an aspiring marathon driver would need to know. They even include an inventory of all the stuff that they took with them, but admit that they were grossly overloaded, the poor Camper weighing a total of three tons at the start of their adventure!

Today, some of these journeys might seem relatively mundane, and hardly worth a magazine article, let alone a whole book. Horizons have broadened, roads have improved, and what was supremely adventurous in the '50s, '60s and '70s now seems almost commonplace. Nevertheless, we should not forget these pioneers and the vehicle which took them on their travels.

▶ On the back roads of Lancaster County, Pennsylvania, the VW Camper of Mr and Mrs Humphrey pauses as an Amish family pass by on a transporter from an entirely different age. (BS)

▶ *Safari for Seven* was the title of the Van Helsema family's book about their 15,000-mile tour of Europe in 1962 in a red and white Microbus. *(BS)*

▲ William Stockdale, his wife and six children (the eldest only 11) pose for the cameras at the 1963 New York Motor Show, around a poster promoting their self-made film of the 10,000-mile pan-American trip that they had just completed, which culminated in 800 miles of bad roads on the Baja peninsula. *(BS)*

▼ Ron and Leon Watts discuss their plans to drive from Greenwich to India in the winter of 1969. Leon was paralysed and the VW Caravette had to carry an iron lung for him to sleep in. *(BS)*

▶ Victor Norwood, with shotgun, leans casually against his VW Kombi on the front cover of his 1967 book *The Long Haul*, describing his 8,000-mile wanderings around Australia. *(BS)*

▶ Jonathan and Theresa Hewat in 1976, outside Corfe Castle in Dorset, following the completion of their circumnavigation of the world in their 1972 Bay-window. *(BS)*

1979–92

PART IV

Twists in the tale

▶ Without presenting a shot of the interior and very little else, identifying a multivan – the dual-purpose vehicle that offered simple camping facilities while also being a fully-fledged people-carrier – isn't easy.

▲ Three generations of Transporter side by side. Note how the new model looks considerably larger than its two predecessors.

After more than a decade of massive change at Volkswagen, few would have anticipated that the third generation Transporter would emerge with an air-cooled, rear-mounted engine; a vehicle very much following in the steps of its illustrious predecessors. After all, the rest of Volkswagen's air-cooled family had either been summarily deposed in favour of the likes of the Passat, as was the fate of the VW 1600 and VW 412, or had been sent into exile, as was the case with the former king of Wolfsburg, the once seemingly immortal Beetle. While those in Germany and other selected European countries with an enduring penchant for the old master could still knock on their local dealers' door and expect to purchase a Beetle, virtually all would have realised that the car was now *hecho en Mexico*, its place at Wolfsburg and more recently at Emden having been taken by a new generation of cars for young and growing families, the shopping-trolley Polo and the hoped for bread-and-butter saviour and cure for all Volkswagen's ills, the Golf. Even the niche market Karmann Ghia, the hand-crafted sporting look-alike, had faced the axe in favour of a water-cooled speedster, the nearly as attractive and certainly more powerful Scirocco. Also, wasn't it the case that not only was the air-cooled engine more expensive to build than a water-cooled offering, but also that without drastic measures such power plants struggled to keep up with the pace of modern living? If it had been necessary for the second generation Transporter to go through an uprated 1600 engine to two litres via both a 1700 and 1800 power plant, what would the future demand if Volkswagen was to stay competitive?

Most have presumed that the seemingly odd decision announced by virgin Director General Toni Schmücker in May 1975, to produce a third generation Transporter with an air-cooled engine, resulted from either lack of knowledge; awareness of Volkswagen's only too recent perilous financial state; or complacency. In the

first instance, Schmücker might have been the new boy at Volkswagen, but the reality of the situation was that he was a car man through and through, having championed Ford's cause for many a year. In the second, although Volkswagen had recorded an enormous loss in the previous year, the stage was set for a full financial recovery, with sales of and predictions for the Scirocco, Passat and particularly the Golf being highly encouraging. The argument for the third case initiates with the German author Randolf Unrah, who said of Schmücker that he 'considered the Transporter to have no direct competition due to its particular design and mechanics'. This may or may not have been his view, but as will be revealed shortly, by the time of his announcement such an opinion was largely irrelevant. Nevertheless, whatever the divergence of opinion among Volkswagen buffs, historians and Transporter addicts, all have united to agree that the third generation Transporter was a product of the Schmücker era, taking roughly four years to develop from caterpillar to chrysalis and, ultimately, the launch of the butterfly in August 1979.

Original research at Wolfsburg, however, paints a very different picture. For starters, work had commenced on a replacement for the second generation Transporter many months before Schmücker's appointment. The minutes of relevant meetings show that his predecessor, Rudolph Leiding, was not only present, but was in essence the driving force in determining the future of Volkswagen's successful commercial vehicle and micro bus programme.

Although Leiding was virtually forced out of office as a consequence of growing concerns about Volkswagen's risky financial state, in part at least brought about by the necessarily huge investments made to create a new range of vehicles, many are now coming to recognise him as the true architect of Volkswagen's successful rebirth, which was already taking shape at the point of his departure. Despite being a child of the Nordhoff era, his hard work having been rewarded by successive and increasingly pivotal promotions, such as head of Audi and Volkswagen's Brazilian operation, on his succession to the top job following four years of Kurt Lotz's misrule Leiding recognised that the day of the Beetle and its siblings was over. Moving at speed was a characteristic of Volkswagen under his command, and it is therefore no surprise that, despite the popularity of the second generation Transporter, diagrams of a vehicle instantly recognisable as the third generation model are revealed in archives dating from 1974, with the first prototype having allegedly been rolled out during the course of September. The heart of the matter was that Leiding had pushed through the need to replace the second generation Transporter in a Board Meeting held as early 4 December 1973. The concept he proposed was of a 'front-steered [vehicle] with rear engine, rear gearbox with 4 gears and auto gearbox', which at first sight might seem to have been uncharacteristically conservative for this vociferous architect of change. Further delving into the records unearths that Leiding's call for change centred upon a new breed of engines. Sadly, although minutes from a meeting held nearly 12 months later, in November 1974, reveal exactly what Leiding had had in mind for EA389 (the project number that the third generation Transporter was allocated), a potential minefield of issues had arisen:

The engine space available and the increase in costs which is expected, rule out a water-cooled diesel engine for EA389. As a priority, however, we will check whether an air-cooled diesel engine (based on the Type 4 engine), or a water-cooled diesel engine (based on the Passat engine) are technically possible in order to meet the competition.'

Leiding might have proposed a conventional layout, but he hadn't foreseen unquestioned survival – or, indeed, continued existence at all – for the traditional flat-four air-cooled engine. Despite the issues that had arisen, in the last months of his tenure of office he demanded – like Nordhoff before him – a tight schedule, planning that the third generation Transporter should enter production during 1977, with the Delivery Van being available from 1 August, the Micro Bus and Kombi following exactly one month later, and the Pick-up, plus models destined for America, coming last on 1 October. To ensure that such targets were met Leiding sanctioned budgets that allowed the Research Department 29 prototypes with diesel engines, and while apparently even this was not enough, it helps to explain the diminution of profits to the point of becoming heavy losses during his four years in the top job.

Undoubtedly, the engine issue was a key factor in subsequent delays; certainly the archives held at Wolfsburg confirm that the matter was the subject of ongoing debate, although the short notice given of Leiding's departure, with the summary crossing out of his name and its replacement in pencil by that of Schmücker's on one Transporter-related document, might also help to explain the apparent slackening of the pace.

At a point when Schmücker had been Director General for 18 months, notes taken at yet another planning meeting indicate a projected production start date of 2 January 1979 for the Delivery Van and 1 March for the Micro Bus and Kombi. Minutes relating to the vehicle's engines reveal further details of Transporter-related project numbers, as well as more than a hint of the extra work necessary to achieve the compromise between ongoing air-cooled units and Leiding's insistence that, to survive, the Transporter, like the rest of the range, must move forward:

'The space for the engine is designed in such a way that apart from the air-cooled flat-four motor, a water-cooled 4 cylinder, and if necessary, a water-cooled 5 cylinder diesel engine (at a 50 degree angle), can be offered.

EA162	*Van, Kombi, Bus, Pick-up, Double Cab.*
EA357	*Camping Vehicle.*
EA162/10	*1.6L (Type 1 based) / 2.0L (Type 4 based) engines with fuel injection or a single carburettor.*
EA162/02	*Diesel Engine (1.5L) 1.6L (EA827 based).'*

Confirmation, if it was still needed, that Volkswagen would have little option but to launch the new Transporter with both 1.6 and 2.0-litre air-cooled engines came from the précised words of a future Director General, Ferdinand Piech:

'Herr Piech repeated his thoughts mentioned during previous meetings. He advised that due to the lowered load floor, installation of the water-cooled engines at an angle was not an insoluble technical problem, but in the first instance would cause an increase in development costs, as practically every water-cooled engine produced by the company would have to be planned with the Transporter in mind. This would also result in making the production programme more complicated.'

With the benefit of hindsight Schmücker might have been wise to delay his 1975 announcement about a new Transporter. The result was an acknowledgement that the days of the second generation Transporter were limited. As Laurence Meredith pointed out in his book *Original VW Bus*, 'by 1976 Volkswagen admitted the development of the second generation Transporter was over'. Brochure copywriters had to go to the lengths of making a virtue out of a lack of development. 'The VW Commercial has nothing new to offer', they proclaimed, 'which is precisely why it is so remarkable.' They wrote of 'the same basic idea' at a time when the boffins behind the scenes were trying their utmost to make a radical change. That such a move couldn't be perfected within one or even two years was serious. The only possible compromise was to launch the third generation Transporter with the old faithful engines and rely on its new body to carry the day. After all, it wasn't unprecedented to change engines part way through a production run, even if such a radical departure had never been planned from the outset before.

Thus in May 1979, and later than all predictions, the new Transporter, the bigger, slab-sided model, that would eventually be rewarded with the somewhat dubious nickname of the Wedge, was presented to the world's press. One month later production began in earnest for release on general sale in August 1979.

Specification of the third generation Transporter

Volkswagen's copywriters had little difficulty in telling a story of a bigger and better Transporter than ever before, as this somewhat heavily edited extract from several pages of an early British market brochure indicates:

'Aerodynamically designed, the new style front now incorporates a sloped windscreen enlarged by 21%, giving greater visibility. New large exterior rear view mirrors finished in black, compliment the black safety door handles and the new black bumpers with matching plastic end caps. New too, are the wrap-round direction indicators, located lower down near the front bumper. The black full width grille incorporating the headlamps adds that touch of distinction to a classic design. … The new shape of the rear allowed a much larger tailgate to be used.

The tailgate window, which has almost doubled in size, gives much greater rearward visibility. New too are the rear lamp clusters, which now incorporate powerful reversing lights and a fog driving lamp … Careful design and comprehensive wind-tunnel tests have enabled Volkswagen to reduce the "drag" which benefit both performance and economy. … As far as alterations to dimensions are concerned, the width has been increased by almost 125mm … and the length by 65mm … The slightly longer wheelbase and wider track give a turning circle of 10.7m. … Height has not been affected. … On lifting the large rear tailgate, now assisted by two gas struts, you will be surprised to see how much lower the rear platform has become. We've lowered it by almost 145mm … thus increasing the volume over the rear engine compartment by 40%. … The spare wheel has now

▼ **With the Delivery Van facing the camera in the background, this image dating from the press launch of the third generation Transporter is dominated by the Bus L – the top-of-the-range model. Many such vehicles carried two-tone paint, the shades in this instance being Liana Green with Saima Green upper panels.**

been relocated to the front, under the cab ... Access to the engine is through a removable hatch in the rear compartment. Notice how much flatter and compact it is. This has released another 0.7m³...'

Running through what the copywriters had to say on the subject of the third generation Transporter in the same sequence, most present-day pundits would argue that the aesthetics of the model were less desirable than those of its predecessor. Without question, the big windscreen lacked the wraparound qualities of the second generation's, while to modern eyes the girder-style bumpers with cheap-looking plastic end-caps – a characteristic of most Volkswagens dating from this era – do little to improve the model's overall appearance. A flicker of a smile must cross the faces of those reminded of the two variations in the position of the front indicators on the second generation Transporter, with the move to a higher location being commended as offering other motorists increased visibility of the Transporter driver's intentions. Nevertheless, logically the third generation model's new low-down indicator location was in keeping with those of the rest of the commercial world, not to mention most if not all cars. What Volkswagen failed to inform its once adoring public of was the visual similarity of the third generation Transporter to its bigger water-

cooled cousin, the LT. A house style had emerged; whether this was a good or a bad thing is for today's enthusiasts to determine. Do the looks of the second generation Transporter outweigh the advantages associated with a newer design?

Reminiscent of the engine compartment lids of the pre-March 1955 first generation Transporter (the so-called 'barn door' models), the third generation Transporter's tailgate at first viewing seemed to be logical in its design. As the copywriters noted, its massive size offered 'protection from the elements' whilst loading, while the very act of stowing larger or bulky goods was much easier. But there was a

▲ This three-quarter front image of the Delivery Van as launched illustrates the good, or bad, points of the third generation Transporter's appearance. Note the girder-style bumpers with simple end caps and the location of the indicators.

T1, T2 and now T25?

Although somewhat irrelevant to the story of the first two generations of Transporter, by the time of the fourth such incarnation the factory terms of T2, T3 and so on had become increasingly important. If there is a nickname for the current model, most are unaware of it, and so it was with its predecessor. Announce ownership of a T4 or a T5 and the number of blank expressions or baffled looks will be counted on one hand. Logically, then, the third generation Transporter should be the T3, and in most European countries this was indeed the case. However, for the British market the trade referred to the new Transporter as the T25. Was this some sort of concession to the fact that here was a new Transporter with old engines, a stepping stone on the path to new technology? Possibly, who knows!

problem, and quite a big one too. Access to the engine was only available through a hatch concealed beneath the rear loading or luggage compartment. Despite a nifty arrangement whereby the oil level could be checked by lowering the licence plate located between the Transporter's rear lights to reveal a filler cap, the danger was one of neglect. Only the Pick-ups escaped this risk, as they benefited from an upward-lifting lid below the platform bed and once again situated between the rear lights.

That the third generation Transporter was usefully larger than its predecessor is without doubt. From a wheelbase of 2,400mm for the second generation Transporter, the increase to 2,460mm made the creation of a longer vehicle easier. Overall length of the third generation Transporter stood at 4,570mm, compared to 4,420mm for the older model, while the all-important width of 1,845mm dwarfed the second generation's 1,765mm. Overall height, as the copywriters pointed out, was more or less unaffected, the new model officially taking a drop of 6mm (1,950mm compared to 1,956mm). The wider front and rear track – up from 1,384mm to 1,570mm at the front and from 1,425mm to an identical 1,570mm at the rear – assisted in the creation of a tighter turning circle of 10.7m. There was also a linked improvement in the stability of the new vehicle in adverse weather conditions, while radial instead of standard cross-ply tyres were offered when the larger of the two engines was selected by potential owners. Best of all, for deliveries of anything from fluffy pillows to the kitchen sink, the third generation's new body afforded an increase in overall capacity, which was up from 5m³ to a useful 5.7m³. In achieving such improvements Volkswagen had been afforded a little help – not by a top-drawer designer imported specially to do the job, but by computers. Such was the ingenuity of their programming that they achieved a 100mm lower entry height for the new model, while at the same time conniving to rid the vehicle of its cumbersome cross-members.

Although the relocation of the spare wheel ensured extra space within the vehicle, its new position under the front must have led to more than a little cursing

and swearing on a wet day on a muddy verge when a puncture occurred.

As for the carry-over engines, both the 2.0-litre and age-old 1.6 survived, as, knowing the background, one would expect. The smaller air-cooled unit suffered most. Almost overnight it succumbed to the suitcase design, with its fan attached to the crankshaft in order that it might be wedged into the third generation's much more compact compartment. This same underpowered engine also endured the ignominy of a further decline in its effective power brought about by the increased weight of the new model. Naturally, unladen weights varied from model to model, but taking the Delivery Van in both instances the second generation model stood at 1,175kg, while its successor bumped down on the scales at 1,492kg, which by anyone's standards was a noticeable increase. Despite Volkswagen's claim that both the old and new models fitted with a 1600 engine were capable of a top speed of 68mph, the truth of the matter was that it took longer with the third generation, and at the expense of the amount of fuel used. Three little plusses, though, came in the form of hydraulic tappets, avoiding the need to make frequent manual adjustments; electronic ignition, which ensured the engine stayed in tune longer; and 'Digital Idling Stabilisation', a computerised way of ensuring that the engine didn't cut out on a cold morning, or refuse to start when hot.

Volkswagen suggested that the revised suspension set-up of the new Transporter was inspired by the desire to make it safer, although cynics would suggest that the demise of the long-lived torsion bar arrangement was at least in part due to the costs involved in their manufacture. A generous analyst would conclude that torsions bars were unnecessarily bulky and consequently intrusive to the design of a vehicle where extra space was deemed a top priority. Whatever the interpretation, the third generation carried double wishbones and an anti-roll bar at its front, as well as progressive coil springs, while at the rear was the by now well established arrangement of semi-trailing link suspension, albeit upgraded through the use of mini block coil springs, which resulted in an improved reaction from the suspension to whatever was thrown at it.

Perhaps sufficient mention hasn't been made so far of the third generation Transporter's design, for this was the first Volkswagen of its kind to have been created, at least in part, by computer; and while more emphasis was placed on 'comprehensive wind-tunnel tests' to reduce drag to much more respectable levels, in essence the passenger safety cell wasn't entirely the work of human hands. Crash-testing organised under the most advanced technological conditions resulted in the impact of a head-on collision being absorbed by the front bumper and transmitted to a

▲ The first Transporter to have been designed at least in part by computer. A safer vehicle without doubt, but one that lacks some of the aesthetic charms of its predecessors.

▶ The High-Roof Delivery Van, although still not the most elegant of vehicles, looked better-proportioned than it had in the days of the second generation. The more angular design of the new body and roof avoided the impression created by the second generation model that the high-top was very much an afterthought.

deformation element running the full width of it. As an enlightened copywriter explained:

'This element, in turn, is mounted on a forked frame with pre-programmed deformation points in the floor assembly. Other safety features include the safety steering column with a detachable coupling and two flexible struts under the dashboard and door reinforcements. All these truly make the cab of the Volkswagen Commercial a "safety cell" which protects driver and passenger alike.'

A slightly later and definitely bolder statement claimed that the new model was:

'Probably the safest commercial vehicle in the world. The Transporter's body construction incorporates "safety cell" cab, reinforced doors, deformable front frame elements. All computer calculated. Proven on impact testing. Safety as a design criteria – not as an afterthought.'

Finally, in this download of the third generation Transporter at its launch, Volkswagen were mightily impressed with the interior they had created, summarising their achievements thus: 'The new Commercial's cab. A saloon car couldn't ask for more.'

Of course, to modern eyes the mass of brittle plastic, right-angles and spindly controls is no more appealing than that of the equivalent Golf or Polo of that era. Indeed, most today would prefer the primitive nostalgia of the painted metal dash of the first generation Transporter. Realistically, though, the nearly all-plastic dashboard was a considerable advance and the closest Volkswagen, or for that matter many

another manufacturer, had come to creating a car-style dash in a commercial vehicle; even the steering wheel was much closer to the near-vertical position of a car. Not only that, but the car-like instrument binnacle, itself a first, housed much more in terms of instrumentation than had ever been the case before, while the generous glove-box was unprecedented.

All variations on the core Transporter theme were available from the start of production, at least on the home market, despite earlier management records indicating a schedule for release model by model. No doubt to the relief of salesmen charged with selling the product range in North America, these countries were bereft of the underpowered 1.6-litre engine option. For Britain both the still reasonably impressive 2.0-litre and the 1600 engines were offered, although the official list of types varied a little, either intentionally or unintentionally, from that of the second generation Transporter. A launch brochure issued in August 1979 offered potential purchasers the following options: Van, High Roofed Van, Pick-up, Double Cab Pick-up, Extended platform Pick-up, Bus and Bus L, all of which were available with 1.6 or 2.0-litre engines. In terms of price differentials, and using the straightforward Delivery Van as the obvious marker, the larger of the two power units added a premium of approximately 10 per cent to the price.

While the dedicated follower of all things Volkswagen might be interested to know that the Double Cab Pick-up was available with or without a rear seat and rear window, of more general interest was the announcement that the Bus range was listed for some markets as being available with seven, eight or even nine seats. The rather more restricted list of options in Britain nevertheless still included both eight- and nine-seat models! Of still more newsworthy interest had to be the dropping of the term 'Micro Bus'. For most markets it was now called either the Bus or the Bus L, while in America all that had to be done was to tweak the terminology to read Vanagon and Vanagon L. (Leaping ahead to 1982, however, and a quick perusal of an American brochure, another complication of terminology arises, albeit in line with other products in Volkswagen's range across Europe and beyond. Enter the GL, a more upmarket version of the L!)

Again using the British market as the guinea pig, it's worth emphasising the difference in price between the basic 1.6 Delivery Van and the then top-of-the-range model, the nine-seat Bus L, fitted with a 2.0-litre engine. While the seemingly tiny figures in pounds sterling are virtually meaningless today, the percentage difference is altogether more revealing, with the latter model costing just short of 46 per cent more than the former.

As before, if there was a vehicle to condemn it was the Bus L. In an age when chrome or shiny

▲ Volkswagen UK's Press Office caption for this image of the Bus, which they refer to as the Micro Bus, contains a boast that no other manufacturer could deny: 'The Volkswagen 8-seater Micro Bus is based on the world's most successful commercial vehicle.'

▼ The Bus L (finished in Bamboo Yellow with Ivory upper panels) incorporated a number of features that many would consider out of step with the mood of the time. These included chromed bumpers, chrome hubcaps and additional brightwork, most noticeably at the front of the vehicle but also discernible surrounding the windows.

brightwork was no longer the height of fashion, this model looked out of place with its additional trim around the windows and the mock grille on the front. Full-size chrome hubcaps and chromed bumpers were equally out of step with the mood of contemporary vehicle design. Even the interior wasn't safe, as brightwork strips adorned the waistline, though the chrome protection bars bolted to the rear door could be excused. On a separate theme, the former opulence of two-tone paintwork was no longer deemed desirable. Towards the end of second generation Transporter production some colour combinations had been introduced for the top-of-the-range model, such as Sage Green with a Mexico Beige roof, which certainly did the vehicle no favours. This theme continued, indeed became more prominent, with the third generation. Perhaps if the second colour had been restricted to the roof, rather than the divide coming at the waistline, it might have bordered on the acceptable, but put bluntly the decision to team bright Bamboo Yellow with Ivory, near tan Aswan Brown with Samos Beige, and striking Liana Green with mushy Siama Green, was inexcusable. The Bus L's only saving grace came in its seats being trimmed with cloth, rather than cold-in-winter, hot-in-summer vinyl.

What the motoring press had to say

That the third generation Transporter met with near universal approval shouldn't come as too much of a surprise; after all it was bigger, better appointed and, of course, a much newer design – but there was the big question of the engines of which Leiding had been determined to rid Volkswagen. Undoubtedly some journalists were surprised by the engine's location in the new Transporter; more still were shocked to find that air-cooling looked as though it was here to stay. The US magazine *Road and Track* set the ball rolling:

'... those who insist on something new will be disappointed. VW has stuck with the tried-and-true layout, the traditional boxer motor behind the transaxle, driving the rear wheels. This despite the fact that, in Germany at least, VW no longer produces a single car of this genre. Now, is that any way to maximise profits?'

Equally typical was the review by the American magazine *Car and Driver* in February 1980:

'The engine chosen for the job is ... surprising, given VW's switch to and promotion of water-cooled power plants. It's a two-liter version of the familiar air-cooled flat four that powered every Vee Dub until the Rabbit. Volkswagen claims it would have preferred to have used a Rabbit-derived engine lying on its stomach, but because of the flood of orders for Rabbits, the VW engine foundry simply couldn't supply enough extra engines for the Vanagon. So that change will have to wait a few years.'

Car South Africa probably liked the Transporter most of all, not even digressing to comment on the old layout or the equally old engines. The entire report is littered with words such as 'magnificent', 'remarkable' and 'handsome', while the summary phrase 'far superior' says it all. Typical in its praise is the section devoted to suspension:

'Gone is the torsion bar suspension which has served so well in earlier models, and in its place is an all-coil spring system using wishbones and anti-roll bar at front, and semi-trailing arms at rear with dual-jointed, half-axles. This new suspension is very good – it has virtually all the resilience and progression of the torsion bar system, and if anything, is even more load capable.'

Motor Trend's opening observation more or less makes it unnecessary for its readers to go any

further: 'VW's new Vanagon breaks with the past and leads the industry into the '80s'. However, there were paragraphs that could have taught other manufacturers a thing or two:

'Much of the handling was realized through arranging certain components so that the weight under load would be 50% over each axle and the center of gravity would be low and over the front section of the vehicle. The 15.9-gallon fuel tank was positioned directly behind the front axle, the spare tire is on a drop carriage ahead of the front axle, and the battery occupies a compartment under the front right passenger seat.'

The following conclusion was inevitable!

'The Vanagon is one of the best utilitarian vehicles ever to take to the highway. Its efficient use of space, attention to ride comfort and sedan-like handling position it as the new high mark the industry must strive to equal.'

▼ Like its predecessors, the T3/T25 soon became available in a multitude of guises, including as a glass carrying vehicle as shown here. (RC)

Third generation Transporter chronology

Sales and production highs for the third generation Transporter never matched those of its predecessor. Whatever the vehicle's merits, times had changed, and the world's manufacturers were now confronted by the unstoppable advance of the Far East. In 1980, the first full year of third generation Transporter production, Volkswagen's records indicate that 217,876 vehicles were built worldwide. The source is official, but doesn't break the models down by type. To draw a direct comparison between the popularity of the third generation model and its predecessor, the table opposite relies on the same source for both. Note, however, that these are worldwide totals and as such don't eliminate Brazilian and Mexican production of second generation-based models.

▼ The Pick-up with tarpaulin and bows as it was presented in the summer of 1979.

Second generation	Total production	Third generation	Total production
1968	253,919	1980	217,876
1969	273,134	1981	187,237
1970	288,011	1982	188,681
1971	277,503	1983	155,500
1972	294,932	1984	157,596
1973	289,022	1985	155,423
1974	222,233	1986	161,712
1975	221,351	1987	145,380
1976	234,912	1988	150,999
1977	211,024	1989	147,539
1978	207,625	1990	Changeover August
1979	Changeover August		

▼ Described in its brochure as a '12 seater Bus', this third generation Transporter carries one or two features from the Bus L, such as chromed hubcaps and additional trim round the front grille, but otherwise both the internal and external specification is more basic. Key to its inclusion here is that it dates from the point when black plastic covers had been applied to the air intake vents. *(RC)*

Before too much in the way of despondency appears, it's worth considering that, for example, in 1986 the third generation Transporter sold in 180 foreign markets, and that Hanover's export quota equated to 56.8 per cent of total production – a very healthy boost to both Volkswagen's and the German economy.

1979–80 model year

June
Production of the third generation Transporter began at Hanover in preparation for the model's official release in August. Full model line-up, including seven-, eight- and nine-seat Bus, and options such as the Pick-up with enlarged platform, all available from day one.

1981

January
Although more significant changes were made in 1981, the addition from January of black plastic covers for the engine air intake vents in the upper rear quarter panel is important in helping to distinguish earlier third generation Transporters from slightly later models.

February
The first stage of a move away from traditional air-cooled engines commenced, over six years after it had been mooted. New on the Transporter scene was a diesel – but it wasn't new to Volkswagen, as this was the Golf's engine.

A brochure designed for the US market outlined the advantages of diesel power thus:

'Vanagon L Diesel: Now there's a fuel efficient alternative with the Vanagon. A diesel.

▲ As the accompanying press notes to this photograph indicate, the home market Bus L was available as a 'seven, eight and nine seater'. The text continues: 'The vehicle has the dimensions of a passenger car and with its considerably larger amount of space available it can justifiably be regarded as a large car. Alloy wheels and broader tyres underline its sporty character.' Note the covers on the air intake vents. (RC)

◄ With the introduction of the diesel engine, a second grille appeared on the front. Somewhat leisurely in performance, Volkswagen of America's copywriters solved any potential problems with a line that ran: 'There's nothing like a diesel to help you save on fuel…' (RC)

▶ Captioned as a Micro Bus, but described by Volkswagen's archive as a Kombi, this image portrays a vehicle powered by a diesel engine.

'By its very design, the Vanagon is economical. With a fuel efficient diesel engine it's even more so. There's nothing like a diesel to help you save on fuel. And, only the diesel can offer you the standard 5-speed transmission for versatility and for greater comfort at cruising speed.'

Despite all the preplanning, the only way the Golf's diesel engine could be accommodated in the third generation Transporter was by tilting the in-line four at a 50° angle.

For anyone wanting a purposeful level of power coupled to decent economy – something not available with either the 1600 or 2.0-litre petrol engines – salvation wasn't forthcoming in the shape of the new diesel. Admittedly the specification for the Golf didn't look bad:

Capacity	1.6 litres (1,588cc)
Bore and stroke	76.5 x 86.4mm
Output	54PS at 4,800rpm
Compression ratio	23.5:1
Maximum torque	73.4lb ft at 2,000rpm
0–60mph	16.8 seconds
Fuel consumption	53.3 at a constant 56mph

However, for commercial vehicle usage the engine was deliberately made more leisurely and delivered maximum power at 4,200rpm, which brought the metric horsepower figure down to 50PS, although torque was boosted to 76lb ft at just 2,000rpm.

The Golf's gross weight with a diesel engine tipped the scales at a healthy 1,280kg. By comparison the much bigger-bodied Transporter in Delivery Van guise and with a diesel engine weighed in at 2,400kg, already an increase of some 40kg over the 1.6-petrol engine Transporter and almost double that of the little car. Perhaps, then, it's no surprise that it's impossible to find a 0–60mph time in any of Volkswagen's literature, and that the 0–50mph figure stood at 24.4 seconds when the engine was mated to a four-speed box, or 25.7 seconds when coupled to a five.

Likewise the maximum speed of the vehicle was no more than the 68mph already quoted for the underpowered 1600 air-cooled petrol engine. However, this figure is for a five-speed box and was reduced to a miserable 64mph with the equivalent four-speed unit.

Despite the diesel option having been available for 12 months, direct comparisons in fuel consumption levels between the Transporter and the car are difficult to determine, with Volkswagen conveniently placing an irritating 'N/A' in the appropriate column for the former vehicle. The most optimistic figure to be detected in print came in at 32.8mpg, this being calculated at 'half permissible payload at a constant ¾ of maximum speed, plus 10%', and as such well behind that of the Golf. However, on the plus side,

and using exactly the same criteria, this compared well to the 1600 petrol's 25.6mpg, and even better against that of the 2.0-litre with just 21.4mpg against its manually geared entry, and a depressing 19.7mpg for the equivalent automatic.

To cope with the demands of commercial usage the Golf Diesel's engine included a larger flywheel and a heavy-duty clutch, while to accommodate potentially heavy load conditions an oil cooler was fitted for the purpose of regulating the engine's temperature.

Contemporary reviews were epitomised by the one that appeared in the December 1982 issue of *VW Safer Motoring* headed 'Diesel – likeable but leisurely'. The article's principal, Chris Burlace, concluded:

'Neither of the 1600-engined vans, petrol or diesel, is for those who want to go places in a hurry. Both are rather underpowered compared with the competition,

yet their refinement does so much to compensate for lack of performance. With a car-like ride and driving comfort, impeccable steering and handling and first class braking, driving a VW Transporter is always a pleasure.'

Until the arrival of water-cooled petrol engine Transporters it was easy to distinguish the diesel model from its stablemates thanks to the addition of a grille for the radiator which sat below the largely decorative grille that had defined the third generation Transporter's looks from its inception. Inevitably, with an engine at the rear and a radiator at the front the mechanics of cooling were more complex. Cooling air was drawn in by the action of forward motion, but was supported by the addition of two fans, both of which were thermostatically controlled. From that point the vital coolant was drawn to the back of the vehicle and the engine

through pipework that was hidden and protected by the Transporter's under-frame.

September
The presentation at the Frankfurt Motor Show of a seven-seater luxury edition of the third generation Transporter, branded as the Caravelle, heralded either a return to the bespoke qualities epitomised at the original launch of the first generation Micro Bus De Luxe, or a step forward in a decade when luxury people-carriers were emerging as the must-have vehicle for an increasing number of consumers. Volkswagen simply described the new model as 'offering all the comfort of a luxury car.'

In addition to the somewhat questionable attributes of the Bus L, such as two-tone paint and a relative abundance of chrome or brightwork, the Caravelle featured frame-style headrests for both the driver and front seat passenger; foldable armrests throughout; improved padding and upholstery for the seats; additional storage compartments; velour carpet; pre-wired radio; and other items that certainly couldn't be taken for granted as being standard at the time.

The success of the concept was to lead to a further rethink on presentation. A sales brochure issued in August 1983 bore the title 'Volkswagen Transporter and Caravelle'. The workaday models, including the Delivery Van, Pick-up and Double Cab (note the simplification), were bracketed together as Transporters, while what would have previously been referred to as Buses became 'The Caravelle C, an ideal minibus'; 'The Caravelle CL, greater luxury in

◀ ▼ **The US-market Vanagon and Vanagon Camper of 1982: Vanagon specifications tended to be higher than those offered to most markets. Note that both images feature vehicles with petrol engines.** *(RC)*

▲ This is an example of the Caravelle GL. According to Volkswagen the most notable features were inertia reel seatbelts, adjustable frame head restraints, rear window wiper and 'protective bars in front of the rear window'.

every detail'; and, at the pinnacle of comfort, 'The Caravelle GL, the executive bus'.

Officially the once pivotal Kombi was dead, even if the small print might still include reference to the term. Although the Caravelle C included features often associated with the Kombi of old, such as a half-height bulkhead, and while a more basic approach to people-carrying was in evidence, such as a floor covering of 'easily maintained vinyl board', the basic versatility of such a vehicle appeared to have been lost.

However, even this was not the end of the story, for what started as another special edition, the Caravelle Carat – an even more luxurious Transporter offering – eventually led to the single word 'Carat' being used to promote a top-of-the-range model defined as 'the executive limousine with space, comfort and performance'. From the special edition model onwards, Volkswagen had launched into the territory of alloy wheels and rectangular double headlamps. Add to this swivelling centre-seats, an abundance of velour upholstery at a time when the return of cloth had become nowhere near universal,

power steering and additional instrumentation, and the intentions were abundantly clear.

As in the latter years of the second generation Transporter but more so, special models and limited edition offerings were to play an increasingly prominent part in overall sales of the Transporter, and would pave the way for the multifarious-model approach that characterised both the T4 and particularly the T5, covered in the next chapter. Significant third generation specials are noted below in relation to the appropriate production years.

1982

What Rudolph Leiding had planned for the third generation Transporter all those years earlier finally came into effect for the 1983 model year, starting in August 1982. As the copywriter of a wordy but nevertheless informative brochure explained, 'the second and decisive phase in the conversion of the Volkswagen Commercial to a new engine technology is the presentation of the brand-new water-cooled carburettor engines.' However, whether these engines

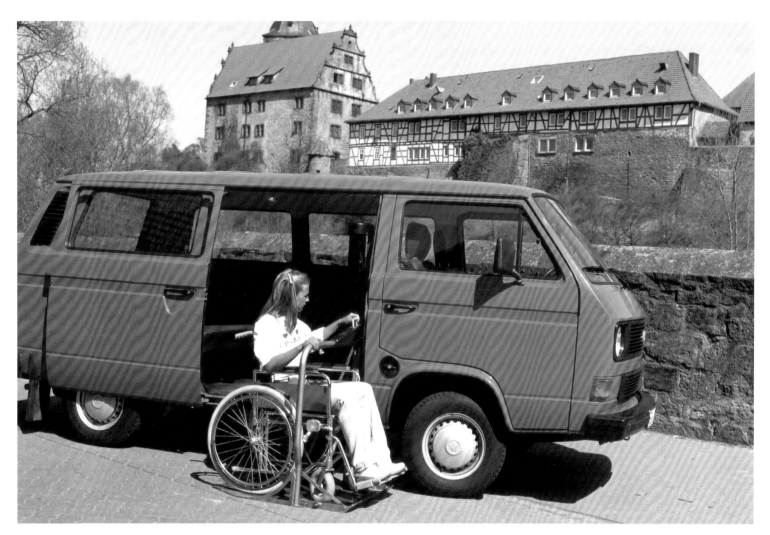

▲ Although Volkswagen's purpose in presenting this photograph was to illustrate the Transporter's capability to be adapted for disabled usage, the vehicle is undoubtedly a Caravelle C, the base model of the people-carrying range.

▶ This official image of the third generation Transporter is listed as depicting a Caravelle Carat.

were literally brand new – or, for that matter, due to their design, entirely logical when compared to the water-cooled blocks offered with all other Volkswagen products – remains debateable.

Returning to and studying the carefully crafted words of the learned copywriter, the answers to any points of debate were obvious to some:

'Requirement-orientated output, economy, comfort and the satisfying of legal requirements as regards less environmental impact were foremost when planning the new carburettor engines. The economy aspect and the utilisation of existing production facilities as well as logistics and the handling of the new engines in practice were also of prime importance for Volkswagen. The company's many years of experience with boxer engines also played a part in the decision in favour of the power unit

concept to be used. In the past 37 years more than 30 million such four-cylinder power units have come off the production lines … All this is backed by an immeasurable know-how potential in terms of foundry, processing and production engineering; a wealth of knowledge which is worth a lot and for which we are envied.'

A quick glance at Volkswagen's bank balance in the early 1980s might suggest that a more determined effort to break away from 'existing production facilities' would have been squashed by, if nothing else, the return of a precarious financial state. From the 438 million DM profit made by Volkswagen AG in 1979, the tide of success had ebbed away to just 120 million two years later. In 1982 the VW group as a whole made a loss of 300 million DM, even though Volkswagen AG clung on to a 33 million DM

◀ **A water-cooled version of the Double Cab Pick-up. Externally the only difference to be seen was the second grille on the vehicle's front.**

▶ **The third generation Ambulance with a water-cooled engine.**

balance in their favour. A year later they too were in the red, and to the tune of 85 million DM.

Thus the advantages of retaining the boxer principle with the suddenly not quite so new flat-four engines had to be broadcast, and were duly summarised thus:

'Compact design in both terms of length and height, thus providing for favourable installation conditions and ease of access to power unit in existing engine compartment.

'The longitudinally mounted engine and its low weight make for even axle load distribution and thus good handling characteristics and suspension under all load conditions.

'Low vehicle centre of gravity and thus excellent directional stability.

'The 1.9-litre capacity and the favourable torque characteristic permit low operating speeds and thus economical fuel consumption and a reduction in noise level.'

Bearing in mind that the above was directed at general prospective purchaser consumption, it would be wise to consider that Volkswagen's 'Self Study Programme – Transporter with water-cooled Boxer engine' was aimed at its employees. Without ceremony the two new water-cooled engines, obviously in their first incarnation, were specified after the following text:

'The water-cooled boxer engines are a further development of the air-cooled versions. In carrying out this development the requirements for higher output, driving comfort, brought about by improved running smoothness, and reduced fuel consumption have been attained.'

Add to this a basic catalogue of the engine's design, and the story is more or less told:

Engine block	Split light alloy case
Cylinders	Cast iron sleeves
Cylinder heads	Aluminium alloy with water jackets
Valve arrangements	Pushrod-operated overhead valves, hydraulic tappets
Cooling system	Liquid-cooled, with belt-driven water pump
Carburettor	
60PS engine:	34 PICT downdraught with automatic choke
78PS engine:	2E3 twin choke downdraught with automatic choke

Specification	1.9-litre 60PS	1.9-litre 78PS
Capacity cm³	1915	1915
Bore mm	94	94
Stroke mm	69	69
No of cylinders	4	4
Compression ratio	8.6:1	8.6:1
Output	60PS at 3,700rpm	78PS at 4,600rpm
Torque	103.1lb ft at 2,200rpm	103.9lb ft at 2,600rpm

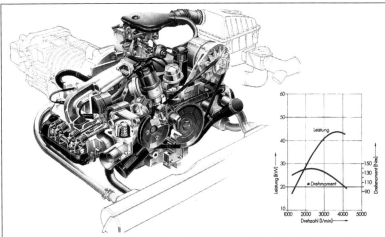

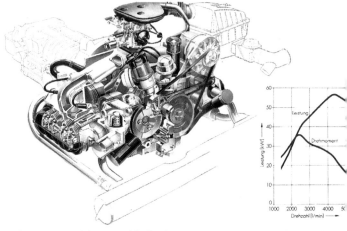

The watercooled flat-four engine has a displacement of 1.9 litres and develops 44 kW (60 bhp). It pulls lustily, runs quietly, and uses very little fuel, making the vehicle economical and pleasant to drive. And it needs only regular-grade (2-star) fuel.

This is the more powerful version of the flat-four engine. Also with a displacement of 1.9 litres and developing 57 kW (78 bhp), it runs smoothly and economically even from cold starts on short trips. It pulls well at extremely low speeds, for low engine noise and fuel e...

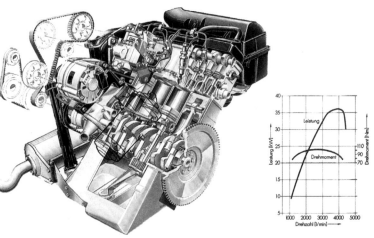

Proved successful a million and more times over, the 1.6 litre diesel engine is unsurpassed for its fuel economy. With an output of 37 kW (50 bhp), this is the ideal unit for short trips and has tremendous pulling power.

The 1.6 l turbo-diesel engine developing 51 kW (70 bhp), is the technical successor to the immensely successful diesel engine. It is outstanding for its greater performance with ...tively low fuel consumption, together ... operating noise levels.

This is the successful double-wishbone front axle layout. Independent suspension all round, with of course the semi-trailing arm rear axle, is the secret of the Volkswagen Transporter's supreme road behaviour.

The semi-trailing arm rear axle, common to all Volkswagen Transporters. Together with the double-wishbone front axle, it is an important element in this technically superior su... concept.

24

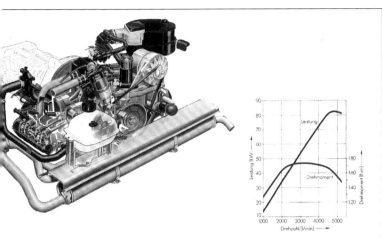

In the generally less detailed offerings describing the new engines, Volkswagen tended to stick to the story that as the engine was at the rear of the vehicle and away from the driver and front-seat passengers, the arrangement kept engine noise to a minimum. However, there was more to the story than this. The new engines' water jackets made for a reasonable reduction in noise:

'In the vehicle itself, it was possible to reduce the noise level by 2-3dB (A), which, for the human ear, amounts to a reduction of over 50%. The engine noise level outside the vehicle was also noticeably improved by 3dB (A) to 77 dB (A).'

2 kW (112 bhp) flat-four engine with a ·cement of 2.1 litres and digitally-con- l fuel injection is an immensely free- revving, flexible unit with outstanding quiet running. Available with Caravelle GL only.

Two manual gearboxes were offered, as well as automatic transmission, the four-speed box being a 'further development of the well-known Transporter gearbox', while the five-speed was 'further developed from the four speed version' as an optional extra linked to either engine. The automatic could only be specified with the 1.9 78PS engine.

The top speed for the respective 1.9-litre water-cooled engines was 73mph for the lower powered unit and 81mph for the 78PS version, the choice between four- and five-speed gearboxes making no difference to the result. As might be expected, a penalty was incurred with the auto box coupled to the 78PS engine, but this only amounted to a total of 4mph.

·olkswagen Caravelle's technical con- supreme suspension design allied to a ·lete range of safety features. Effective distribution of axle loads means excellent road behaviour.

Acceleration for either engine was hardly earth-shattering, as the reluctance to print anything more than a 0–50mph might have served to indicate. The four-speed 60PS engine was the slowest as might be expected, offering a yawningly drawn out figure of 19.1 seconds. The five-speed box improved on this slightly, but only to the tune of 18.2 seconds. The bigger engine coupled to a four-speed box gave a 0–50mph time of 15.7 seconds, while with a five-speed box this was reduced to 15.1 seconds. Curiously even a 0–50mph time was unavailable for the automatic!

Fuel consumption was definitely healthier than for the old air-cooled engines, but wasn't as good as that offered by the leisurely diesel, the 60PS engine clearing 25.9mpg, and the 78PS engine with a four-speed box offering 24.1mpg, or 24.7mpg with a five, in comparative tests. Volkswagen were eager to note that both engines used regular fuel.

·onally rigid floor pan frame ensures ·assive safety in the Transporter and ·elle. Impact energy is withstood by the bumpers and absorbed progressively by a full-width deformation element.

25

◀ **With the later third generation Transporter, Volkswagen was keen to illustrate all the salient points of what they believed to be its advance over previous generations – from petrol and diesel water-cooled engines and double wishbone front suspension to enhanced safety features.** *(RC)*

Volkswagen's manual for its employees noted that the higher output of the water-cooled boxers was attained by 'higher compression ratio giving improved efficiency', and 'reduced internal losses due to the discontinuance of air-cooling', while the increased output achieved by the 78PS engine resulted from 'cylinder heads with larger ports and valves, new twin choke carburettor, intake manifold with larger passages, modified camshaft'

The American market was not unusually only offered the larger of the two new engines. Comparing it with the 2.0-litre air-cooled block, the results appeared impressive (recall that fuel injection had been the norm for US specification Transporters for the best part of a decade):

'Although the new engine is more compact than its air-cooled predecessor, it's also more powerful – with 22% more horsepower. But the new engine is not all brawn. It has brains too. A unique "Digi-Jet" fuel injection system digitally monitors the fuel and air mixture for maximum power output. Just as comforting, the EPA estimates that the new engine is 19% more economical than the old one, and 23% more economical on the highway.'

Press reaction to the new engines was more or less universally positive. For example, *Road and Track* included all the details Volkswagen would have liked to hear – such as three seconds quicker on the 0–60mph sprint, smoother, quieter, less likely to 'plug away' on a lengthy incline – before offering the following summary: 'The new engine's power, flexibility, economy and quietness are delightful and give the VW van a level of performance that is commensurate with its design.'

For *Car and Driver* there was plenty to write about, despite the subheading of 'Just add water'

◀ As with previous generations, the Transporter in its third guise was a multi-tasking vehicle. In this Volkswagen publicity shot it is seen as a Pick-up with hydraulic lifting platform.

▼ While *Car and Driver* might be content to describe the new water-cooled third generation Transporter as a commercial Porsche, it's doubtful if many potential purchasers saw them in such a light!

"*The Porsche 911 of Vans*"
Car and Driver

for their June 1983 article. The author also neatly landed on Volkswagen's challenge for the future while highlighting the advantages of water to cure, once and for all, a gripe afflicting all air-cooled vehicles:

'The water-boxer has enough strength to run all the way to 86mph – an 11mph improvement. That translates into more relaxed 65-to-75-mph cruising and some extra power for passing that wasn't there before. They haven't yet invented the Vanagon that will crack sixteen seconds in the zero-to-sixty dash, so the VW is still no threat to your average Subaru. Luckily, though, the Vanagon has the gift of feeling quicker than it is. It always seems to have more than enough oomph to keep traffic from breathing down your neck...'

'...Not only is the cabin more peaceful, it's also more cosy now. The water coursing through the engine and the radiator hidden behind the lower front grille can now be diverted through two heaters: one under the dash and one nestled beneath the rear seat. They should keep the cavernous cabin at least as toasty as the old model's optional gasoline heater did...'

Road and Track were more specific concerning challenges to Volkswagen's people-carrying crown while its fortunes were tied inextricably to the third generation Transporter. For the writer, the 'Wasserboxer' engine was Volkswagen's salvation:

'We've always thought the Volkswagen to be the best of its kind, especially when pitted against Detroit's offerings in recent years. But now the people-hauler market is rapidly changing. Toyota is entering the fray with its Van Wagon and Chrysler has recently introduced its T-115 and Vista (nee Mitsubishi Chariot). After living with the Vanagon and its air-cooled engine's deficiencies ... we question whether VW could have maintained its advantages against the newcomers. But with the new Wasserboxer engine, the king of vans has a good shot at retaining its crown.'

The final word has to go to the American magazine *Car and Driver.* Such was the nature of their compliment to the new water-cooled Vanagon that Volkswagen immediately went to press with a brochure built entirely round those five immortal words:
'The Porsche 911 of vans'
Having transferred lock, stock and barrel to water-cooling, Volkswagen didn't rest on their laurels, as they were no doubt mindful of the threats raised by Japanese manufacturers. Via the special edition Caravelle Carat of September 1983 vintage with its 90PS fuel-injected engine, the line-up for the 1986 model year included two new introductions.

For the British market at least, the 112PS 2.1-litre engine with digitally controlled fuel injection was only available with the top-of-the-range Caravelle GL. The 2,109cc engine achieved maximum output at 4,800rpm, while maximum torque of 174Nm was available at 2,800rpm. Elsewhere it was also available with a catalytic converter, the result of which was that power output dropped to 95PS. Around the same time the 90PS engine mentioned in relation to the Caravelle Carat was quietly dropped.

Described as the 'technical successor' to the leisurely 50PS diesel, which remained on the books as 'an ideal unit for short trips', being 'unsurpassed for its fuel economy', for the '86 model year there was also a new turbo diesel engine. The 1,588cc unit was boosted to a maximum of 70PS at 4,500rpm thanks to indirect injection and a turbocharger. With a compression ratio of 23.0:1, bore and stroke stood at 76.5mm x 86.4mm. Maximum torque of 138Nm was achieved at 2,500rpm.

August 1987 saw the original diesel engine given a much-needed boost through an increase in the bore from 76.5mm to 79.5mm, which resulted in an increase from a maximum of 50PS at 4,200rpm to 57PS at 4,500rpm.

Following what would be the final revisions to the engine range for the 1990 model year in August 1989, which involved a reduction in the output of the 2,109cc fuel-injected engine to 92PS (or 95PS for syncro applications), the full line-up included two diesel engines offering 57 and 70PS respectively, plus three petrol engines, the 2.1-litre supplemented by the 60PS and 78PS derivatives.

As a final comment, tuning firms pumped out the water boxer engine further still. Take, for example, the German Oettinger wbx6, a six-cylinder 3,164cc, 165PS offering capable of 0–62mph in just 11.8 seconds. That the third generation Transporter could cope with such power was testament to its design and undoubtedly sent messages back to the development engineers working on the fourth generation prototypes in Hanover.

1984
August
While considerable play had been made on the safety aspects of the third generation Transporter's

▶ This photograph was taken to illustrate a brochure produced in 1984 covering all aspects of Volkswagen's Transporter range. In the back row are a Delivery Van (left) and a Caravelle, while at the front are (from left to right) a Kombi, a single cab and a Double Cab Pick-up. Note the engine inspection covers on the flatbeds of the two Pick-ups.

computerised design, it hadn't been possible to make too much of its anti-corrosion measures. From August 1984 for the '85 model year protection was considerably enhanced, leading to the complete listing consisting of galvanised sheet steel employed for the cab doors, sliding door where fitted or rear cab door in the case of the Double Cab Pick-up, the drop sides, tailboard, storage compartment and maintenance access covers (again relevant to the Pick-ups); stone impact protection, relating to the front panel and all wheelarches; PVC stone impact protection for the floor-pan and wheelarches; undersealing of the floor-pan: and cavity protection treatment for the frame's longitudinal and cross members, plus the doors and flaps and the lower body section on the inside.

1985

September
At the IAA held in Frankfurt, Volkswagen presented the 'Multivan' camper study, a desirable cross between a full-blown camper and a passenger-carrying vehicle. Built by Westfalia, there was sufficient interest for the vehicle to go into production, which it duly did during the course of 1986.

At the time Volkswagen described the Multivan concept as a vehicle that 'closes the gap between the working week and the weekend', adding decisively that 'a versatile multi-purpose vehicle is born.'

1986

January
Toni Schmücker had resigned in 1981 shortly after suffering a heart attack, and his post as Director General had been taken by Carl Hahn, with effect from 1 January 1982. The one-time Nordhoff prodigy, and from 1959 until 1965 head of Volkswagen's business in America, had followed the fortunes of the Transporter from almost its earliest days.

Dr Hahn's praise for the Transporter as an enduring but still innovative genre was wholesome, as the following extract from an address to an invited audience made on 15 January 1986 (on the occasion

◀ This image of the complete range of commercial vehicles available in the mid-1980s includes, in the case of the Transporter, the passenger-carrying options. The larger LT models towards the back of the photograph were first introduced in April 1975, and when the full chronology of the third generation Transporter is appreciated the similarity in appearance between it and the LT is all the more understandable.

▲ On the Devon stand at one of the shows held in the mid-1980s. Apart from the 'Devon 12 seater bus', the eagle-eyed will spot a Moonraker to the left of the photograph. (RC)

of the six-millionth Transporter coming off the Hanover production line) serves to confirm:

'Our Type 2 has always represented to an extraordinary degree the essential characteristics of Volkswagen's products, these being: progressive technology; quality; economy; and robustness, as well as being efficient, undemanding and holding their value. Since 1979 we have been producing the third generation of the Type 2. As the technical press confirms again and again, we have a concept whose main characteristics ensure a unique position.'

February
February 1986 saw the start of the Syncro story. Reasonably well-known images exist of a second generation Transporter clambering over terrain that no two-wheel-drive vehicle could ever countenance, apparently confirming that Volkswagen's first thoughts of a production four-wheel-drive model dated back to the mid 1970s. Unfortunately, the project wasn't official, despite it being allocated the internal project number EA 456/01. Two of Volkswagen's most

passionate engineers developed and tested a vehicle in the Sahara desert, which in turn led to the production of five all-wheel-drive prototypes in 1978. These vehicles all had switchable front-wheel drive, while transmission was via a four-speed manual box and a torque converter. A combination of the imminent arrival of the third generation Transporter and the grey nature of the project meant that no moves were made towards series production, but the knowledge gained from the exercise was useful when it was determined that, to combat the threat from American and, particularly, Japanese off-roaders, Volkswagen would produce its own such vehicle in conjunction with specialists Steyr-Daimler-Puch of Austria.

The third generation Transporter with four-wheel-drive capabilities was marketed as the Syncro and built by Steyr-Daimler-Puch at their factory in Graz, with bodies and engines coming from Germany. Unlike a conventional four-wheel-drive vehicle where the second drive had to be activated manually, the requirements of the Syncro, or rather its driver, were controlled completely automatically.

With accordingly modified running gear, power

was still directed to the rear axle, but also, via the propshaft, to the viscous coupling, which lay at the heart of the new technology. The front axle was a completely new subframe structure with front final drive and integrated viscous coupling. The coupling was capable of monitoring and regulating required additional front-wheel drive, detecting even slight differences in speed between the front and rear axles, and transferring the propelling force to the front axle accordingly. It was filled with a highly viscous silicone fluid and acted on a number of plates, some of which were splined internally, the rest externally. Given a difference in speed, the driving power was transmitted from the externally splined plates via the silicone fluid to the internally splined ones. These latter plates were connected to the pinion of the front axle differential. As a result the coupling started to lock and power moved to the front wheels. Differences in speed between the two axles, albeit minimal, were virtually constant; hence four-wheel drive was virtually always in action, although the degree of power transmitted to the front wheels varied according to the driving terrain and conditions.

Volkswagen hailed the advantages of syncro technology as being too obvious to be missed:

'Exceptional directional control particularly on smooth, slippy road surfaces with little grip.

'Optimum off-the-road performance and improved tractive power on difficult terrain, unpaved roads and on building sites.

'Outstanding tractive power particularly on snow and ice and for moving off and tackling steep difficult mountainous routes, for instance.

'Essentially neutral cornering with improved safety reserves in marginal areas.

'Positive influence on braking performance even in winter road conditions.'

The syncro system was coupled to a four-speed manual gearbox which benefited from an additional gear described as either a cross-country or off-road gear. Front and rear differential locks could be specified for use in particularly extreme conditions. The advantage of the inclusion of this feature was that each pair of wheels became rigidly locked so that the entire

▲ **Dr Carl Hahn addresses his audience on the occasion of the production of the six-millionth Transporter in January 1986.**

OVERLEAF: These two images from a brochure produced specifically to promote the Syncro models, in both Transporter and Caravelle guise, show the vehicle eating up the territory on which it came into its own. Photographed and printed before the Syncro range was officially introduced, the vehicles pictured lack some of the decals destined to make the four-wheel-drive models stand out from the rest of the crowd. *(RC)*

◀ ▼ Typical press shots of Syncro models in action – with the aid of a magnifying glass, it's possible to confirm that the vehicle has a Multivan badge on its tailgate.

▶ Although an apparently less dynamic image of the Syncro, that the vehicle is towing a yacht, and will therefore encounter off-road conditions, results in a more subtle message being presented.

tractional force might be utilised to the full. The differential switches were conveniently located on the dashboard. As might have been expected for a vehicle that could be taken off-road, an 'undertray device' was fitted forward of the front wheels, while a similar arrangement protected the engine and gearbox, and protective rails were positioned on either side of the propeller shaft. Likewise, the petrol tank was relocated to an even safer position directly ahead of the rear wheels. Little reference was made either to the wider wheels adopted by syncro models (6J x 14 compared to the normal 5½J x 14), or perhaps more significantly greater ground clearance, which in the case of Caravelle models equated to 35mm, but just 10mm where the more basic Transporters didn't have lowered suspension. Equally, it was only when the technical specification of the vehicle was listed in the small print that there was an obvious reference to 'heavy duty suspension', or the more adroit could work out that the braking system was more robust.

While it might have been assumed that the syncro option would be restricted to carefully selected models, this was not the case. Bearing in mind the rapidity with which Volkswagen changed names and options during the production run of the third generation Transporter, for the '87 model year it could be specified on the Caravelle in GL, CL and C guises, and on both the Delivery Van and the High Roofed Delivery Van, not to mention the Pick-up and Double Cab Pick-up, which in reality was the entire core range. Similarly, the Syncro ran in conjunction with a number of engine options, so

using 1987 as the example once more it was offered with the 78PS petrol engine, the 70PS turbo diesel and the 112PS fuel-injected option.

Finally, for anyone wanting to distinguish a syncro model from the rest of the pack, reliance on prominent lower-side decals reading 'syncro 4 x4' coupled to an under-the-windscreen 'syncro', would be dangerous. Earlier models lacked such trimmings, as did some of the much later examples.

As might be anticipated there was not only a special edition model based on Syncro technology but it was a Double Cab Pick-up, undoubtedly the model in the range that leant itself more than any other to the combination of load-lugging, people-carrying, off-road antics. Launched in September 1988, the Volkswagen TriStar oozed luxury and extras, ranging from alloy wheels as standard, to headlamp washers and thick pile carpet throughout the cabin area. Volkswagen's copywriters wrapped up the TriStar in the following manner:

'Externally TriStar really looks the part with large black bumpers front and rear, plastic protectors around the wheel arches, matching black skirting and twin headlight grille with high pressure headlight washers.

'For really heavy duty applications front nudge and roll bars are available as options.

'Internally TriStar is "practical" luxury for five people.

'The seats are covered in a durable cloth trim, the front seats having integral armrests, head restraints

Finding carefully posed or action-packed photographs of the third generation Transporter isn't the easiest of tasks, and it's to Volkswagen of America that homage has to be paid for these three images dating from 1987, depicting a Vanagon, a Vanagon GL and a Vanagon Syncro. (RC)

Volkswagen TriStar

▶ The cover of Volkswagen's special brochure to promote the inspirational 'TriStar' limited edition model. *(RC)*

◀ Syncro publicity shots don't come much better than this! Look more closely and the TriStar decal is evident on the metalwork below the windscreen.

▶ This carefully posed shot of the TriStar launches it as a luxurious people-carrier with which owners and friends can indulge in their favourite pastimes no matter what the conditions.

and map pockets. The floor is fully carpeted, there is a separate heating unit for the rear passengers. The rear bulkhead is lined and sound proofed...

'All four doors have armrests for comfort and open wide for easy entry and exit.'

1987

October

The Caravelle Coach special edition was launched, a vehicle that featured power steering, wide wheels, suspension lowered by 30mm, twin headlamps, anti-dazzle day and night rear-view mirror, additional heating for the passenger compartment, heated rear window and full wheel trims amongst its other attributes.

1988

August

The Multivan Magnum special edition made its debut. Apart from an under-the-windscreen decal announcing its pedigree, the external appearance of the Multivan Magnum was enhanced with rectangular-shaped twin headlamps, and heavier bumpers and lower-body side trim in black plastic. Inside, the van included Volkswagen's multi-purpose seat and bed system, a foldaway table, a slide-back window in the side door, an under-the-seat refrigerator and storage cupboards, plus general additional luxuries such as power steering, rear wipers and intermittent wipe settings for the windscreen. Like some other special editions, the Multivan Magnum could be specified with four engine options, while nine choices of exterior paint demonstrated that the colour of the vehicle wasn't a part of the limited edition's make-up.

1989

Such was the diversity in the range of third generation Transporters that the British market even went so far to add an 800kg Van to the vehicles it offered. Available only in Pastel White, the Transporter 800, as the badge proclaimed, was available with either the 1.9-litre 60PS

petrol engine, or the 1.7-litre 57PS diesel option – both offering least in terms of power within their relative segments.

With smaller wheels and tyres than the one-tonne van and a similarly downgraded anti-roll bar, the side-loading height stood at just 455m from the ground, which Volkswagen was keen to note was one of the lowest of any van. Other cost-cutting measures, such as an unglazed rear tailgate, had the effect of not only keeping the overall cost down, but also of cleverly engineering a payload of 875kg including the

▼ The Multivan Magnum made its debut in August 1988 for the 1989 model year. *(RC)*

driver, which could then be sold as being specifically designed for a new segment of the market.

1990

July

Although production of the third generation Transporter ceased at the end of the month to make way for the T4, the Syncro models continued to be built by Steyr-Daimler-Puch for a further two years.

1992

March

The final third generation Transporters with Syncro were promoted as 'Limited Last Edition' models and included decals indicating individual numbers in sequence from 1 to 2,500. The last example of all, '*2500 von 2500*' resides in the Stiftung Museum in Wolfsburg and is finished in Tornado Red, although most were painted in Orly Blue Metallic. 6J x 14 alloy wheels, body-coloured bumpers and lower-side trims, and suspension lowered by 30mm, were all aspects that helped to set the Limited Last Edition apart from most of its predecessors. Additional items such as external heated mirrors contributed to the vehicle's luxurious specification.

Although dwarfed by its predecessor in terms of production numbers, and outrun by the first generation model too, a more than creditable total of 1,227,669 third generation Transporters were nevertheless manufactured and sold around the world.

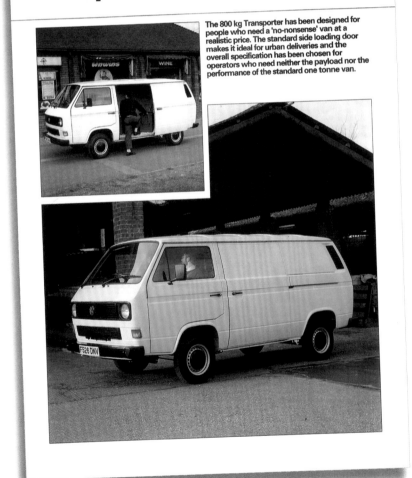

Volkswagen Commercial Vehicles

Transporter 800 kg Van

The 800 kg Transporter has been designed for people who need a 'no-nonsense' van at a realistic price. The standard side loading door makes it ideal for urban deliveries and the overall specification has been chosen for operators who need neither the payload nor the performance of the standard one tonne van.

◄ A less powerful and less expensive member of the Delivery Van line-up – the Transporter 800kg Van – theoretically opened the brand up to an additional sector of the market.

▶ An attractive publicity shot of the Limited Last Edition model, showing the vehicle finished in Orly Blue metallic paint.

1990 on

Thoroughly modern Transporters

▶ In safe but dynamic hands. The current generation Transporter, the T5, ensures that Volkswagen is ahead of the rest of the field. Sales of the vehicle in Britain for example regularly outstrip those of all other imported models..

For this account of the Transporter to be an accurate and informative celebration of its 60-year history, the exclusion of the current model and its immediate predecessor, both conventionally up-to-date vehicles, would amount to sacrilege.

Of equal validity has to be an acknowledgement of the fact that both the fourth and fifth generation's multifaceted natures – at least in comparison to those of the simple line-up of days gone by – are no more than an essential ingredient in an increasingly competitive marketplace.

Fortunately, although the fourth generation

Transporter's story is more complex than that of its predecessor, it is at least finite and can be tailored to some extent into comparatively few words without compromising the narrative.

As for the fifth generation models, make no mistake about it, the T5s are awesomely well-equipped beasts, whether in workaday clothing, on a mission to convey passengers from one point to another in the lap of luxury, or – for the first time in six decades of Volkswagen Transporter production – as a home-built Camper, the California, as discussed in the section allocated to campers generally (page 330 onwards).

The T4 – 'Now a complete range of vehicles'

The T4, as the fourth generation model is widely known – no nickname having been adopted, at least as yet – was a product of the Hahn era at Volkswagen. As we have seen, Volkswagen's fifth Director General succeeded Toni Schmücker on 1 January 1982, and left office 11 years later. His strategy as the man in overall charge was one of growth and multi-markets, a policy that raised the VW Group of companies to new heights amongst European manufactures, and one that

allowed them to develop a wider variety of vehicles to cover every taste and demand conceivable. Specific to the Transporter, it would have been difficult to imagine anything other than a message of conventionality and conformity emerging from Hahn's office. Leiding's oddball tactic of retaining the Transporter's engine at the rear, inevitably coupling it with rear-wheel drive, had no place in the Volkswagen story devised by Hahn for the 1990s.

Overview of the fourth generation

What was widely expected, Hahn delivered: vehicles with front-wheel drive, front-mounted engines, and completely flat loading beds. It was no revelation that a new and entirely conventional range of engines ensured that all models were both sufficiently powerful to keep up with the offerings from other stables, and fuel efficient. That the Pick-ups, single and Double Cab, of old had been superseded by a new breed of chassis cabs as a result of such changes did not come as a shock. Nor was there any surprise that, in line with the norm for other commercial vehicle manufacturers, there was now the option of a long-wheelbase version.

An official although retrospective utterance had a particular way of telling the story of the by now necessary conventionality of the new arrival, as the following extract on the T4 from Wolfsburg's *Snapshots of a Legend – 50 years of the Volkswagen Transporter* demonstrates. Note how the key message falls in the last sentence!

'Commercial users benefit from the now fully flat cargo floor, the wide sliding doors, which open effortlessly, and the massive tailgate also requiring very little force to use. But they also wonder what made Volkswagen put so much comfort into a commercial

▼ Volkswagen confirm the Transporter illustrated to be a Kombi, but perhaps of most interest is the TDI badge on the grille – a symbol of powerful, responsive, yet economical engines that were effectively to eclipse the supremacy of most forms of petrol power.

vehicle? You only need to look at the now increasingly Asian competition to see how it can be done in a simpler, harder, less durable and less safe way.'

In expectation of the new model, the Hanover plant underwent a rather drastic, if entirely beneficial, makeover. With the automation of axle, engine and gear installations, overhead work became more or less obsolete, to the immediate advantage of the plant's employees, while steps had previously been taken to remove chemical solvents with a new automated paint facility reliant largely on water-based products.

Production of the fourth generation Transporter began on 6 January 1990 some months in advance of the vehicle's official press launch, which occurred in May, and even further ahead of the showroom debut across the world in August of the same year.

Unlike its immediate predecessor and the second generation Transporter, the T4 range was incomplete at launch, despite assertions from eager copywriters to the contrary. As examples, singular by its absence at the time of launch was any form of double cab, previously a volume seller, while the relatively niche market option of a long-wheelbase High Roofed Van was also missing. Also, despite genuine excitement about the new range of engines offered, Volkswagen later deemed that there was room for further improvement, as the following additional extract from *Snapshots of a Legend* confirms:

'As soon as it was launched the T4 again set a new standard in its market segment. But it still fell a little short of perfection. The engines were good enough, they were frugal in fuel consumption and durable. But they were not exactly punchy.'

The days of the turbo diesels and, of course, the immensely powerful VR6 were still a few years ahead.

Five possible engine options

The engines available at the time of the new Transporter's launch were five in number, although one was offered in two guises, while each was coupled to a five-speed box. All were transversely mounted, with access enhanced by the use of a moveable radiator to make servicing as easy as possible. Similarly, the routine check elements of the engines were accessed from the top of the engine compartment, while a standard equipment under-bonnet light helped improve visibility.

Designed for use in the workhorse models only, there was a 1.9-litre, four-cylinder diesel engine with an output of 61PS achieved at a maximum of 3,700rpm, and producing maximum torque of 127Nm between 1,700 and 2,500rpm. To complement this option, and for those who preferred petrol, a 1.8-litre engine developing a maximum of 67PS at 4,000rpm and 149Nm of torque at 2,200rpm was also offered.

Two of the larger engines, one diesel and one petrol, could be found not only in the Transporter but also in the Caravelle, the two distinct brand names – one for the workhorse models, the other for the people-carriers – having been retained from their introduction during the production run of the previous generation. The top of the range Caravelle GL could be specified either with the big diesel engine, or its own exclusive petrol engine.

The five-cylinder, 2.4-litre, 2,370cc diesel engine, with a compression ratio of 22.5:1, and a bore and stroke of 79.5mm x 95.5mm, developed a maximum of 78PS at 3,700rpm, with maximum torque of 164Nm occurring between 1,800 and 2,000rpm. Maximum speed, according to Volkswagen, ranged between 79 and 87mph, the latter being pertinent to the Delivery Van and the Caravelle, the former to the chassis cab, with an auto-box option sliding between the two at 83mph. Fuel consumption varied similarly, the best figure of 39.8mpg being given for a Caravelle travelling at a constant 56mph, although this could easily soak away to as little as 26.1mpg for a Transporter with an auto box and half payload, operating at three-quarters maximum speed plus ten per cent.

The 2.0-litre petrol engine was available with, or without, a catalytic converter, and was offered on all models in either guise, with the exception of the Caravelle GL already mentioned, and, in the case of the 'Cat' version, the 800kg payload Delivery Van. With a cubic capacity of 1,968, bore and stroke of 81.0mm x 95.5mm, and a compression ratio of 8.5:1, the engine produced a maximum of 84PS at 4,300rpm, with maximum torque of 159Nm being achieved at 2,200rpm. It was capable of a top speed of 91mph, but fuel consumption, whichever way the figures are assessed, was hardly sparkling. Volkswagen quoted 19.3mpg for the urban cycle, 29.7 at a constant 56mph, and 20.3mpg at a constant – if in some countries lawbreaking – 75mph. Alternatively, for the load-carrying models only, with half payload, and running at three-quarter maximum speed plus ten per cent, an overall figure of 20.9mpg was announced.

Briefly alluding to the exclusive property of the Caravelle GL, here was a five-cylinder 2,459cc in-line, transversely mounted petrol engine that developed 110PS at 4,500rpm and stimulated a driver to attempt a top speed of 110mph. The penalty, excluding the presence of a three-way

Publicity shots showing work in progress moving towards the completion of more T4s.

catalytic converter, was undoubtedly in the form of heavy fuel consumption, although at least there was a little sting in the tail for those who had chosen less luxury and a smaller engine. The urban cycle figure was calculated at just 18.0mpg, and at a constant 56mph a straight 30mpg was the result. At a constant 75mph, consumption was heavier as might have been expected, with the figure being shown at 21.1mpg. While not suggesting that the big five-cylinder

engine was a definite way forward, it is undoubtedly interesting to note that both at a constant 56mph and at 75mph the 2.5-litre engine was slightly more frugal than its smaller sibling.

As a footnote, the fascination with syncro of a few years earlier seemed to have more or less evaporated, although it did remain on the list as a choice, tending to be available mated to the largest engine option associated with a given model.

Bigger and better than its predecessor?

That the fourth generation Transporter was a longer vehicle with an extended wheelbase compared to that of its predecessor, there can be no doubt. If there was any controversy, it regarded the amount of usable space, with the protagonists of each model arguing their respective cases.

From the single wheelbase of 2,460mm offered with the third generation Transporter, even the new model's shorter option of 2,920mm made it appear a much larger vehicle. (The long-wheelbase option rolled in at 3,320mm.) Using the short wheelbase fourth generation Transporter in Delivery Van guise as the object for comparison, at 4,707mm the new model was some 137mm longer than its predecessor. However, the T4 was marginally narrower than the third generation Delivery Van, albeit by just 5mm (1,840mm compared to 1,845mm), while in terms of overall height there was a drop of 10mm for the new model, which stood at 1,940mm compared to the third generation's 1,950mm. The wider front track, up from 1,570mm to 1,589mm, and narrower rear track, down from 1,570mm to 1,554mm, did little for the turning circle, which now stood at 11.7m for the short-wheelbase T4 and an expected 12.9m for the long-wheelbase options, compared to the tight 10.7m of the third generation Transporter.

Despite the increase in both overall length and wheelbase, even with the shorter versions of the fourth generation Transporter, in terms of load space the new model could only offer 5.4m³ compared to the third generation's 5.7. Of course, aficionados of the front-wheel-drive, front-engined T4 could quickly point to the 'impressive' 6.3m³ of loading space afforded by the long-wheelbase model, and to the lack of an obtrusive humped floor at the rear, a characteristic of the old third generation Transporter and its predecessors, which was bound to make the heaving of parcels through the tailgate more difficult. On a suitable roll, they might also refer to a wider side door of 1,092mm compared to 1,060mm, the minimal wheelarch intrusion, leaving a handsome space of 1,220mm between them, and to the load-floor height of just 520mm, 'one of the lowest available on any van'. As a couple of final blows,

they might mention the cab step height of 408mm, before pointing out the economy associated with a Cd coefficient of 0.37. The problem, if there was one, came in explaining away the proportions of the cab, for after all, part of Volkswagen's marketing strategy centred upon the fact that 'all the major running components – engine, gearbox, final drive and fuel tank' were 'now incorporated within the cab area of the new Transporter'. There was no getting away from it: there was more bulk at the front of the vehicle, a mass which resulted in a longer vehicle overall but one with a slightly smaller loading area.

Volkswagen played the card of 'technical superiority' over the third generation Transporter and particularly over that of other manufacturers' products with consummate ease. Everything is neatly locked together in the following extract, but note how the copywriter includes aspects that might best be described as traditional to the specification of earlier generations:

'The new Transporter is unique amongst commercial vehicles in having independent suspension front and rear. The compact front suspension uses double wishbones and torsion springs together with short shock absorbers so that none of the components project into the footwell area.

'At the rear, diagonal trailing arms and coil springs are used. Again a compact arrangement has been achieved by mounting the shock absorbers below the load floor. … The rack and pinion steering is connected via universal joints and collapsible struts so that in the event of a collision the steering wheel cannot be pushed back towards the driver.

'Disc brakes are used at the front and drum brakes at the rear. According to model either 14 inch or 15 inch wheels are fitted. Ventilated discs are used with 15 inch wheels. A dual circuit system with load sensing valve ensures that the correct brake pressure is applied over varying load conditions.

'Extensive anti-corrosion treatments are applied during manufacture including dip-degreasing, zinc phosphating and catopheretic priming. In addition cavities are flooded with hot wax as a further protection against rust.'

▲ ▷ Two examples of the fourth generation Transporter in workaday guise: each bears company branding – one well-known and the other not so well. As an aside, note how the bodywork of the Coke van has been damaged thanks to crates hitting bare metal in the vehicle's loading area. *(RC)*

Launch-day options

Analysis of publicity material produced at the time of the fourth generation Transporter's launch confirms what Hahn and his team had already predetermined what was most important about the new model:

'Much thought and care has gone into every aspect of its design. From the front engine with front wheel drive, to the low flat load floor and wide opening rear doors. From the moulded dashboard and door panels, to the independent suspension front and rear. From the aerodynamic shape, to the extensive anti-corrosion treatment … Two wheelbases, four engines, three payloads and a variety of body styles can all be added to Volkswagen's enviable reputation for reliability and economy to make the new Transporter a real success.'

Despite this apparent whirl of complexity, the range on offer – at least for the British market – was relatively straightforward, with a straight spilt between Transporters and Caravelles. Taking the latter first, compared to the specification of models produced not all that long ago luxury was inherent, and at the lowlier CL level of trim, in the tradition established during the run of the third generation

▲ ▶ Earlier Delivery Vans may have enabled goods to be placed in the rear, but never with such ease as now. The double doors were standard, the tailgate was a useful option.

model. Cloth upholstery and carpeted floors were now the norm. The GL specification added to the package such luxuries as contoured seats, an array of armrests, and such trivialities as 'full diameter' wheel trims. The CL could be specified with either eight or nine seats, while the GL came with seven.

As for the workaday models, essentially there were three core variations on the Delivery Van theme, ranging from the 800kg short-wheelbase option, via the 1,000kg offering, again on a short wheelbase, to the long-wheelbase 1,200kg model. At each vehicles' rear, and in addition to the by now normal sliding side door, the fourth generation model was the first to benefit from double doors which opened on stays to hold them at 90° or, by using the quick-release mechanism, to 180°. A tailgate could be specified as an alternative, as could either choice in unglazed form. Specific reference was made to the option of a 'hardboard load-lining', while a full bulkhead might also be requested.

New to the range was the chassis cab, a body option – or possibly the lack of it – that was set to replace the Pick-up, however much brochures and other documentation implied that a model of that name was both part of the range and a separate entity.

An abundance of publicity shots were produced to illustrate both the single and double chassis cab models.

While just a single copywriter referred to the cab units as having a 'clean, bodybuilder-friendly chassis', not one omitted mention of its independent rear suspension, or its versatility: 'The perfect base for a wide variety of bodies from simple drop-sides and boxes, through tippers and refrigerated bodies and on to more specialised applications.'

The chassis cab was only available in conjunction with the long wheelbase, and initially a double cab option wasn't included. However, with that choice included it became easier to suggest that the vehicles listed as having a drop-down wooden-sided load area were, indeed, Pick-ups.

The construction of the chassis centred upon U-section longitudinal and cross members. These were closed by the combination of the floor plate of the cab and inverted U-sections for the chassis rails, which in turn formed a rigid box construction. The net result was a blend of minimal weight, great strength and torsional stiffness. Volkswagen must have known that they had chosen a winning design when they could proclaim with surety that the chassis allowed body lengths of up to 3,100mm. This in turn allowed one copywriter to announce in a 'Volkswagen based Motor Caravans' brochure that:

'A coachbuilt motor caravan gives you the freedom to live in style. The space provided by the coachbuilt body enables the converter to fit in all the comforts of home including a separate shower/ toilet compartment, a comprehensive kitchen and comfortable dinette, and seating areas which convert to luxury beds at night.'

Research at Wolfsburg confirmed that the Hanover plant always 'shipped' cabs in pairs for ease of handling, and that the 'low bed frames' were added by the bodybuilder.

▼ Coachbuilders Karmann produced amongst other models this attractive Colorado – the essence of luxury on wheels, and only practical with a chassis cab arrangement.

The tradition of a host of officially approved special models continued unabated, as did the availability of optional equipment.

▶ With modifications for use by the AA in Britain.

▼ The Caravelle was commonly adapted for use as a taxi.

▲ Two Caravelle-based ambulances.

◀ A chassis double cab with additional storage.

▶ A 'party service' Transporter.

▲ The latest on a low-loader theme.

◄ The VW 'Glaswagen'.

Continual improvement

Just because a conventional approach was now deemed appropriate didn't necessarily mean that Volkswagen were going to break with another tradition, as a glance through a brochure promoting the T4 in its final years, compared to one covering the model at launch, instantly confirms. However, it went further than that, as even by the 1995 model year something as simple as the British Transporter Range line-up held one or two surprises. The number of variations on the theme had increased, while the variety in engine options was equally plentiful:

Delivery Van – short wheelbase		
800 Special	1.9-litre Diesel	61PS
1,000kg	2.0-litre Petrol	84PS
1,000kg	2.5-litre Petrol	110PS
1,000kg	1.9-litre Diesel	61PS
1,000kg	2.4-litre Diesel	78PS
900kg syncro	2.4-litre Diesel	78PS

Delivery Van – long wheelbase		
1,200kg	2.5-litre Petrol	110PS
1,200kg	2.4-litre Diesel	78PS
1,100kg syncro	2.4-litre Diesel	78PS

High Roofed Delivery Van – Long Wheelbase		
1,200kg	2.4-litre Diesel	78PS
Chassis Cab		
1,200kg	2.4-litre Diesel	78PS
1,100kg syncro	2.4-litre Diesel	78PS
Double Cab		
1,000kg	2.4-litre Diesel	78PS
900kg syncro	2.4-litre Diesel	78PS

▼ Like many a modern engine, there isn't a great deal to be seen when the bonnet is opened. Nevertheless, Volkswagen produced a series of publicity shots. This is the 150ps TDI unit.

Then compare this 1995 listing with that of the 1998 model year reproduced below and bear witness to the age of the turbo diesel and additional payloads:

Delivery Van – short wheelbase		
800 Special	1.9-litre TD Diesel	68PS
1,000kg	2.0-litre Petrol	84PS
1,000kg	1.9-litre TD Diesel	68PS
1,200kg	2.5-litre Petrol	114PS
1,200kg	2.4-litre SD Diesel	78PS
1,200kg	2.5-litre TDI Diesel	102PS

Delivery Van – long wheelbase		
1,000kg	2.0-litre Petrol	84PS
1,000kg	1.9-litre TD Diesel	68PS
1,200kg	2.5-litre Petrol	114PS
1,200kg	2.4-litre SD Diesel	78PS
1,200kg	2.5-litre TDI Diesel	102PS

High Roofed Delivery Van – long wheelbase		
1,200kg	2.5-litre Petrol	114PS
1,200kg	2.4-litre SD Diesel	78PS
1,200kg	2.5-litre TDI Diesel	102PS

Chassis Cab – long wheelbase		
1,200kg	2.4-litre SD Diesel	75PS
1,200kg	2.5-litre TDI Diesel	102PS

Double Cab – long wheelbase		
1,000kg	2.4-litre SD Diesel	75PS
1,000kg	2.5-litre TDI Diesel	102PS

The notes accompanying this chart are equally interesting:

'Window Vans – Many of the models listed are also available as window vans suitable for minibus conversions or special applications.'

Such terminology seems to sound the death-knell for the once highly popular Kombi option. However, this subject will be covered in more depth when we come to the fifth generation Transporter, but for the moment a further footnote reaffirms the status of the Pick-up, now termed the 'dropside':

'All of the models listed are available as chassis for locally built bodies or with a factory built dropside body.'

Such footnotes tended to be covered in the main text penned by the ever-enthusiastic copywriter:

'Many operators find they do not need to specify a special body. A standard pick-up is all they require. Volkswagen have the answer with a strong, versatile pick-up body that can be fitted to the Transporter at the time of manufacture. With a choice between ribbed steel or alloy for the dropside, a large load area and compact overall dimensions, these purpose built commercial vehicles have become the hardworking favourite of many trades and businesses.'

By this time too, the Caravelle had moved forward significantly, even spawning what had now become a definite sub-species, a type which had first seen the light of day as a special in 1985 during the time of the third generation Transporter. Fortunately for our purposes here, Volkswagen summarised the updates particularly succinctly:

'Caravelle and Multivan –
'The Caravelle is the ultimate MPV ... The Caravelle GL now includes air conditioning as standard ... The range has been extended to include the new seven seat Multivan, which has been specifically designed to offer even more flexibility on the move with the addition of a folding seat that converts into a full size double bed. All Caravelle models benefit from a number of refinements to ensure that it stays in a class of its own. To house an impressive VR6 engine option, a longer bonnet has been introduced which, when coupled with new foam-filled bumpers, upholstery and paint colours, brings a complete new look to Caravelles. There are also some technical improvements including disc brakes at front and rear, improved suspension for better ride and handling, and two new engines. ABS braking and traction control come as standard with the new 2.8 litre 140PS VR6 engine, and is optional with other engines.'

The redesign of the bonnet and the new bumpers had the effect of increasing the overall length of both the short- and long-wheelbase models. From the 4,707mm overall length recorded for the short-wheelbase Transporter when it was launched (and, incidentally, used for comparison purposes between the fourth and fifth generation models), the changes in specification meant an increase of 82mm, or a total length of 4,789mm. However, it is worth pointing out that the workhorse Transporters retained their original look, the differences between the two genres proving useful to enthusiasts if no one else when wanting to identify the type of fourth generation they had encountered.

▲ ▶ Caravelles with the VR6 engine (above in the background and right), as indicated by the badge on the grille.

Standard equipment on all Caravelles now encompassed engine immobiliser, power-assisted steering, collapsible steering column, rear wash/wipe, heated rear window, pollen filter, stereo radio cassette, rear luggage cover (short-wheelbase only), recirculating ventilation control and a windscreen aerial. The Caravelle was available as a short-wheelbase model with either seven or eight seats, or as a long-wheelbase with either nine or ten seats. Syncro remained an option with just about every model.

Over and above the standard specification of the Caravelle but lacking some attributes of the Caravelle GL, the Multivan – which for the British market at least was only offered in conjunction with a short wheelbase – benefited additionally from two removable rear-facing seats, a folding rear bench which could be converted to a bed, a folding table and electric cab windows and door mirrors. All the engine options afforded to the Caravelle, which at this point included everything other than the 68PS 1.9TD diesel, were available for would-be Multivan owners too.

As an indication of just how luxurious and sophisticated the GL, or top-of-the-range, model was becoming, in addition to the already referred to air conditioning other standard items included

Numerous promotional images were made available of the Caravelle, the Multivan and the California camper sporting the new-look bonnet and bumpers.

◥ No VR6 badge, no diesel indicator, therefore it's a straightforward petrol engine model!

◀ The Caravelle with TDI engine.

▲ The Multivan was now a standard part of the range.

▶ The California Advantage special edition.

▲ The Caravelle with a VR6 engine can be identified by an appropriate badge on the grille.

▼ The redesigned dash and interior of 2000 vintage.

central locking, armrests on all but the folding seats, tinted glass all round, velour upholstery and carpeted interior, colour-coded bumpers and mirrors and electric cab mirrors and door mirrors.

However, the most exciting aspect of the latest line-up had to be the new VR6 engine, originally developed for the Passat syncro and certainly a power plant which took the Transporter into a different league in terms of performance. The transversely mounted, six-cylinder, narrow angle V produced a maximum of 140PS at 4,500 rpm, while greatest torque of 240Nm was achieved between 3,000 and 3,400rpm. The 2,792cc engine had a bore and stroke of 81.0mm x 90.3mm, and a compression ratio of 10.0:1. Even when linked to an automatic gearbox, which was the norm for the UK market, the VR6 was capable of a top speed of 109mph, although with an overall fuel consumption figure of 21.7mpg it could hardly be considered as particularly fuel thrifty.

For the millennium model year, a further redesigned dashboard brought the fourth generation Transporter more in line with the rest of Volkswagen's by then particularly well-crafted passenger interiors. Makeovers, including name changes, were commonplace and for 2000 the range of Caravelles were identified as the 'Sedan', a distinctly luxurious eight-seat short-wheelbase or nine-seat long-wheelbase starter model; the 'Variant', where potential purchasers could choose between a standard eight-seat model, three different seven-seat packages, and what Volkswagen described as a 'roomy' six-seat vehicle; and the 'Multivan', which seemed to have acquired an additional strata of clientele in the form of the 'busy executive', who would have loved 'the rear facing seats which form[ed] the ideal mobile office or meeting place'.

However, the ultimate T4 of the age was the 'Caravelle Limousine', a vehicle which when mated to the VR6 engine and an automatic box cost nearly twice as much as Volkswagen's legendary two-door Golf GTI with a 1.8 turbocharged engine. The specification included:

Full luxury leather interior, armrests for all seats, remote central locking, electric front windows, electric heated door mirrors, full climatronic air conditioning, ABS and EDS, twin sliding doors, Gama stereo radio cassette player, twin airbags, multi-function indicator, cruise control, electric sunroof, luggage compartment shelf, dark tinted glass to the rear windows, front fog lights, headlamp washers, six spoke alloy wheels, metallic or pearl paint.'

The humble box on wheels had indeed come a long way, and yet there was still more to come for eager customers with the fifth generation Transporter.

Number crunching

Finally, no overview of the fourth generation model would be complete without an indication of production numbers. While the heady days of the second generation weren't revived, at least annual figures continued in the same vein as those of the fourth generation's predecessor. In 1991, the first full year of production, 137,682 such vehicles were produced. In 1992 this increased to 167,830, but dropped back sharply the following year as recession struck not only Germany but other countries too: just 129,779 Transporters were produced. A revival followed in 1994, as the figure crept back up to 135,444, a number slightly bettered by the 141,355 Transporters produced in 1995; 1994 had also borne witness to the 500,000th fourth generation model being built. The following year, 1996, saw little change, with a total of 141,454 vehicles being recorded, but in both 1997 and 1998 production passed the 150,000 mark, with 155,436 T4s leaving Hanover in the first year and 154,982 in the second. Both years were also significant for other reasons, 1997 heralding the eight millionth Transporter, and 1998 the millionth fourth generation Transporter. Sadly, 1999 saw production drop back to a rather more lowly 148,886, while 2000 bore witness to the best year of all for the T4 with 162,699 Transporters of one kind or another being produced. The drop of over 10,000 vehicles down to 151,722 experienced in 2001 must have been a little disappointing for Volkswagen, if not as alarming as the final full year of T4 production, when the figure slipped further to 131,913.

▶ The cover of the brochure produced to promote the luxurious Caravelle Limousine.

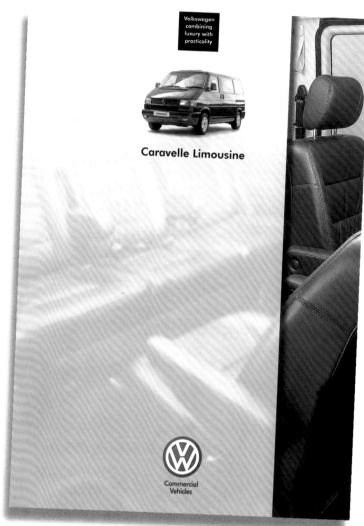

Volkswagen combining luxury with practicality

Caravelle Limousine

VW Commercial Vehicles

◀ The Last Edition – the T4 bows out in style!

The T5 – at the forefront of van production

The fifth and current ambassador of Volkswagen's Transporter brand, the T5, made its public debut at the Auto Mobil International held in Leipzig in March 2003. In the most recent version of *Volkswagen Chronicle*, published in 2006 – one of a growing number of volumes produced by VW's Corporate History Department – writer Markus Lupo is proud to announce that with the T5 'the Volkswagen brand is able to maintain its market leadership in the van segment in Germany and Europe'. Certainly with annual production running at 148,552 units in 2004, followed by 177,956 vehicles in 2005, there is little doubt that Transporter sales will never simply ebb away until competitors in the market usurp the lion's share. It can also be predicted with some confidence that when the T6 emerges – and on present and past form

this is likely to be at least five, if not more, years in the future – this as yet hypothetical vehicle will take centre stage, once more ahead of the competition.

One minor point regarding model years needs to be clarified in relation to the T5. Part-way through the production run of the T4, a practice introduced in the summer of 1955 whereby the new model year ran from the beginning of August through to the end of the following July was discontinued. Hence, although the model year 1999 began in August 1998 in what had become the time-honoured manner, it finished at the end of April 1999. The inevitable result was that model year 2000 and all subsequent ones have run from 1 May of one year through to 30 April of the next. The T5 is in reality a product delivered for the 2004 model year and onwards, despite the calendar date already given for its unveiling.

▼ **Multivan Business.**

▶ The T5 is the perfect ambassador for Volkswagen – the latest in a long line of models forging the way ahead and a vehicle for other manufacturers to emulate.

▼ Launching the Transporter at the Auto Mobil International in March 2003.

Numerous images are available to tell the T5's story. Startlines rub bumpers with Comfortlines, even if the Multivan Business is a cut above the rest!

▲ Startline.

◀ Comfortline.

▼ Startline.

◥ Comfortline.

▶ The luxurious interior of the Multivan Business.

The product range

Set foot on the forecourt of a German dealership, or delve into the appropriate Volkswagen website written in the mother tongue, and a vast array of T5 offerings will greet you. For the 2009 model year the full line-up of what might loosely be termed commercial vehicles encompasses a variety of standard vans in both low- and high-roofed guises, a flatbed or chassis truck subdivided into single and double cab versions, and what Volkswagen describe as 'combos', vehicle transporters, sales vehicles, crane cars and tipper trucks. Ignoring the somewhat curious spelling of the word 'combo', accept with a degree of caution that basic Transporter models include vans with windows and removable seats as in days of old.

Neatly displayed in an adjacent line, and – as it will be covered elsewhere – ignoring the VW California, there are also the familiarly termed Caravelles, now presented in two guises, the Trendline and the more upmarket Comfortline, both described as a cross between a minibus and a people-carrier. Deigning to rub shoulders with the overalls and working boots brigade on the one hand and taxi drivers and minibus operators on the other, are the Multivans, described by Volkswagen as sitting in the 'exclusive niche of multi-utility vehicles' (MUV). From the Startline, the series progresses to the Comfortline, and then to the Highline (a term previously used to describe the high-specification models often offered as a Volkswagen car approached the end of its natural production run) and the Multivan Business, a vehicle summarised by the factory as possessing 'extraordinary luxury above the Multivan Highline and offer[ing] exclusivity which is peerless.'

Only one complication apparently exists after such a cavalcade of variety in fifth generation models, and this comes in the form of Volkswagen's propensity for limited edition models packed with extra goodies to entice would-be buyers to stay with the marque. In the summer of 2008 these included the luxurious Multivan Concert and the Multivan United, plus the California Biker and the California Beach. If audio plays a significant role in the specification of the Multivan Concert, while the California Biker is adorned with a prominent cycle rack across its rear hatch, perhaps the storyline is obvious.

So far limited edition special models have abounded during the reign of the T5. A search through Volkswagen's archive reveals the following:

▼ Multivan 4 Motion Beach.

▶ Kombi Sport Edition.

▼ Kombi Concert.

▲ The Panel or Delivery Van – no frills!

◀ Is that a short-wheelbase Delivery Van trying to hide a high-roof long-wheelbase model?

▲ No publicity shot of a high-roof
Delivery Van would be complete
without someone loading a bulky item
through the cavernous door.

Sadly, though, for lovers of simplicity, a smattering of specials does not spell the end of the story. Aficionados of the T4, if not the owners of earlier generation Transporters, will be unsurprised to find that long- and short-wheelbase options are available on a variety of models, while even followers of the first generation Transporter of 1960s vintage will be conversant with the notion of a high-roofed Panel van, though the diversity of roof options – particularly when linked to more than one wheelbase – will come as something of a surprise. Couple such factors to a group of four diesel engines, each providing progressively more oomph than its smaller relative, supplemented by two petrol offerings ranging from run-of-the-mill to now well-established V6 technology, and degree-level learning courses loom large.

Perhaps, then, the time has come to turn to British market simplicity. Possibly; but even then the emergence of different terminology and name confusion demands concentration! Irritatingly for the would-be purchaser or simple enthusiast, such a roll-call of commercial and MPV metal is not to be found on the forecourt of the Volkswagen car dealer, but only in the showrooms of the relatively few – 70 in number – dedicated Van Centres. Panel van, yes, cab and platform without question – but the California

and a genuine people-carrier seem a little odd, even from the perspective of Volkswagen's wider sales pitch.

First out of the Transporter pod for 2009 are the Panel vans, closely followed by the Chassis and Double Cab. So far no problem, despite a slight repositioning in terminology, but next comes the 'Window van', summarised as 'Volkswagen's heavy duty answer to passenger carrying', or, slightly more confusingly, as 'a van for specialised passenger carrying or conversion'.

One click further into the van website, or a quick flick to a different brochure, reveals the Volkswagen Transporter shuttle, and yes, the small 's' is not a proof-reader's oversight. Available with an 'S' level specification, for which read attractively appointed base model, or the familiar – at least in VW circles – SE package, as found throughout the passenger car range with the exception of the Brazilian-built baby Fox and the much larger and incredibly popular Passat.

Then arrives the Transporter Sportline, an as yet unheard of variation on what appears to be a popular theme, on the German market at least. Finally, if the California is excluded, there are the Caravelles, the well-trimmed SE and the even more luxurious Executive.

▲ ▶ When is a Kombi not a Kombi? The answer appears to be when it is a Window van with, or without, a higher top.

◀ From straightforward chassis … to a single cab … and the Double Cab.

However, while nowhere near as complex as the line-up offered in Germany, there are complications. For 2009 the Sportline has side windows in the Window van style, whereas an earlier and impeccably cleanly designed brochure of great panache implies these are exclusive to the Panel van.

Then there's the VW UK press release of March 2007 for the 2008 model year, dangled in front of the noses of journalists, talented or otherwise, which heralds 'extra value' in the form of S and SE packs for Panel van drivers and passengers, not to mention the earlier special edition Transporter Trendline, a limited run short-wheelbase Panel van bearing the brand name of a Caravelle model – or at least, such a model when offered in Germany.

Clearly, prudence would dictate a ruling to all parties of 'back to basics', but unfortunately there has to be one more detour away from the core story. Most if not all Transporter markets these days will be found to include an automatic option, either in the style of the auto-boxes produced before the arrival of direct shift gearboxes (DSG), Tiptronic, or the ability to shift manually upwards or downwards. Likewise, mention has to be made of 4MOTION.

◀▼ **Enter the Volkswagen Transporter Shuttle – a further variation on the Kombi theme.**

▲ The Transporter Sportline Kombi made its debut at the 2008 CV show as far as the British market was concerned.

▶ The Transporter Trendline, for the British market, with a package of luxuries such as air-conditioning and electric windows.

▲ 4MOTION is available for most T5 incarnations, as the following lively action shots indicate. One giveaway is the badge on the rear.

▼ Many Volkswagen press shots merely indicate that the vehicle pictured is blessed with 4MOTION, and rely on a spray of mud to do the rest.

▶ Double cab in 4MOTION guise.

◄ **Comfortline causes discomfort for passengers!**

▼ **The Shuttle 4MOTION out on an autumn stroll.**

This permanent four-wheel-drive system made its debut in Britain coupled to a Golf, the appropriately named V6 4MOTION, a spring introduction in the first year of the current millennium. Employing a Haldex coupling – a medium incapacitated in terms of influencing the drive to the front wheels, but also

unable to push the rear wheels faster than those at the front – the primary additional advantage of the coupling arrangement is in the adjustable nature of the amount of torque that is sent to the back wheels, directed through electronically controlled hydraulic actuation of its clutch plates.

Engine options

True to the spirit of the current millennium, or at least its first decade, the fifth generation marks a further advance in the invasion of advanced diesel technology. Never at a Transporter's launch had the number of diesel options so completely flooded the market once dominated by petrol models. Only a few years previously it would have been unthinkable that a workaday delivery van with a petrol engine was no longer an option for the British market, or that back in Germany only one plodding petrol option and one rather desirable if undoubtedly thirsty V6 could be specified across the entire voluminous range.

As a general guide, but certainly not exclusively, most of the options below relate to the British market, but not necessarily at launch, while the intricacies of an option with one type of T5 and not another have to be skimmed over for reasons of space if no other. As an example of the first type, reference to 4MOTION and the 130PS engine is not to be found in the earliest British market line-up, but by 2006 this position had altered. In the second instance, while the 174PS engine couldn't be specified with all-wheel drive in straightforward Transporter guise even by 2006, it was a key option when the California made its debut in the UK during the course of the same year. Turning to the petrol engines, British customers were only offered the Caravelle with a V6 at launch; another petrol engine existed and still does, but this was a preserve of the home market. Reference to this less powerful option's make up is as a result brief.

Justifiably described by Volkswagen as 'powerful' and 'extremely' economical, the four TDI engines contain at their hearts *Pumpe Düse*, or PD, technology, which translates as 'unit injector'. PD fuel injection indicates a system that can operate at pressures of up to 2,050 bars or 30,000psi. Such a high injection pressure ensures better mixing of fuel and air, and allows more to be burnt cleanly in each cylinder. The finer adjustment of the fuel-injection process and much higher pressure results in higher torque without detrimental results to fuel consumption, or CO_2 emissions. Each of the four engines are transverse water-cooled in-line units, with variable turbine geometry turbochargers, featuring direct injection and intercoolers.

The starter or baby of the less powerful 1,896cc engines produces 84PS at 3,500rpm, and develops maximum torque of 200Nm at 2,000rpm. Mated to a five-speed box as would now be expected, when allocated to the short-wheelbase Panel or Window van with a low roof, the engine is capable of a top speed of 91mph and offers a leisurely 0–62mph time of 23.6 seconds. Volkswagen suggests a combined fuel consumption figure of 36.2mpg.

The other 1,896cc engine develops 102PS, again at 3,500rpm, with maximum torque of 250Nm, once more achieved at 2,000rpm. This larger 1.9TDI, again mated exclusively to a five-speed box, offers a combined fuel consumption figure of 34.9mpg. Using the short-wheelbase Panel van or Window van with a low roof as the baseline to measure top speed attainment and acceleration capability, the 102PS engine offers 99mph, and achieves the magic 0–62mph in a still somewhat leisurely time of 18.4 seconds.

Two 2,460cc, or 2.5-litre, five-cylinder engines are offered, both engineered to make the T5 perform in a manner equal to that of many medium-sized cars designed for people on the move. The less powerful of the two develops 130PS at 3,500rpm, with maximum torque of 340Nm being achieved at 2,000rpm. Available with a six-speed manual box, or with the option of six forward ratio auto Tiptronic, this is the only engine which in Transporter guise can be paired with Volkswagen's versatile all-wheel-drive 4MOTION. Again using the Panel or Window van in its short-wheelbase, low-roofed guise as the example, the 130PS engine achieves 0–62mph in 15.3 seconds and a top speed of 104mph in manual guise. The luxury or laziness of Tiptronic knocks just one second off the 0–62mph sprint and only 2mph off the top speed. Permanent four-wheel drive, in reality an over-simplification of the attractions of 4MOTION, has the effect of extending 0–62mph acceleration to 16.3 seconds, although, perhaps a little surprisingly, the top speed of 103mph is only 1mph behind that of the straightforward manual vehicle with front-wheel drive. Fuel consumption figures offer few surprises, with penalties for both the Tiptronic and 4MOTION options. In straightforward manual guise the T5 with a 130PS engine offers drivers a combined consumption figure of 33.6mpg according to Volkswagen's statistics; this drops to 30.7mpg with four-wheel drive and to 29.4mpg when the clutch pedal is absent.

Volkswagen's most powerful diesel engine option for the fifth generation develops an impressive 174PS at 3,500rpm and really beefs up the pace, with an impressive 400Nm maximum torque level achieved at 2,000rpm. Available only with a six-speed manual gearbox in the comparatively lightweight Panel or Window van with a low roof, the top-of-the-range engine accelerates from 0–62mph in just 12.2 seconds, and in Volkswagen's cautious phraseology is capable of speeds of 117mph 'where the law permits'. Despite such scintillating performance for what once would have been considered as nothing more than a

▶ **Body and engine due to meet.**

dirty diesel van, overall fuel consumption is recorded at a healthy 32.8mpg. With eyes turned to the California as an example, however, the 174PS engine is offered mated to either 4MOTION or Tiptronic.

Undoubtedly the German owner of a T5 Panel van fitted with the 2.0-litre petrol engine they specified at the point of purchase will be quite happy with their lot. Although such an owner will be foregoing the extravagances of six gears and any notion of Tiptronic, as this is the base option five-speed model, most of the figures look good on paper at least. The four-cylinder, eight-valve overhead cam engine develops maximum output of 115PS at 5,200rpm from its 1,984cc motor, while maximum torque of 170Nm is available between 2,600 and 4,000rpm according to a launch press pack, or from 2,700 and 4,700rpm if the spec guide for the 2009 models is referred to! The same brochure indicates a 0–100kph (0–62mph) time of 17.8 seconds – considerably better than that of the smallest diesel engine – while a top speed of 101mph can only be classed as highly respectable.

Is V6 terminology synonymous with walnut veneer, leather and luxury? Certainly both the Golf Mk3 VR6 and the Mk4 V6 4MOTION were models ranked in the upper echelons of their respective ranges, with price points to match. But when such a power plant was to be found lurking under the bonnet of the somewhat bland people-carrying VW Sharan, itself a joint project with Ford and Seat, the question has to be reconsidered. For the British market Volkswagen's top-ranking petrol engine is only linked to the Executive version of the already luxurious Caravelle, and even then can only be specified with the lazy or outwardly opulent option of an auto-box. Head for the home market and the V6 is to be found nestling in the lowly Panel van – such is life! Described as 'state-of-the-art-petrol-power' in a British market launch brochure for the Caravelle, the transversely-mounted narrow angle V6 complete with variable valve timing has a cubic capacity of 3,189 and develops maximum output of 235PS at 6,200rpm. Maximum torque of 315Nm is achieved at 2,950rpm. Recalling that an automatic box always has an effect on an engine's performance, the V6 is still capable of the 0–62mph sprint in just 10.5 seconds and has a top speed of over 127mph.

Comparing the fifth generation Transporter to its predecessor

The days of signwriting are long since gone, as the vinyl graphics attached to these two fifth generation Transporters demonstrate. For the hardened enthusiast, capturing the artwork of a variety of companies on camera is a pleasure not to be missed! *(RC)*

The Delivery Van, bigger in all respects than its T4 predecessor.

As might be anticipated, the fifth generation model, using a straightforward short-wheelbase, low-roofed Panel van as the example in all instances, is not only longer than its predecessor, but also wider and taller. From a starting point of a short wheelbase of 3,000mm compared to the T4's 2,920mm, and an overall length of 4,890mm against 4,707mm for the older vehicle, the T5 looks convincingly beefier. Add an expansion in width, up from 1,840mm to 1,904mm, to a growth in height from 1,940mm to 1,969mm, and the muscular and distinctly fully-fledged appearance of the latest Transporter is instantly apparent.

Volkswagen's stylists are unquestionably amongst the cleverest not only in the world of commercial vehicles, but also across the entire production range. As an example, if the question is asked whether at a cursory glance a Mk6 Golf can be mistaken for a Mk5, the answer is undoubtedly in the affirmative. However, take a closer look and every aspect of the two cars differs. And so it is with the fifth generation Transporter and its predecessor. The fifth generation Transporter at a distance could be a fourth generation model: Volkswagen is, by intention, the master of recognisable design branding. An aim throughout has been to build on past glories and to remind would-be purchasers of the latest model that they are buying into a lineage that has made it the world's most recognisable van. The introductory text in the fifth generation UK launch brochure illustrates perfectly Volkswagen's ongoing message:

'Part five of the legend is here. From generation to generation the Transporter (the world's best selling van) has made its mark and demonstrated the legendary Volkswagen qualities of reliability, economy, and efficiency ... The all new Transporter continues to build on the successful traditions of its predecessors, while setting new standards for the commercial vehicle market.'

Workaday options

▲ Transporters continue to carry out every conceivable role imaginable.

Familiar to aficionados of the fourth generation Transporter is the notion of long- and short-wheelbase options, although the near infinite variety in roof height choices serves to demonstrate that to stay ahead of the game, ever more variety has to be offered. Thus, the Panel van is available with a 3,000mm wheelbase and a low or medium roof affording 1,410 and 1,626mm height in the luggage area. The long wheelbase option adds 400mm in length to the storage area, up from 2,543mm to 2,943mm, while a third roof option – not available with the short-wheelbase T5 – gives an overall loading height of 1,940mm, or an additional 314mm over that of the medium-roofed Panel van.

The Chassis cab and Double Cab are only offered as long-wheelbase vehicles, and in straightforward Chassis guise the available space behind the cab is more or less irrelevant. Add the optional drop-sides and the available loading platform is defined as 2,939 x 1,940mm in the case of the single cab and as 2,169 x 1,940mm for the versatile six-seater double.

The Window van is offered in exactly the same guises as the Panel van. While it would be difficult to amend the two more basic models' lengths there is a variance in available space between the passenger floor and the headlining compared to the load area and the roof. The key, of course, is in the terminology, with the padding and insulation of the headlining accounting for most if not all of the 16mm difference.

What is different, and in certain instances explains apparently mysterious tailgate badges, is the way in which not three, as in the case of the

fourth generation Transporter, but four gross vehicle weights/payloads are designated. Volkswagen defines the T5's various payloads as the gross vehicle weight in each instance minus the unladen weight, itself specified to include a full tank of fuel, but to exclude both the driver and attendant passengers.

With a gross vehicle weight of 2,600kg, the 'starter' model, only available as a short-wheelbase Panel van with the 84PS engine, is known as the T26. The T28 has a gross vehicle weight of 2,800kg, and again is offered on short-wheelbase Panel vans only, but with all engine options through to and including the 174PS unit. By now the 'T' designations should be apparent. The T30 therefore has a gross vehicle weight of 3,000kg and the T32 3,200kg. The T30 is available as both a short- and long-wheelbase Panel vans across the range of engines and includes the 130PS unit linked to either a Tiptronic box or with 4MOTION. In Panel van guise the T32 is restricted to the 102 and 130PS engines in both short- and long-wheelbase variants.

The Chassis cab and Double Cab are only available as T30s, the former with all engines except the 174PS unit, the latter with either the 102 or 130PS options. At launch the Window van and Kombi were likewise only available as T30s, but all sizes of engines could be specified. Later the Window van was also offered as a T32, restricted to the 102PS and 130PS engine with a short wheelbase, or including the 174PS unit with a long wheelbase.

The T26 Panel van has a payload of 802kg, while its T28 counterpart offers a payload of 1,002kg with either the 84 or 102PS engine, but only 928kg with

▶ The coachbuilt ambulance. (RC)

▶ A low-loader for two vehicles. (RC)

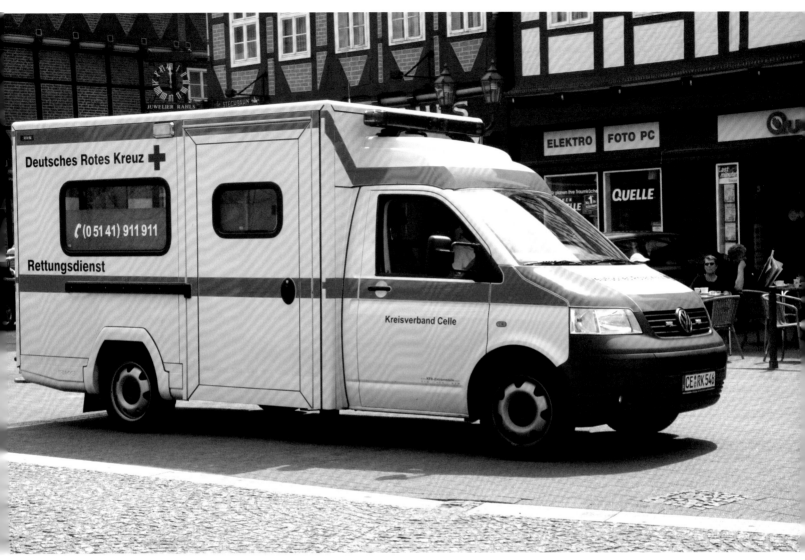

Safety first

In terms of driver and passenger safety, the latest Transporter comes with an impressive list of letters after its name – a collection of features that once upon a time even the top-of-the-range Volkswagen passenger saloons would have lacked. Admittedly, it's hard to locate a vehicle without an anti-lock brake system (ABS) these days, but to this is added an electronic differential lock (EDL) and a traction control system (TCS). Better still, there is an engine braking control (EBC), a device that prevents the driving wheels breaking away on a slippery surface when either taking your foot off the accelerator or re-engaging the clutch. Albeit at added expense, and restricted to the 130PS and 174PS Window van and such-like vehicles, an electronic stabilisation programme (ESP) and a brake assist system can be specified.

the two larger engines. The T30 short-wheelbase affords a payload of 1,202kg with the 84PS or 102PS engine, and 1,128kg with the 130 and 174PS units. The only exception is the short-wheelbase T30 130PS TDI PD 4 MOTION, which has a payload of 996kg. T32 payloads are comparatively easy to relay, with the smaller engine affording a payload of 1,383kg in short-wheelbase guise and 1,351 in long. The 130PS engine by comparison results in payloads of 1,309 and 1,281kg respectively for the short- and long-wheelbase options.

If the complexities of wheelbases, roof heights and engine options appear confusingly multitudinous, they are unfortunately by no means the end of the story as far as the T5 is concerned. For would-be Panel van owners there is the well-known option of a second sliding door, plus the choice between the standard unglazed twin rear doors and a glazed, or for that matter unglazed, rear tailgate. Then there is the decision to make between a single or dual passenger seat, the latter including an integral storage area; the additional cost of air conditioning; the benefits of a pleasant constant temperature; and much, much more.

Included in the standard specification for the most basic workhorse is a whole host of functional equipment that could well make the owner of a previous generation model green with envy. Who would have thought that one day a simple Panel van would include remote central locking with deadlocking, a warning buzzer that sounds if the lights are accidentally left on, a heater with a dust and pollen filter, a lockable glove compartment, or two-speed wipers that also feature a variable intermittent delay, to name but a few of the extensive goodies listed in each successive promotional brochure?

Trim packages

From March 2007 the Transporter has been offered with both an S and an SE pack, each of which offers a treasure trove of additional equipment at around 15 per cent less than the total value of the individual components. The S pack incorporates an alarm, a full-height bulkhead, and electrical goodies consisting of electric windows, heated and adjustable wing mirrors and internal central locking. As might be anticipated the SE pack goes further still, incorporating manual air conditioning and a driver's comfort seat with armrest, in addition to all the elements of the S pack.

Perhaps such a move was inevitable as, at least for the UK, Volkswagen had produced successive, near identical limited edition models in 2005 and 2006 featuring extra comforts and branded in each case as the Trendline, with badging to that effect on the tailgate. The essence of the Trendlines was a specification that included air conditioning, electric windows, electrically heated and adjustable door mirrors, internal central locking controls, driver's seat armrests, a full bulkhead without window, full diameter wheel-trims rather than plastic hub caps and Reflex Silver metallic paintwork. Version one was restricted to a short-wheelbase T28 with the 104PS engine, while the second edition of 500 vehicles was based on the same vehicle but with the 130PS engine added as an option

Also in 2006, for the '07 model year, there emerged a Transporter that Volkswagen describe as 'range topping' but for which the accolades of executive, luxury and limousine are equally apt. This is the Transporter Sportline, complete with a bespoke tailgate badge proclaiming some of its attributes. 'T30 174 TDI Sportline', with Sport picked out in red and the word 'line' duly underlined in the same colour, might appear a little over the top, but then for the average business looking for a practical means of conveying a variety of goods reliably and economically so too is the Sportline concept! As the specification is unfurled, undoubtedly most will wonder just who exactly the vehicle is directed at. Pre-empting such questions, Volkswagen advise us that the Sportline will appeal to 'user-chooser van operators, allowing them to select a more dynamic form of transport', while adding that bikers, surfers, snowboarders and skiers with equipment to move could well be looking to the Sportline as 'something a bit different from the usual run-of-the-mill van'.

Available in both short- and long-wheelbase guise, as should be surmised from its badge, the Sportline is only offered with the 2.5-litre 174PS engine. Volkswagen's press release summarised the extensive list of goodies that 'distinguishes it … from "lesser" vans':

'At the front you can't help but notice the colour coded front bumper and lower spoiler combined with chrome grilles. The polished theme continues with chrome side rails and body-coloured mirrors and door handles. At the rear is a roof level spoiler, colour coded bumper and unique Sportline badging … A sporting chance is achieved with a combination of Eibach suspension springs, which lower the Sportline by 30mm compared with the standard Transporter. Imposing 18" "Borbet" five-spoke alloy wheels and low profile tyres complete the look. Inside the Sportline is generously equipped with a height and reach adjustable steering wheel; comfort driver's seat with armrest; electrically adjustable and heated door mirrors; electric windows; ABS; air conditioning; remote central locking; stereo with CD player; and special Sportline gearshift cap fitted as standard'.

Three colour options are available – stunning Diamond Black pearl effect, trusty Reflex Silver metallic and suitably sporty Tornado Red. Could it be more than a coincidence that all three shades equate with those of Volkswagen's hot hatch, the market-leading GTI? Sadly, as is Volkswagen's nature even with a luxury offering such as the Sportline, both pearl effect and metallic finishes incur a premium charge, which for the British market equates to some £500 plus! Although the price tag stands well above that of any other van from the Volkswagen range, current or past, extra cost options and accessories including GTI-style leather upholstery complete with Sportline headrests and an iPod adaptor abound.

Reasonable mention has already been made of the Window van, but less of the once fundamental Kombi. But turn the pages of a launch brochure and there it is, the T5 Kombi. As previously, the Kombi is described as 'the ideal choice when you need a vehicle with the flexibility to combine load carrying and the ability to carry up to six passengers in comfort'. Succinctly, that is three 'up front', if the dual passenger seat is specified, and three on a bench seat behind that incorporates both a folding and a tipping motion. The T5 version of the Kombi featured a tailgate with heated window, rather than doors, which was by no means unusual. However, in a break with tradition the rear row of passenger seats weren't removable, while the vehicle lacked any form of window in the rear side panels. In other words, still very much a Kombi, but no longer in the recognised sense of the term.

Whether the Window van at launch could be described as a direct successor to the Kombi is also debatable. All appears well when Volkswagen refer to seating for nine people including the driver: 'Standard

What might have been! On the back of the euphoria surrounding the New Beetle a design study was created loosely based on the first generation Transporter and designated as the 'Microbus'. Despite the clamour of excitement from a cross-section of enthusiasts nothing more came of it.

cab seating consists of single driver and passenger seats (with the option of a dual passenger seat), while behind the cab, there's the option to specify seating for up to six passengers along two rows of seats'. However, a complication arises in Volkswagen's next utterance. 'Flexibility extends to the body of the Window van, with the option to delete windows and include metal body panels'. Here, then, is a lowly version of the Caravelle, nothing more!

Perhaps potential purchasers of the new fifth generation found the situation equally obscure, for within a relatively short time the 'multi-purpose' Kombi was no more, its functions being amalgamated into the 'flexible choice' Window van. Still described by Volkswagen as the 'heavy duty answer to passenger carrying', a neat row of illustrations shows the front seat options of single or dual passenger seats, followed by 'seat pack K' through to 'seat pack P', each rear seat option adding to or varying the layout until the magical six seats is achieved with the final 'pack'. As before, 'flexibility extends to the body of the Window van, with the option to delete windows', but now 'rear wing doors ... either with or without windows' can be specified. And in answer to customers' needs for a multi-purpose vehicle to carry both a load and passengers, Volkswagen suggest 'a kombi pack on T32 models, which adds first row seating, deletes rear seat windows plus sliding windows in side door and opposite.'

1950–20

PART VI

The cult of the Camper

▶ Camping has been part of Volkswagen's Transporter heritage from the early 1950s and it still is in the 21st Century.

The Camper's place in the Volkswagen story

Say to someone outside the enthusiasts' circle or the dealer network that you are interested in, or own, a Volkswagen Transporter and the response is likely to be a blank stare. On the other hand, if you acknowledge ownership or love for a VW Camper then most people will understand instantly. Some will even confess to owning trinkets or souvenirs associated with the enduring cult of the first two generations of weekend getaway homes based on the Transporter.

Without question, over the years the Camper must have contributed countless millions to Volkswagen's coffers, and yet only recently has the company become directly responsible for the manufacture of such a product. Admittedly, Volkswagen has often given official approval to selected conversions both at home and abroad, and even gone so far as to endorse such products through the Camper's inclusion in their promotional literature, but that was where the line – the American market excepted – had always been drawn.

To be bluntly honest, would Volkswagen even be producing their own Camper, the California, today, if – just before the launch of the current generation Transporter – its premier partner on the home market of over 50 years' standing, Westfalia, hadn't been absorbed into the encroaching empire of VW's deadly rivals, the Daimler/Chrysler/Mercedes-Benz group?

While it would only be reasonable to expect any celebratory anniversary volume to concentrate largely on the Campers officially endorsed by Volkswagen, the opportunity has been taken to look at some of the other manufacturers who produced models based on the Transporter. Similarly, the issue of supply and demand in the North American market in the early 1960s, and the ingenious solution to the enviable problem of having too great a success on their hands, have not been overlooked. Some of the innovations of more recent times are also assessed.

Westfalia-Werke KG, Wiedenbrück

Able to trace their origins back to 1844 as blacksmiths and agricultural toolmakers, and later as cart builders and then high-quality carriage makers, the Knöbel family started to produce caravans in the 1920s, when they registered the trading name of Westfalia. Bombing during the Second World War nearly destroyed the factory in the state of North Rhine-Westfalia, but by 1948 sufficient progress had been made for the company to exhibit at the Hanover Motor Fair. The straitened circumstances of most post-war Germans meant that few could afford the luxury of more than one vehicle, but a US

officer approached the works with a request for them to build an interior for a VW Transporter based on the design of a typical caravan. From this one-off commission, Westfalia went on to build in the region of 50 further examples over a period of two years, each of which used the Kombi as its base.

The Kombi's undoubted flexibility as both a workhorse, with its seats removed, and a weekend passenger-carrying vehicle, with its seats installed, led to the introduction in 1951 of the Camping Box, essentially a series of self-contained units that could be added for leisure purposes and removed when the

▼ Two exceptional images direct from Volkswagen's archive depict early camping layouts. Logically, both photographs date to the period before April 1951, as from that time the Transporter was fitted with a rear window, which it is unlikely any converter would wish to obscure.

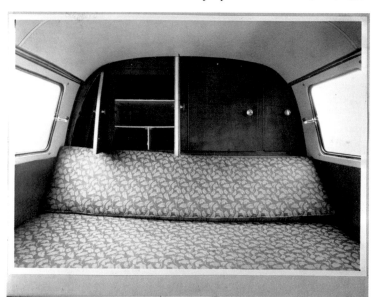

drudgery of the weekly grindstone resumed. One unit fitted to the loading door, another in the shape of a large cupboard sat at the rear, while the third and most important was positioned against the front bulkhead. This unit contained not only a two-burner cooker and a rail for towels and tea cloths, but also a central removable door which could double as either a table or a bed support. The cushions or sections of the made-up bed were carried in the middle section of the same unit. The washing and shaving unit attached to the rear of the two side doors, was complemented by a large cupboard designed to hold both clothes and bed linen. As the brochure writer said, 'Your country house on wheels will accompany you wherever you want to go – into the mountains, to the seaside...'

Despite the Camping Boxes' obvious attributes and the introduction in 1955 of both standard and export versions, sales were relatively subdued. Undeterred, Westfalia pressed ahead with its first fully-equipped production line conversion, known simply as the Westfalia De Luxe Camping Equipment. Released in 1956, the new model was exquisitely kitted out with birch ply panelling on both the side and roof panels, while the interior cabinets were meticulously finished in light oak.

Co-operation between Volkswagen and Westfalia increased to the extent that new introductions were allocated SO numbers just like any other special model developed either in-house or in conjunction with a *Karosserie* or coach works. Under contract from Hanover, Westfalia started to convert used vans,

while in 1958 the Camping Box was revised and given the designation SO22. Towards the end of the same year, the De Luxe Camping Equipment – the full conversion – was revised once more. Allocated the code SO23, the latest conversion was marketed in America as 'The Volkswagen Camper with Westfalia De Luxe Equipment', complete with a special brochure in the Volkswagen house style of the day.

1961 to 1965 saw the SO34 and SO35 models reign supreme. Both were full conversions as opposed to kits, the former being finished in a white and grey laminate and the latter in a dark Swiss pear wood.

▲ Is this a genuine Camper, or have the owners of a Kombi taken their flexible companion away for the weekend? *(BS)*

▼ The Westfalia camping boxes of 1955, now split between Standard and Export specification, were among the first to define a pattern that would develop in succeeding years. Note, despite the apparent luxury of the vehicle's finish, that the door and other internal areas remain unclad.

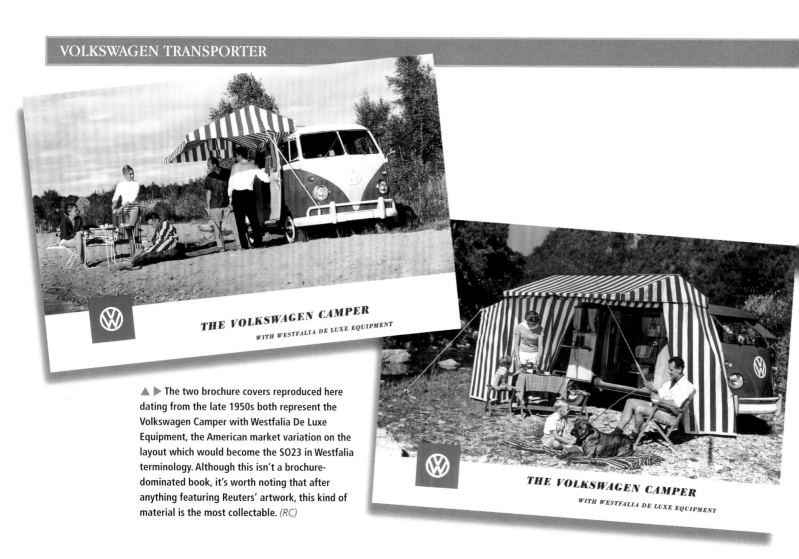

THE VOLKSWAGEN CAMPER
WITH WESTFALIA DE LUXE EQUIPMENT

THE VOLKSWAGEN CAMPER
WITH WESTFALIA DE LUXE EQUIPMENT

▲ ▶ The two brochure covers reproduced here dating from the late 1950s both represent the Volkswagen Camper with Westfalia De Luxe Equipment, the American market variation on the layout which would become the SO23 in Westfalia terminology. Although this isn't a brochure-dominated book, it's worth noting that after anything featuring Reuters' artwork, this kind of material is the most collectable. *(RC)*

◀ In this well-known staged brochure cover shot, the Camper depicted would have carried the designation SO34, an interior layout run from 1961 to 1965. Note the submarine-type roof hatch and the characteristic plaid upholstery. *(RC)*

The Volkswagen Camper

Is it a boat?

◄ The cover of a second brochure designed to attract purchasers for the SO34 was decidedly quirky, at least as far the cover went, although the interior pages concentrated on life with a Camper as before. (BS)

▼ Compare the details and look of the Camping Mosaic 22 – for mosaic read a kit of individually purchasable items – with those of the US-produced Campmobile Kit on the next page. (BS)

VW Camping Car 33 and VW Camping Car Mosaic 22

They say that three is a crowd. Well, we've got four. Four versions of the VW Camping Car, that is to say. You have already read about versions 34 and 35. But there are two more.

The illustration above shows the VW Camping Car Mosaic 22. With this version, you can purchase each item of the equipment separately. Piece by piece you take the items you need and can afford. Piece by piece you put them together, gradually. Until your "Mosaic" equipment's complete.

Of course this equipment is removable. It can be installed easily. And taken out as easily. So you can make any VW Kombi or Micro Bus—old and new—into a Camping Car.

Six days a week your VW Kombi or Micro Bus assists you in earning money. It transports. It caters. It delivers and returns. On weekends it is your bungalow on wheels. It helps you rest and relax wherever you please.

If you install two benches with upholstered seats and backs and two head rests, curtains, and a plastic-topped table you've got a spacious living room. And bedroom. The seats convert to a 5'8" x 3'9" double bed. If you add wardrobe, linen cupboard, and two cabinets

▼ Volkswagen produced some highly entertaining material during the 1960s. While many of the attributes of the Westfalia SO34 can be seen clearly, the distraction of family entertainment concentrates the eye on the image for longer than would normally be the case. (BS)

Their most distinctive feature was a cab seat with a back that could be flipped through 180° so that it could be used as dining room seating one minute and go back to being a cab seat the next.

From 1965 to 1967 the SO42 and SO44 replaced the earlier models. Before their introduction, Westfalia Campers had been fitted with what was known as a submarine roof hatch, a small but distinctive affair primarily intended as an aid to ventilation rather than as a means of extending the vehicle's living space. In the sometimes quirky way that Volkswagen chose to promote their products, a brochure featuring the SO34 model depicted nothing more on its cover than the roof of the camper with the hatch open and part of the often included roof rack (see illustration), under the heading '*Ist e seine Jacht?*' ('Is it a boat?'). However, the SO42 and SO44, the former being geared to the increasingly important American market in its specification, were available either as a simple standard fixed-roof model, or with the full-length roof manufactured by Dormobile, or, most significantly with Westfalia's own new, if rather small, pop-top elevating roof.

Despite the need to supplement Westfalia's conversions in northern America during the mid-'60s, much higher peaks were still to be encountered. As such, the arrival of the second generation Transporter coincided with a notable increase in the popularity of campers generally, and particularly so in the USA, where the explosion in demand for Westfalia products ensured that specific models were introduced and updated to cater for such markets. Less than 12 months into the production run of the second generation Transporter, on 8 March 1968 Westfalia celebrated the occasion of the 30,000th Camper coming off its assembly line. Considering this achievement had taken over 15 years to accomplish, the scale of Westfalia's success in the early years of the second generation Transporter can be seen in the completion of the 100,000th conversion just three years later, during the course of 1971. Daily production had grown to 125 conversions with 22,500 vehicles emerging from the Wiendenbrück

▲ Some of Volkswagen's publicity shots and brochure images told so much of the lifestyle story that the specification of the Camper, indeed the vehicle in total, was more or less obscured. On the other hand, perhaps the intention was to advertise the small tent awning. The picture dates from the period 1961–5.

▼ The Campmobile Kit seen here in situ and removed, as VW of America intended it to be, was a very necessary supplement to the Westfalia vehicles supplied from Germany. *(RC)*

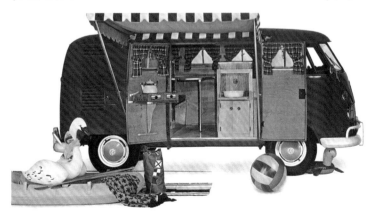

▲ Clearly on parade at a gathering of car manufacturers –
note the Opel flags in the background – this early second
generation Camper appears to be being used as a mobile
office and hospitality 'tent'.

works annually. In 1968, 75 per cent of production
was exported; by 1971, 84 per cent of all Westfalia
Campers were bound for the USA. Clearly, Westfalia
were riding on the crest of a wave, but, and perhaps
inevitably, circumstances dictated that a downturn
would occur. The first oil crisis of 1973 not only
hit the motoring world badly – recall, for example,
Volkswagen's precarious position, with a 555,000,000
DM loss looming for 1974 – but also had serious
repercussions on the global economy. One knock-on
effect was that US Camper sales plummeted, with a
drop in 1973 of a horrifying 35 per cent. Although
the crisis period was relatively short-lived, the heady
days of the late 1960s and the early 1970s were never
equalled again.

In January 1968, only a few months after the
debut of the second generation Transporter in
August 1967, Westfalia launched a whole range of
models based on the new vehicle, starting with the
SO60, 61 and 62, followed during the course of

1969 by six derivatives of the SO69, each of which
was allocated the name of a major Continental
city. Also new for the era of the second generation
Transporter was another highly distinctive elevating
roof, on this occasion being much larger, hinged at
the front and running two-thirds of the length of the
vehicle. The remaining roof area was allocated to a
moulded, built-in roof rack, complete with integral
struts, which could be easily accessed from within the
vehicle by a convenient flap in the rear of the material
which formed an integral part of the lifting roof.

Following the launch of the restyled second
generation Transporter in the summer of 1972,
Westfalia revamped its range to include three options

specifically designed with the American market in mind, and as a result bearing names pertinent to that country. Hence, in addition to the Luxembourg, the Helsinki, and the Madrid, there was now the SO72/2 Los Angeles, the SO72/4 Houston and the S074/6 Miami. Curiously, despite Westfalia's time and efforts, once they had been established in America Volkswagen chose to market all three models simply as the Campmobile. In Britain the Continental was launched at more or less the same time, the model it matched most closely being the SO72/3 Helsinki, Westfalia's new top-of-the-range model.

Further updates during the era of the second generation Transporter were understandably a little less numerous thanks to the dramatic fall in demand created by the oil crisis. US models included items specific to their market, such as both mains and water hook-up points.

Some time late in 1973 Westfalia's elevating roof was redesigned so that it hinged from the rear rather than the front, a useful change for latter-day enthusiasts, if no one else, by assisting their endeavours to identify a particular model year.

▼ This brochure produced by Volkswagen in 1971 to promote Westfalia's latest 'campingwagon' range follows the style of other publicity material. Hardly inspirational on its own, when offered as part of a matching series the effect was much better. *(RC, copyright Volkswagen AG)*

▲ Such Campmobile imagery might not go far towards showing the attributes of the vehicle, but its evocative nature undoubtedly encouraged the undecided to buy, and to buy quickly! *(RC, copyright Volkswagen AG)*

▼ The cover of this brochure produced in the USA confirms two points – home-built Campmobiles were needed if Volkswagen were to have any chance of meeting the demands of their customers; this conversion was based on a Delivery Van, a solution that would become increasingly popular as the years passed by. *(RC, copyright Volkswagen AG)*

Der VW-Campingwagen

Today, it's your second car... **but tomorrow, or next weekend**

▲ 'The 1974 VW Campmobile with Pop-up top option contains two double beds. The upper one folds out of the way during the day for more space in the galley area (foreground) while the lower one serves as a couch.'

◄ The 1974 Campmobile included 'such homey features as an electric refrigerator, an LP gas range and a pressurised water system. There is also a 120-volt hook-up for a TV set, a hair dryer or an electric can opener for those who can't do without them.'

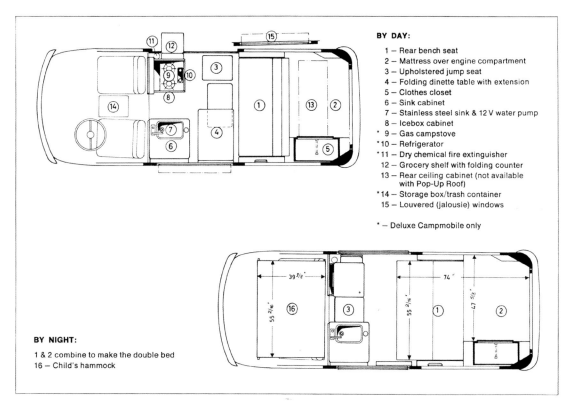

BY DAY:

1 – Rear bench seat
2 – Mattress over engine compartment
3 – Upholstered jump seat
4 – Folding dinette table with extension
5 – Clothes closet
6 – Sink cabinet
7 – Stainless steel sink & 12 V water pump
8 – Icebox cabinet
* 9 – Gas campstove
*10 – Refrigerator
*11 – Dry chemical fire extinguisher
12 – Grocery shelf with folding counter
13 – Rear ceiling cabinet (not available with Pop-Up Roof)
*14 – Storage box/trash container
15 – Louvered (jalousie) windows

* – Deluxe Campmobile only

BY NIGHT:

1 & 2 combine to make the double bed
16 – Child's hammock

▶ 'Flexibility and comfort are features of the 1974 VW Campmobile. Drawings show how the unit converts from day to night configuration. Up to five people – four adults and one child – can be accommodated.'

Between 1975 and the end of second generation Transporter production in the summer of 1979, Westfalia offered two conversions, the Berlin and the Helsinki, both of which were luxuriously appointed compared to earlier designs. The former also broke with tradition in that both the kitchen and cooking facilities were down one side, under the windows opposite the sliding door. Although not a part of the standard package in either instance, a new option was to mount the spare wheel in a box attached to the front of the vehicle above the girder-style bumper. More than any other attribute, although not entirely foolproof, this box remains a means of identifying not only a Westfalia but either of these two models as well.

The advent of the third generation Transporter led Westfalia to introduce a new and extremely popular conversion known as the Joker. Two options were available in 1979; Joker 1 was a four-seater, while

Joker 2 had a full-width rear bench transforming it to full five-seat mode instantly. In keeping with the spirit of the age, cabinetwork was finished in a light teak laminate. Joker 1 boasted two tables, while the layout of Joker 2 resulted in the inclusion of a single table and an extra single side-seat under the window in place of the usual storage cupboards. Although an elevating roof was standard on both models, a fixed version was an option. Curiously, after the turnaround in roof design by Westfalia in the mid-'70s, the former harked back to the style favoured in the earlier days of the second generation Transporter, being hinged at the front. During the course of 1980 three roof options became available, with both a higher-profile elevating alternative and a fixed high roof being added.

It wasn't long before Jokers 1 and 2 were joined by the slightly more upmarket Club Joker and the somewhat dubiously named Sport Joker. Nowadays

▶ Production of the Joker in the Westfalia factory during the 1980s. *(BS)*

▼ The Joker was without doubt a high-quality, best-selling product from Westfalia, and is seen here in the days before the advent of a second grille and water-cooled engines. *(RC)*

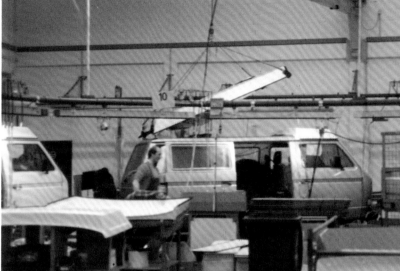

a sport level of trim would be taken to indicate either a vehicle aimed at the younger end of the market, or possibly a higher specification than most. However, the Westfalia Sport Joker was essentially a basic weekender. An altogether more modern light grey covering with attractive contrasting dark grey trim replaced traditional Teak laminate.

The last Jokers were manufactured in 1987, being succeeded by the California and Atlantic the following year. Although these models retained the same basic layout as the Joker, even greater emphasis was placed on luxury, while the materials used were once again updated. By 1990 the Atlantic could be specified with either the 70PS turbo diesel engine or the 88PS petrol engine. An automatic was also on offer. External paintwork ranged from Alpine White to Calypso – a silvery, blue-green metallic – while the seats were upholstered with a remarkably attractive fine check material comprising grey, blue, and red.

The California survived the transition to conversions based on the T4, while a series of special editions, primarily geared to the US market, where Westfalia models were still marketed as Campmobiles, ensured a healthy level of sales in a very competitive market. In 2001, to mark the 50th anniversary of the first Westfalia camper, a special edition known as the California Event was produced. The accompanying brochure included images taken from publicity material produced by Volkswagen in the late 1950s and early 1960s.

▶ Although the style is not exaggerated like that of Reuters a couple of decades previously, the brief return to the use of artwork to promote Westfalia's Joker has a certain charm. (RC)

Von Volkswagen und Westfalia: Der Joker-Spaß ohne Grenzen

▲ One of many publicity shots produced by Volkswagen to promote the Joker – seen here in water-cooled guise.

▼ 'Der Volkswagen Atlantic' by Westfalia. *(RC)*

▶ ▼ Westfalia campers based on the T4. The red example is a California Advantage.

The T5 California – Volkswagen's first Camper

With the advent of each new generation of Transporter, from the second to the fourth, Volkswagen had liaised with Westfalia, supplying as many details as possible of production changes, and even delivering prototypes of the new model for Westfalia's design engineers to work on. Following the Camper company's acquisition by the Daimler/Chrysler/Mercedes-Benz group, this was clearly no longer appropriate when the fifth generation Transporter was about to make its debut, despite the 53-year partnership between Volkswagen and Westfalia. Although a limited number of T4 models continued to be produced after the takeover, Volkswagen had little option but to either find a new associate or take the seemingly bold step of advancing into the Camper business itself. Retaining the California name, Director General Bernd Pischetsrieder and his colleagues chose the latter option.

'Flexibility comes as standard. Anyone who likes to go in search of wide open spaces will feel happy in the California. The bench, which can be moved smoothly to the rear of the vehicle on rails, can be quickly converted into a bed measuring 114 x 200cm. At the touch of a button, the electrically powered roof rises to reveal the spacious upper berth. With mosquito nets to give you all the fresh air you need and a blind to separate it from the lower cabin area, you can be sure of a great night's sleep – leaving you refreshed for the next adventure.

The swivelling front seats and an adjustable free-standing table (which is conveniently stored in the sliding door) mean that mealtimes in the California are always a sociable affair. For times when more seating is needed, the optional fifth seat can be placed in the living area, and removed when no longer needed. And during those warm, summer evenings, why not relax outside and watch the sun go down in the two standard folding seats, which are cleverly stored in the tailgate.' – 'The California', June 2006, www.volkswagen-vans.co.uk/California.

Volkswagen's T5-based California made a considerable impact when it was launched first in Germany and then, to some pundits' surprise, in right-hand-drive form for the British market. It therefore seems apt that a relatively brief rundown of the California's specification should be included, although, as a note of caution, a cursory glance at British sales figures for 2006, when California euphoria was at its greatest (at least in enthusiast circles), makes somewhat dismal reading. 13,817 Transporters 'found homes in the UK' according to the Milton Keynes-based Volkswagen press office. Additionally, 398 'motorhomes' built by Volkswagen's partners in Britain and based on the T5 were registered. However, just 142 California models were brought in from Hanover. Although expensive – the cheapest option within the range was considerably more than double the cost of a five-door Polo GTI, itself the priciest car in that range – California prices were not unrealistic when compared to those of other conversions. Clearly, the reason for the lack of sales had to be attributed elsewhere.

Volkswagen were at pains to stress that the California was not only Caravelle-based but also 'special in being a full factory-designed and produced vehicle'. The British VW press office explained that 'this means it benefits from the expertise which is given to every other Volkswagen product, and is the only recreational vehicle of its type available officially in the UK with full European Vehicle Type Approval.'

Available with the fifth generation Transporter's 130PS or 174PS 2.5-litre TDI PD engines, the latter version can also be specified with 4MOTION. As might be expected of a Caravelle-derived vehicle, the specification is high, with electric windows, air conditioning, remote central locking with alarm, and alloy wheels all being offered as standard. Even the front seats demonstrate how luxurious the California is, for not only are they fitted with support, reach and rake adjustment, plus armrests, but they are also heated.

▼ **Volkswagen's own California.**

As might be expected of a Camper built for 21st century usage, the list of camping attributes is similarly impressive. In addition to straightforward but exquisitely made items such as virtually mandatory curtains, a clothes cupboard, kitchen worktop, cutlery drawer, two-burner gas cooker and the inevitable kitchen sink, the California boasts a 42-litre fridge with a −18°C capability, a 30-litre fresh water container complete with submersible pump, remote control parking and auxiliary heaters, plus the luxury of double glazing in the living area.

Carefully designed, two sleeping areas are available, one being in the main body of the vehicle virtually in the style of Campers dating back to the early days, the other in the form of what Volkswagen describe as a 'private area' in the roof, 'accessible via an electro-hydraulic raising mechanism'.

Cleverly conceived additions include light alloy chairs, which when not in use are conveniently stored in the tailgate, plus a table and awning that 'borrow design cues from the aerospace industry', the result being 'low weight and clever storage solutions'.

Volkswagen's demand upon themselves to produce the very best in state-of-the-art campers is epitomised in a brochure description of the interior dating from the model's launch:

The interior of the new California meets even the highest expectations. All the components have been designed using innovative ideas and materials. For example, the wood trimmed cupboard fittings are made of lightweight material to reduce the overall weight of the vehicle, whilst the corrugated inner core of the aluminium panels ensures the stability of the cupboard surfaces with curves instead of sharp edges. The fresh water and waste tanks are protected against frost and each has a capacity of 30 litres.'

For the British market, the California is available with two engines as previously mentioned, but with four variations on the theme. These are the clear-cut 130PS engine model, the equally straightforward 174PS engine model, plus this latter engine with either a 'Tiptronic' auto-box, or with 4MOTION, Volkswagen's permanent four-wheel drive system.

In Germany, by comparison, the California can be specified with the 1.9 diesel engine, and it is also available in both Trendline and Comfortline versions, plus there is a fixed high-top option, or, for the California Beach model specifically, an alternative without an elevating roof. The California Beach, as the name might imply, is angled towards the more affluent members of the surfing community, and it is undoubtedly the most striking model in the range thanks to its as yet unique duo colour appearance.

Clearly, Volkswagen intends to ensure that, in the best of traditions, their Camper remains an integral part of the Transporter business for the foreseeable future.

▷ California models available on the home market include a fixed high-top option (right).

◀ A particularly attractive image of the California taken on a sunny evening in August 2005.

▼ Three generations of California photographed side by side to mark the 20th anniversary of California production in 2008. From left to right: the T5 California, the T4 California special edition Freestyle and the original California – the water-cooled third generation model.

Volkswagen's North American Camper story

Reference has already been made to the enormous demands placed on Volkswagen and Westfalia as the demand for their Campers in North America reached epic proportions in the early 1960s. The American market more than any other was destined to remain at the core of the Volkswagen-Westfalia partnership's success for a considerable time, until long past the period about to be described.

It was in the years following the debut of the SO34 in the spring of 1961 that the problem of availability of supply first began to really make itself felt. Realistically, both Volkswagen of America and Volkswagen Canada Limited had little option but to take matters into their own hands if they were not to lose sales on a grand scale.

The result in each instance was the introduction of so-called camping kits, units manufactured in both the United States and Canada either for the DIY enthusiast to fit, or for ordering by a customer at a local Volkswagen dealership where fitting was subsequently undertaken by an employee of the garage.

Almost incidentally, the derivation of the word Campmobile is revealed too, for while in later years Westfalia products were branded with this title, originally the name pertained only to those vehicles fitted with a US-manufactured kit. An extract from a brochure designed to sell the Campmobile explains all in the entertaining style which had developed since the DDB advertising agency had become involved with Volkswagen:

'Any Standard Station Wagon, Kombi or Panel Truck we make can be a Campmobile. It's just a matter of getting one of our Campmobile Kits. For super de luxe living get our Super De Luxe Kit. Beds for four big people and two little people. Icebox. Stove. Running water. Dinette. Shower. And john. … The nice thing about any of our Campmobiles is that when you return home (if ever you do), it will happily settle down and become itself again. All you have to do is remove the main components. (Once installed. They can be quickly taken out or put back in.) And you have a station wagon or delivery truck again.'

By 1963, four kits of varying cost were available. Most expensive was the Campmobile Kit for the VW Panel Truck, as this included five windows with gear operation, plus a wealth of panels intended to cover the bare metal of the 'ceiling' ('set of four') and sides of the vehicle. The Campmobile Kit for the VW Kombi Station Wagon was the next most expensive, the only real difference between the two options being the lack of a need for windows for the latter. The Campmobile Kit for the VW Station Wagon was the cheapest of the full-blown kit options, as logically neither windows nor ceiling/side panels were required. The kit that sold at the lowest price of all was described as 'The Campmobile 20-Minute Kit for the Panel Truck, Kombi, and Station Wagon'.

Volkswagen Canada Limited's brochures were considerably more mundane than those of their American counterparts, but for the purposes of explaining to today's generation of enthusiasts what was on offer at the time are probably far more specific. Against a backdrop of black and white images of unadulterated Transporters, boxes marked 'Made in Canada' and cosy cottage interiors, the only words required in a brochure entitled 'Introducing the Canadiana, Volkswagen's unique Camper conversion kit', were: 'Take a Volkswagen Van – or a Window Van – a new one … or … used one – buy this kit (for only $395.00) install it yourself and you have a cottage on wheels.'

Admittedly, more detail was included on the back page of such brochures, and it's worthwhile to include at least a part of it here. Not only does the text illustrate beautifully that the product outlined was a kit, but it also demonstrates that Doyle Dane Bernbach's influence had not necessarily extended to Canada by 1964:

'The "Canadiana Camper Conversion Kit" can be installed with ordinary household tools in a

▼ **Who else but the Doyle Dane Bernbach advertising agency could have captured the appeal of the Volkswagen Transporter in Camper guise in just two words. As always, stunningly simple and enticingly effective.** *(RC)*

Getaway car!

Volkswagen Window Van or Delivery Van. It fits either a new or a used Volkswagen with easy to follow instructions supplied.

'Walls and ceiling panels are constructed of high quality attractively finished plywood – all pre-cut. You get upholstered foam rubber seats, curtains for the windows, table, tile on the floor, and roomy cupboards. The seats and table easily convert into a full size 6' long bed which will accommodate two or three adults. A child can even have his own bed on the front seat … The "Canadiana" is made in Canada, of course…' – Volkswagen Canada Limited, Golden Mile, Toronto 16, Ontario.

The realisation that both the Campmobile kits and the Canadiana were born out of the need to supplement the genuine article, but more particularly that in terms of design and the choice of materials used they exhibited a remarkable similarity to what was being produced in Germany, has led to more than the odd wit describing such products as 'Westfakias'. However, despite such amusing terminology both Volkswagen of America and of Canada had every reason to be proud of their products; Campmobiles and Canadianas had avoided acute embarrassment on the part of all concerned, and ensured that customer perception of Volkswagen's reputation as a company remained high.

During 1970, Volkswagen of America introduced a Camper unique to its market. As with the '60s kits, their intention was to supplement the capacity offered by Westfalia, and decades later it isn't entirely clear whether Westfalia made and then exported the fittings, or sanctioned manufacture under licence. What is apparent is that the Westfalia style was adopted in the design of the conversion layout, despite the fact that the elevating roof on such models was supplied by the American camping conversion specialist Sportsmobile. Early examples of the second generation VWoA-manufactured Campmobile were modelled on the Delivery Van.

The story of Westfalia models specifically designed and named for the American market has already been covered. The complete integration of Campmobile terminology and later of another US exclusive, the Vanagon Camper, is more than adequately demonstrated in the following extracts, taken respectively from brochures produced in 1977 and 1982:

'A full size family car, a cross-country Camper. Campmobile Bus may well be the most versatile vehicle your family can own. Commute to work, carry the crowd or roll around town running errands. All in a vehicle short enough to park in the space required for a sub-compact car … And when you want to get away from it all, the perfect

▲ Believe it or not, the image above forms the entire front cover of a brochure dating from 1965. In reality what can words add? The theme was used in various guises over a number of years. *(RC)*

▼ More from the creative studio of DDB; the brochure from which this image forms the cover dates from 1967. *(RC)*

Next time you go for a drive in the country

Even with all the equipment left in, you've still got twice as much room as the average station wagon, and at least twice as many ways to use it.

Our home on the range

And when you're not camping.

Your Campmobile becomes a commuter, a shopper, a car-pool taxi or whatever. A little over a foot longer than the beetle —the Campmobile is easy to maneuver in traffic—easy to park.

Even with all the equipment left in, you've still got twice as much room as the average station wagon, and at least twice as many ways to use it.

Printed in U.S.A.   33-23-18010   Specifications subject to change without notice.

▷ The 1973 Westfalia Campmobiles were similar in layout to their counterparts manufactured for the European market. Specific US items included water hook-up and mains. *(RC)*

◁ Early second generation Campmobile brochures told of the freedom of being able to take a holiday anywhere the whim might take a Volkswagen owner. Note the brochure's title, revealed in the top left image – 'Our home on the range' – and the back-to-earth-with-a-bump practicality of the Campmobile becoming transport to take the kids to school, bottom right – 'and when you're not camping'. *(RC)*

▽ Although not instantly recognisable as such, this late model second generation Campmobile based on the Helsinki was given the designation P27 Deluxe Campmobile. *(RC)*

1973 Campmobile

second car turns into a spacious second home. Complete with everything from the kitchen sink and 12-volt refrigerator to a 110-volt outlet for your TV and appliances ... There are comfortable sleeping accommodations for four adults and a child, and spacious storage space that includes a roomy storage locker, large concealed clothes closet with a mirror in the door, a big, deep storage bin and a couple of large overhead storage areas...' – Extract from 'The VW Campmobile Bus. Everywhere you look, you find more things to like', 1977.

'Vanagon Camper: All the comforts of home when you're away from home. Now you can travel with just about all the conveniences you'd find at home even where there are no conveniences to be found. Precisely designed with careful attention to detail, the Vanagon Camper encompasses the precision engineering of the Vanagon. Not just your usual camper, the Vanagon is trim and compact outside. So compact, you'll be amazed when you get inside. All the features you'd expect in a camper plus all the features of a standard Vanagon make the Vanagon Camper not just for camping. – Extract from 'Vanagon and Vanagon Camper', 1982.

The Campmobile Australian-style

The story of the Camper in Australia bears similarities to that of America, where the lack of availability of Westfalia-produced conversions led to homespun action. In this instance when Volkswagen of Australia changed from CKD assembly to full manufacture, in addition to building both Beetles and Transporters the Clayton works also produced a Camper that bore a remarkable similarity to the then-current Westfalia models.

Following the decision to return to the earlier arrangement of assembly from completely knocked down kits supplied from Wolfsburg, rather than full manufacture – an occurrence that more or less coincided with the replacement in Germany of the first-generation Transporter with a new model – it was deemed expedient to hand over the creation of Campers to an Australian firm with sufficient expertise to achieve the necessary standards. E. Sopru and Company was chosen to produce the vehicles, which like their American counterparts were branded as Campmobiles. Sopru's other major activity was the preparation of Dormobile models under licence, although owners of British conversions would not have been instantly at home in the Australian version. Gone were the characteristic front-seat cooker arrangement and the traditional striped elevating roof canvas – in came a fold-out two-burner hob and grill located by the vehicle's sliding door, and plain material was revealed when the roof was put up. White, tan-trimmed cabinet work prevailed, and the spare wheel was mounted on the vehicle's front.

Generally, the range was tweaked on a regular basis, as was – and remains – the practice of many firms offering conversions. By 1976 Volkswagen Australia Pty Ltd, through the auspices of their designated 'agent', could justifiably claim quite an accolade for themselves: 'With the experience we have gained in manufacturing and servicing over 5,000 Campmobiles in Australia, we believe our models for

1976 offer the ultimate in practical design, materials and versatility.'

As a preamble to a range description, this would be hard to better. Four models were on offer in 1976, each of which featured a 'big 2000cc engine'. The starter in the range was the Adventurer Basic, described by Volkswagen as an economy model but which nevertheless featured an elevating roof, ample seating, a cupboard and sleeping arrangements, not to mention a stainless steel sink, a 240-volt power outlet, curtains and bright interior panels. In common with the more luxurious models, the Adventurer Basic package also included a kangaroo bar and a spare wheel relocated to the outside of the vehicle, where it was protected by a padlocked cover.

The Adventurer Traveller scored over the Adventurer Basic in that it included 'comforts like a comprehensive kitchen with modern cooking and refrigeration facilities. And yes, even the kitchen sink.' Summarised as the 'go anywhere camper', other attributes included a roof-mounted pack rack for bulky equipment, an additional portable seat and a retractable step.

The Adventurer Deluxe was described by Volkswagen as 'the ultimate five star motel for a family of four'. In addition to all the features of both the Basic and the Traveller, it included 'all the trimmings for you to get away in style'. With the emphasis definitely placed on luxury, the specification included upper and lower berth light fixtures, an additional folding table, a bottle rack attached to the utility cabinet, and special cloth trim panels and armrests.

The Wanderer Deluxe was in reality a variation on the Adventurer Deluxe, the only difference being that the Wanderer lacked both a roof rack and pop-top. Instead, as the promotional literature tells us, 'Wanderer gives you just on 6' of headroom with a fixed fibreglass roof with additional windows and extra large top cupboards front and rear. Come to think of it, the Wanderer Deluxe is not so much a motel – but your mobile home for those "across the country" tours.'

▲ The Wanderer Deluxe's identifying feature was its fixed fibreglass roof with side windows. *(RC)*

▼ The 'ultimate' model in the range, the luxurious Adventurer Deluxe, depicted here on the move. *(RC)*

With 'official' approval – Volkswagen campers in Britain

Turn the pages of any brochure designed to promote the range of Campers produced by a series of manufacturers – Devon from the late 1950s onwards, Dormobile from the early 1960s and Danbury in the final years of the same decade – and assurances of official status will be prominent. However, an equivalent perusal of catalogues designed to promote the attributes of the now highly sought-after Campers produced by Canterbury Pitt will reveal that references to Volkswagen are more or less singular by their absence.

What has to be taken into account is that, unlike the home market where Volkswagen and Westfalia were essentially partners, the United States where Wolfsburg controlled all the activities of their subsidiary, and Australia where either manufacture or assembly was not only the order of the day but also went hand-in-hand with Camper preparation, the British VW market was nothing more than a franchise managed by a number of different companies over the years. From the well-known tale of Stephen O'Flaherty and the formation of Volkswagen Motors Ltd on 1 January 1953, leading to the arrival of 200 Beetles on British soil some seven months later, and the acquisition of the company by Thomas Tilling Limited in 1957 and the Lonhro Group, headed by the colourful 'Tiny' Rowlands, in September 1975, direct control by Wolfsburg was avoided. Indeed, it was only in 1989 that Volkswagen AG came to wholly own the British operation.

Of this 35-plus years of semi-independence, the most interesting period as far as the present narrative is concerned was undoubtedly the 1970s, when Volkswagen GB Ltd appeared to assimilate Devon Campers into the family lock, stock, and barrel.

Early Devon brochures included information such as this extract, taken from literature produced in 1960:

'Designed and produced by J.P. White Ltd, Sidmouth. Distributed by Lisburne Garage, Torquay … See the "Caravette" at your local dealer or write to Lisburne Garage, Babbacombe Road, Torquay and you will be given the address of your nearest Agent where a "Caravette" can be inspected.'

However, within a very short time the emphasis on official status had been strengthened to:

'Fully approved by Volkswagenwerk in Germany and V.W. Motors Ltd, Volkswagen Concessionaires for Great Britain. … Open up a whole new vista of motoring by investing in a Devon Caravette … your local Volkswagen Dealer will be pleased to show you one.'

When Dormobile first started offering conversions on Volkswagen bodies in the early 1960s its literature was incredibly formal, but immediately demonstrated the vehicle's 'official' status:

'The vehicle described herein is the joint product of VW Motors Ltd., London and Martin Walter Ltd., Folkestone. Marketed in the UK through Volkswagen Dealers. … Ask your dealer for a demonstration or communicate with … VW Motors Ltd., Lords Court, 32/34 St. John's Wood Road, London, N.W.8.'

The third officially approved converter, Danbury, failed to capitalise on its status in the literature it produced, making little – or rather no – reference to the tie-in with Volkswagen dealers across the country. Fortunately, at least until 1972 – when Devon were successful in negotiating an exclusive contract with Volkswagen Motors Ltd – some VW brochures produced for the British market *did* include reference to the company, as an extract from 'Our Home is not a House', of 1968 vintage, serves to illustrate:

'Volkswagen Motor Caravans are converted by three of Britain's most experienced caravan specialists. J.P. White – Sidmouth, Danbury Conversions Limited, and Martin Walter Limited. They're all equally proud of their high quality craftsmanship, each providing a range of styles – one of which is made just for you…'

March 1970 saw the publication of a brochure entitled 'We make the VW Microbus for all sorts of people'. After allocating several pages to the general benefits of Micro Bus ownership, the three nominated converters were each allocated a page, the sequence following strict alphabetical order. Each conversion – or in Devon's case, range of models – was illustrated with images taken from the converter's stock pictures, while the otherwise pithy but witty text of the other pages was reduced to a more general description of what was on offer. For Danbury, the key message was 'getting away from it all', while for Devon the emphasis was on the variety of conversions available. Dormobile was probably awarded the biggest compliment, with an opening statement that said: 'The Volkswagen Dormobile Motor Caravan is custom built – bags of space with nothing forgotten'.

Following Devon's successful bid for exclusivity in 1972 – which they were to retain until 1977 – Volkswagen GB Limited's marketing changed dramatically. A rapid succession of brochures were launched, all with the corporate heading of 'Volkswagen Motor Caravans', and at one stage even extended to accessories such as, for example, 'The VW Motent … Hitch one to your Wagen'. For Devon, although their business inevitably received a boost, the blaze of publicity did not extend to usage

▶ ▼ Unusual in size, and more importantly in content, a brochure entitled 'Our home is not a house', which was released in 1968 specifically for the British market, contained endearing images particularly for those today who lived through such times, while also in a cleverly understated way sold the concept of the Volkswagen Camper in a most effective manner. *(RC)*

of their name. Initially featuring just one model from Devon's range, the Caravette, extensive coverage was also given to Volkswagen's German partner Westfalia and their Continental model. With the subsequent arrival of a new version of the Eurovette, Volkswagen added this to their catalogue but still steadfastly made no allusion to the Devon name.

Reference to contemporary Devon literature also shows that the company added Westfalia's model to its list of options, allocating just as much space to the interloper as to each of its own products. Cynics might say that Volkswagen GB Ltd drove a hard bargain!

'What's in a Volkswagen Motor Caravan for you? – Sure, a VW Motor Caravan is a holiday home. But that's the last reason for buying one. Let's face it, unless you're one of the fortunate few, life isn't one long holiday. So, we've built our Motor Caravans to be useful all 52 weeks of the year. Because you can do so much in one of our Motor Caravans, you'll get more out of owning one than any other type of vehicle. A VW Motor Caravan puts the fun back in motoring. You'll be doing things you've never been able to do before. Because, inside every one we make there's a saloon car, an estate car, a minibus and a delivery van. In fact, some people find them so handy to have around they even take them on holiday!'

'The Caravette is dual purpose with a capital D. Because all the time it's a Motor Caravan it's an estate car. With eight comfortable forward facing seats, that enable you, your family and some friends to get out and about in style. When it isn't seating eight, Dad can use it as a pick-up and delivery van. When it comes to getting away with things there's nothing to touch a VW Motor Caravan ... The Eurovette is the latest addition to the VW range of Motor Caravans. So, we've built in the latest thinking in Motor Caravan interior design. It'll carry a total of seven. Thanks to a wide front seat, a removable rear facing seat and a removable central front seat ... Whether you are a serious camper or a first timer, you'll get attached to the Volkswagen Continental. It's so well planned. And ingenious. While the Continental possesses all the virtues of an estate car it has been designed with the camping enthusiast in mind...' – 'Volkswagen Motor Caravans', September 1974, for Volkswagen (GB) Limited.

Following their own return to the fold, Danbury was much more careful to ensure that it made use of its status in Volkswagen circles. A new model, the Danbury Volkswagen De Luxe, complete with a layout very different to days of old, demonstrated by its very name the importance that the company placed on the renewal of its 'official' status. 'Danbury and Volkswagen – the perfect team – bring you a new luxury conversion...'

Such a pattern would continue as long as Danbury continued to trade – in other words until the latter part of the 1980s. Indeed, in the early years of the third generation Transporter, Danbury went to great lengths to emulate the style of Volkswagen's own brochures, its designers mimicking the font employed and the use of Volkswagen's then house-style of a large double-spread image and a series of thumbnail shots below, with technical specifications on the final page. Best of all, though, from Danbury's point of view had to be the three short paragraphs quoted below, one covering the warranty, another finance, and the third insurance:

'Volkswagen Danbury Warranty – The quality of the craftsmanship and materials of both Volkswagen and Danbury Conversions gives us confidence to cover all our vehicles with a 12-month, unlimited mileage warranty.'

'Volkswagen Finance and Leasing – Financial arrangements can be made for the purchase or lease of your Volkswagen Danbury through A.U.F. Ask your Volkswagen dealer for details.'

'Volkswagen Insurance – Not only does Volkswagen supply vehicles of a high standard, it provides the insurance for them as well. V.I.S. insurance is dependable and very competitive. Ask your Volkswagen dealer for details.'

For Devon, however, the golden days of their relationship with Volkswagen were over. While models from the VW fold still formed an essential part of their business, as the following extract from a press release dating from October 1978 indicates, moves were afoot to broaden the portfolio:

'Devon Conversions are one of the leading motor caravan manufacturers in Britain. They have been building motor caravans for more than 22 years and bus conversions since 1973 ... Until this year, they were exclusively involved in building conversions on the Volkswagen range of vehicles. But they have now expanded into converting the vehicles of other manufacturers including Mercedes-Benz and Ford.'

Throughout the era of the third and fourth generation Transporters, Volkswagen in Britain endorsed a number of companies and produced lavish brochures to promote not only the goods emerging from Hanover, but also those from an array of specialist converters. Literature produced in the mid-'90s inevitably referred to the fourth generation Transporter's acclaimed victory in 1992, when it won the coveted International Van of the Year award, but also embraced Volkswagen's motor caravan partners in a generous way:

'We believe that at the heart of the best motor caravans can be found a Volkswagen. The UK's leading motor caravan builders use the Volkswagen Transporter as a base vehicle for both traditional van conversions and increasingly popular coachbuilt motor caravans.

'It's easy to see why. The Volkswagen name has been synonymous with motor caravans since the early days. The original "camper" concept was based on the first generation "split windscreen" Transporter. Now, more than 40 years on, the range of Volkswagen based motor caravans has expanded considerably...'

In 1994 Volkswagen Commercial Vehicles VAG (United Kingdom) Ltd endorsed the products of six manufacturers. These were Auto-Sleepers Limited of Broadway in the Cotswolds; Autohomes of Consett, County Durham; Auto Trail based in Immingham; Compass Caravans of Durham City; Richard Holdsworth Conversions Ltd of Reading; and the Swift Group of Cottingham, North Humberside. A couple of years later there was only one change to the list: Richard Holdsworth Conversions Ltd had gone into receivership, but the remnants of the company had been purchased within days to re-emerge as Cockburn Holdsworth Limited.

The final years of T4 production almost inevitably saw changes to the approved list. In 2003 just four companies were included in Volkswagen's literature; Auto-Sleepers and Compass were still there, but Bilbo's Design of South Godstone in Surrey, and Reimo with bases in Hythe, Kent and Manchester, were more recent additions to the list.

'For nearly half a century Volkswagen has dominated the leisure vehicle market. Indeed, our name alone epitomizes both the motorhome and touring tradition.

'The popularity of the T4 Kombi as both a chassis cab platform for coachbuilt motorhomes or as a van conversion, has ensured Volkswagen retains the enviable position as one of the leading vehicle options within an increasingly competitive and demanding industry.

'Volkswagen supply the T4 to a number of specialist converters. It is these conversion companies that are represented within this brochure. Each has met the highest standards of build, expertise and service to gain Volkswagen's coveted endorsement ... Each finished vehicle is unique and benefits from well considered design, build quality and a range of features that add up to a package as individual as any prospective owner.

'So, whether you require a vehicle for extended periods of touring or simply days out, whether you need to cater for family or friends, whether you want to pack golf-clubs, a surfboard or a picnic

They work at home.

◀ ▼ The relatively subtle message behind the two images taken from British market brochures produced in the mid 1970's work better out of the context they were intended for and away from the paragraphs of text that would have surrounded them. From the pictures would it be obvious that Devon as a company and Westfalia's Continental were being marketed? *(RC)*

▲ Without this 1975 model year brochure's heading, only the detail of an elevating roof suggests that this is not a piece of literature to promote the Micro Bus. *(RC)*

▲ Brochures produced by Volkswagen UK in the era of the fourth generation Volkswagen appeared to use inviting imagery from at home and abroad. *(RC)*

hamper, then a Volkswagen conversion is available to meet your exacting needs.' – 'Volkswagen Based Motorhomes – The 2003 Range', brochure for Volkswagen Motorhomes, Yeomans Drive, Blakelands, Milton Keynes.

With the debut of the T5-based California in right-hand-drive form, Volkswagen inevitably had to distance itself at least slightly from the conversions developed by other Camper and motorhome manufacturers. While Bilbo, for example, continued to include the famous VW roundel on their adverts, with the words 'Volkswagen Motorhomes Specialist' appended, and Reimo elected likewise to display the celebrated V over W symbol and the words

'Volkswagen Compatible Design Manufacturer', there was no escaping the message conveyed in Volkswagen's press office release to journalists at the time when the California was hot news:

'Volkswagen continued a long-standing tradition of producing recreational vehicles when it launched the new Caravelle-based California in October 2005.

'Unlike many "camper vans" which are essentially conversions, the California is special in being a full factory-designed and produced vehicle. This means it benefits from the expertise which is given to every other Volkswagen product, and is the only recreational vehicle of its type available officially in the UK with full European Whole Vehicle Type Approval...'

The best-known names in Britain

Four key players from the days of the first generation Transporter deserve more than a cursory mention when it comes to the important British market and its Camper conversions. Three of the four companies still exist today, although in two instances gaps of many years duration in which the brand lay dormant confirm more than a simple change of ownership. Only one out of the four can claim a direct, if adopted, lineage to its founding father. The alphabetic order of presentation of Canterbury Pitt, Danbury, Devon and Dormobile works well, for the first and, sadly, the only name not in current usage played a pivotal role in making the Camper a viable proposition for those living in Britain.

CANTERBURY PITT

As early as 1956 Peter Pitt, a one-time refugee from Austria, created a modular 'Moto-Caravan' from the Volkswagen Transporter. The nature of the design allowed Pitt to promote the vehicle as 'perfect for one' and 'wonderful for the family.' Available as a conversion based on the Kombi (although the brochure Anglicised this to 'Combi'), this Camper looked Spartan even by the standards of the 1950s, with a good deal of bare metal still in evidence with the conversion fully in place. Fortunately, Pitt also listed the Micro Bus and the Micro Bus De Luxe as appropriate vehicles, and for all options Pitt itemised the attributes likely to tempt people to buy his products:

'All this…
Ample locker space for bedding for four people.
Ample locker space for food, crockery and cooking
*   utensils.*
Wardrobe. 2 ring enamel Calor gas cooker.

Bright interior lighting.
Single table arrangement. Separate table
*   arrangements for 3 and 4.*
Single bed – double bed arrangement and day sitter.
Full travelling accommodation in Pullman comfort,
*   for 6 or 7 adults.'*

However enticing such a package might have been to a potential purchaser, however, legislative obstacles lay in the way of sales, for in Britain the Transporter was regarded purely and simply as a commercial vehicle, and as such was restricted to a maximum speed of 30mph. Not a man to shrink from controversy, Peter Pitt took his Volkswagen 'Moto-Caravan' to Windsor Royal Park and deliberately drove through the grounds, knowing that commercials were banned. His goal of being arrested so that his argument might be heard in court not only paid off but also resulted in a victory for common sense and the infant Camper industry. The judge declared that the Volkswagen

▼ Early Pitt brochures made use of the image shown as a cover statement. Note the absence of an elevating roof and the single colour paintwork of the vehicle. *(RC)*

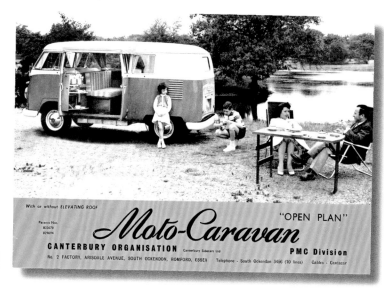

▼ Pleasant though this cover image scene is, it is in its comparison with that overleaf that most interest is aroused. Note the size of the rear window – correct for the 1962 model year and when this brochure was released. *(RC)*

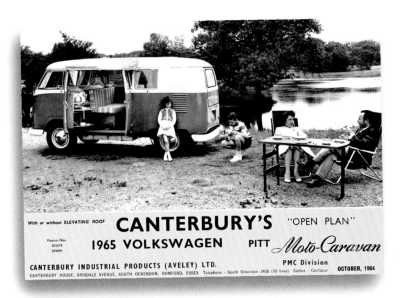

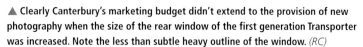

▲ Clearly Canterbury's marketing budget didn't extend to the provision of new photography when the size of the rear window of the first generation Transporter was increased. Note the less than subtle heavy outline of the window. (RC)

▲ Sadly, despite Canterbury's confirmation that Peter Pitt's conversion worked well in conjunction with Volkswagen's second generation Transporter, it was not destined to be a long-lived affair. (RC)

should no longer be classified as a commercial vehicle, meaning that it could travel at the same speed as any car on the road and, with its new status as a motorised caravan, would be exempt from purchase tax. Admittedly, qualifying for this status meant that the fittings had to be permanent, which ruled out a Westfalia-style camping kit, and each design had to be submitted to HM Customs and Excise for approval, but an enormous step forward had nevertheless been taken. Makers such as Devon were in Pitt's debt; but, curiously, while they pursued quality conversions on the Volkswagen with renewed vigour, Peter Pitt himself turned his attentions to British manufacturers such as Thames, Commer and Austin, thus avoiding the import duties associated with a Volkswagen, then the only serious contender when it came to vehicles manufactured in Europe or beyond.

Peter Pitt reintroduced his Volkswagen-based Camper in 1960, by which time his literature had become a little more adventurous. Now he claimed a series of 'unique features' that gave rise to 'over thirty "easy to arrange" layouts', while also promoting the fact that the best things in life came free: 'Free accommodation anywhere you choose … Free from timetable restrictions … Free to take your office with you … Be carefree on the open road.'

Peter Pitt's business merged with, or rather was taken over by, Canterbury Sidecars Ltd in 1961, leading to highly convoluted model designations such as 'Canterbury's "Open-Plan" Pitt Moto-Caravan'. Under Canterbury's wing, Pitt successively revised his designs until the point came in 1963 when the

layout scheme was so successful that it ran to the end of first-generation Transporter production without further alteration.

Camper enthusiasts today whose main ambition is to seek out and retain originality are more likely to search for a Canterbury Pitt conversion than just about any other model. Beautifully crafted, expertly finished, exquisitely designed, such conversions typify the workmanship of a bygone age. Yet Canterbury's marketing material was duly modest throughout, as the following extract illustrates:

'The "Pitt Open Plan" preserves space for free movement, and for your comfort. Look at the thought given to the domestic equipment. When not in use – which is most of the day, most days of the year – it disappears! The furniture is in mahogany, all corners well rounded, with a satin finish that is easily maintained. The flooring is soft underfoot, non slip and insulating. Easy to clean and requires no polishing. There is a choice of colours for cushions, each contributing to your personal note and to the elegant harmony of your home on wheels.'

Sadly, following Peter Pitt's death in February 1969, shortly after he had adapted his conversion to suit the second generation Transporter, Canterbury ceased production of Campers. The arrangements between Pitt and Canterbury were such that his designs were produced under licence, making it impossible for the South Ockendon firm to continue without resorting to the employment of a new design team to generate new models.

DANBURY

Unlike the pioneering work of Peter Pitt, and the groundbreaking activities of J.P. White, Danbury Conversions only made their debut in the final years of first-generation Transporter production, offering its first conversion, the Multicar, in 1964 on a Transporter dating from 1963.

Even as late as November 1966 the Essex-based firm was still only offering glorified typed-up paperwork to sell their wares to customers. Nevertheless, the contents made interesting reading, as the company's own Camper layout was sufficiently different to those of the established conversion firms for Danbury to prosper and grow. Conversions were available on the Delivery Van, the Kombi, the Micro Bus and even the Micro Bus De Luxe, while two styles of elevating roof were offered on all but the last. One was the Pitt elevating roof, the other the option favoured by Devon. The 1966 promotional literature declares:

'This conversion of the famous range of Volkswagen Commercial series vehicles represents a new approach to the design of motor caravans: it has been evolved to provide a comfortable touring and staging vehicle for a family, while still retaining all the advantages of a fast cruising car … The Danbury Multicar is based on a new principle, that of making those essentially bulky fittings, the sink, refrigerator and storage units, moveable and interchangeable so that a variety of basic layouts can be used to make the most of the space available, with no unwanted equipment in the way. Other interior fittings have the same common dimensions, making detailed variations possible and allowing items not in use to be stowed quickly in convenient positions…'

Less than a handful of conversions from this era are known to have survived, so details of the colour schemes available at the time are bound to arouse the curiosity of the enthusiast:

'Colour Schemes
The standard exterior colours are Pearl White, Blue, Pale Grey or Green Velvet. Two-tone combinations are available to special order and at an extra charge.

Interior Colour Scheme

Headlining	*Grey-white*
Side lining	*Light Grey*
Rear seats	*Light Grey*
Stove, sink and storage units	*Light Grey exterior*
Spare wheel cover	*Light Grey*
Metal work, fascia etc.	*As exterior or Pearl White*
Upholstery	*Light Grey with mosaic black, white and grey panel*
Locker tops	*Varnished natural birch*
Curtains	*Daffodil Yellow*
Floor	*Patterned Daffodil Yellow or Tweed Green*
Rear compartment carpet	*Black and white mottle*
Table top	*Light woodgrain'*

▼ From the early days of little more than type written sales sheets, Danbury evolved to properly printed brochures. However, note that the printer couldn't spell Volkswagen and a sticker had to be placed over the original 'Volkeswagen'! *(RC)*

▼ By 1971 full colour adorned the cover of Danbury's literature. Inside black and white pictures illustrated 'a few of the attractive possible arrangements for your conversion'. *(RC)*

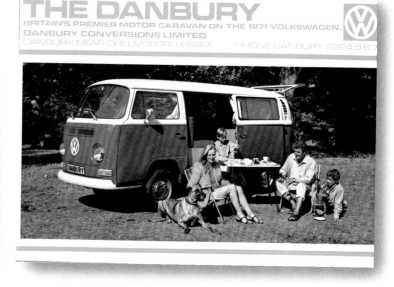

▶ Despite the loss of its official status as a converter of Volkswagen Transporters to Campers, Danbury's work continued unabated. Larger format brochures were commensurate with the times, although a winter image could have been improved upon! *(RC)*

▼ Danbury's good fortune in regaining official recognition as a converter approved by Volkswagen was demonstrated with the inclusion of the famous VW roundel on the cover of this brochure dating from 1978. *(RC)*

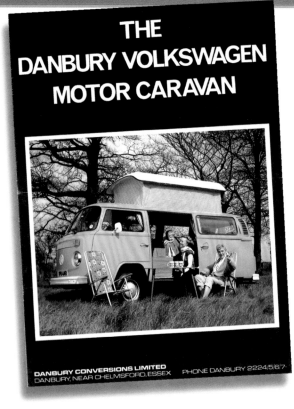

THE
DANBURY VOLKSWAGEN
MOTOR CARAVAN

DANBURY CONVERSIONS LIMITED
DANBURY, NEAR CHELMSFORD, ESSEX   PHONE DANBURY 2224/5/6/7

The arrival of the second-generation Transporter led Danbury to reassess its conversion, dropping the term 'Multicar' in the process, but retaining the flexibility of usage. Without question, the biggest innovation on the second-generation walk-through Kombis and Micro Buses was the inclusion of moveable twin middle seats, allowing a walk-through living option and L-shaped seating arrangement. For travelling, the seats could easily be made to face forwards, while for dining around the Danbury table they could be placed against the bulkhead with the backrests in an upright position. The options were multitudinous, but the package was simple in appearance and cost. Indeed, in 1970 Danbury went to the lengths of having a single-side flyer produced that proclaimed the one-line message: 'Still the cheapest VW Caravan and still the Best.'

From the closing years of the 1960s through to 1972 Danbury, along with Dormobile and Devon, had official Volkswagen approval for their conversion. This ended in 1972 when the already mentioned exclusive agreement with Devon came into being. Five years later, though, Danbury regained its official status and launched a new De Luxe conversion with

The Danbury Volkswagen De Luxe

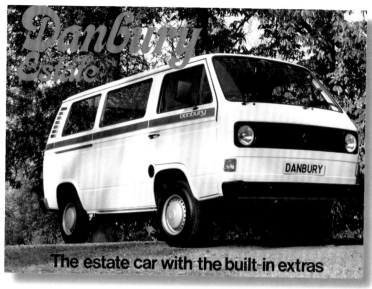

▲ Danbury were justifiably proud of the 'first-ever motorised caravan to have an electrically-operated fully automatic elevating roof' – the Danbury Volkswagen Series 2. *(RC)*

▲ Once upon a time named the Danbury Standard, the base model in Danbury's range of conversions was cleverly reborn as the Danbury Estate – very much a load mover and people carrier with extras. *(RC)*

a different layout and a more upmarket package at more or less the same time:

'Danbury and Volkswagen – the perfect team – bring you a new luxury conversion but at a standard price … The list of standard equipment is so long – but here are just a few items:-

1   *Elevating roof, complete with two full length roof bunks*
2   *Two rear opening sliding windows for extra ventilation*
3   *Stainless steel ring cooker and grill, plus a compact and practical oven – both housed in an aluminium lined teak cabinet which slides and locks back onto the engine deck when not in use*
4   *Sink with pumped water supply*
5   *Attractive melamine crockery – place settings for four*
6   *Stainless steel cutlery set in its own neat folder*
7   *Portable cool box with freeze pack*
8   *Easy to clean vinyl floor*
9   *Removable needle punch carpet*
10 *Three fluorescent lights – two over the kitchen unit, and one over the dinette…*

'Danbury has always made its watch words simplicity and comfort. Now we add luxury and class.'

The arrival of the third-generation Transporter in the summer of 1979 presented Danbury with the opportunity to develop its luxury theme, as the language of an extract from a brochure issued in 1981 indicates:

'The Volkswagen Danbury Series II is a quality motor caravan that has been superbly designed to give you maximum comfort and versatility. It's generous in space, tasteful in décor, ideal for relaxing or dining in and packed with thoughtful fitments to make life easy…'

Elsewhere the company wrote of the Danbury Volkswagen Series II as being 'the first-ever motorised caravan to have an electrically-operated fully automatic elevating roof'.

Topping the range above both the standard model – now named the Volkswagen Danbury Estate – and the De Luxe, or Volkswagen Danbury Series II, there was the Danbury Showman. Danbury's own marketing sold this model simply as 'everything you expect from a Danbury Volkswagen Series II … and much more.'

Danbury retained official Volkswagen approval for its products until it ceased trading at the end of the 1980s. Not that this was the end of the road for the Danbury name, for Beetles UK, famous for their import of Mexican Beetles, bought it early in the present century and set about converting Brazilian-built Transporters into Campers. It will not come as a great surprise that the reborn Danbury brand has no links with Volkswagen in this country!

DEVON MOTOR CARAVANS

Jack White, an entrepreneurial builder from the little seaside town of Sidmouth in the county of Devon, became a Beetle owner almost as soon as the cars became available in Britain. Following the birth of a third daughter, Jack and his wife Anna decided that the saloon was no longer big enough to meet their needs. However, as highly satisfied Volkswagen owners they had little desire to quit the brand and turned to the Transporter in Delivery Van guise as the only other option. While affording the necessary space to accommodate their growing family, long journeys – some of them to Germany, where Anna's family lived – proved uncomfortable to say the least. Jack therefore spent Christmas 1955 researching the options for turning their Transporter into a more comfortable machine.

With the aid of Pat Mitchell, a designer and master craftsman employed by White to create kitchen units for his construction business, February 1956 saw the humble Delivery Van transformed into a multi-seated vehicle, with a laminated table which, with a couple of swift actions, could be transformed into a double divan in the centre of what had once been the load space. A single bed was added across the vehicle's rear, while a little later a fourth bed was devised, this time to be suspended above the bottom of the double divan. If this one-off conversion had ended there, perhaps its very existence would be a dim distant memory to just a handful of the more elderly residents of Sidmouth and no one else. However, Jack White added a cooker, washing amenities complete with a built-in four-gallon container, an array of beautifully crafted fitted cupboards, plus luxuriously deep Dunlopillo cushions, window curtains for night-time privacy and both a Calor gas supply and six-volt DC electricity. Leaving the best till last, an Osokool food storage cabinet completed the package.

The completed vehicle was driven to the local main VW Distributor, Lisburne Garage Ltd of relatively nearby Torquay, to await inspection by the combined forces of the Ministry of Transport and the Board of Customs and Excise, who needed to approve the vehicle – or not, as the case may be – since its living accommodations exempted it from purchase tax. Such was the interest in the vehicle that the General Manager at Lisburne suggested displaying it in the main showroom. Once it went on show it wasn't long before Jack realised that the creation of Campers on a commercial business could be a serious business proposition.

Never one to knowingly miss an opportunity, the marketing man in Jack devised the term Caravette to describe his new product. Within a short time, and certainly by July 1956, orders had started to flow in, resulting in a number of workers from Jack's building business being redirected towards Camper work. After operating initially from his garden shed, Jack had little option but to transfer the work to his building premises at Stevens Cross, before finding an appropriately large workshop, or so he thought, in another part of Sidmouth. With 56 vehicles built and sold, by the early months of 1957 J.P. White (Sidmouth) Ltd was on the lookout for an even larger workshop, and the freehold interest of the old gasworks was acquired, a five-acre site of fields and woodlands which included a direct link with the adjoining railway. After a little gentle persuasion of the town council, Jack obtained the necessary planning permission to construct a new factory, to be known as the Alexandra Works. Not only was his own workforce diverted onto the Caravette project, but 16 workers were also recruited from other local builders, with a promise of triple pay for work done on Sundays.

The Alexandra works opened officially on 20 May 1960, and not a moment too soon, as by this point there was a staff of 75 mainly skilled carpenters and craftsman producing in excess of 1,000 Caravettes annually, consisting of four conversions based on the Transporter and two on either Austin or Morris vehicles every day.

Without question the Devon Caravette designed and manufactured by J.P. White and sold, marketed and distributed by Lisburne was a product of the highest quality even by the seemingly exacting standards of the day. The interiors were made of light oak throughout and were hand French-polished. Early promotional literature referred to a catalogue of attributes. The following is taken from a brochure dating from 1958:

'Generous locker space for the family, Calor gas 2-ring easy clean cooker, wardrobe for your suits and dresses, three interior lights, double bed with Dunlopillo mattresses – in addition – accommodation for two children, mattresses fitted with loose covers for easy cleaning, table tops fitted with Formica no scratches or marks, conversion from day to night use in a moment, fitted curtains throughout, designed by experts fitted with heater and air conditioning units, built throughout by cabinet makers.'

Jack White worked exceptionally hard to put the Devon brand on the map, with a great deal of success. He ensured the company was represented at the London Motor Show at Earl's Court, the Caravan Show and Outdoor Life Show both held at Olympia, and constantly thought of new ways to improve the product. Apart from the somewhat curious conversion of 1959 vintage designed as 'the answer for the gentleman of the road', he was the driving force behind a new budget model of 1962 vintage called the Devonette – a vehicle based on the Kombi rather than the Micro Bus – and the inspiration behind the Gentlux elevating roof, Devon's own design of pop-top fibreglass roof complete with skylight, which, when in the up position, gave 6ft 6in (almost 2m) of standing room. In 1963 he added Dormobile's elevating roof to the options, while revising the specification of both the Caravette and budget Devonette so that each could be ordered using either a Micro Bus or Kombi as the basis for conversion.

Sadly, but perhaps not unexpectedly in the light of his extensive workload, Jack White collapsed and died at the factory in November 1963 at the early age of 51. During the course of 1964 the business was sold to the Renwick Wilton and Dobson Group. They chose to continue trading under the name of

▶ ▼ **Although Devon's range evolved almost continually, their publicity images varied little for the best part of a decade. The picture on the right is from a brochure made available in 1962, while the one below is from November 1964.** (RC)

▶ This brochure, offered for the first time during 1966, demonstrated a considerable leap forward in marketing tactics with a clever cover, featuring the weekday work of a Transporter in dull black and white compared to a vibrant full-colour image of the Camper and its occupants soaking up the warmth of the sun on holiday or at the weekend. *(RC)*

A hardworking Devon motor caravan earns its holidays in the sun

▼ Devon produced a good number of press releases and images for journalists to use. This series of pictures was taken in anticipation of the London Motor Show held at Earl's Court in 1970. *(RC)*

J.P. White (Sidmouth) Ltd for a number of years, while also expanding the range and pumping funds into the Alexandra Works, thereby ensuring the further development of the site.

1965 saw the arrival of a new budget model, the Torvette, a conversion which duly replaced the Devonette, while the following year a walk-through version (*ie* from the cab to the main body) of both the Caravette and Torvette was introduced. Branded as the Spaceway, this option was offered in addition to the standard model. By the late 1960s, following the arrival of the second generation Transporter, Devon models accounted for one quarter of the total UK motor caravan market, despite having to share official approved conversion status with both Danbury and Dormobile.

Conversions on the second generation Transporter were updated with ever-increasing rapidity and a whole new range of names made their debut. Generally, top of the range was either the Eurovette or the Moonraker, with the Caravette sticking to the middle ground. The Torvette gave way to the Sunlander, designed to be a people-carrier and basic

▲ Devon Moonraker with roof elevated and cooker swung out.

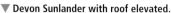

▼ Devon Sunlander with roof elevated.

▲ Devon Moonraker ready to drive away.

▼ Devon Sunlander. All four pictures depict conversions based on a VW Micro Bus.

camper, while a new version of the Devonette was soon to replace it.

The press release announcing the debut of the Devon Sunlander and Moonraker models at the 1970 London Motor Show ran as follows:

'Devon Conversions, Britain's most famous producers of motor caravan conversions on the Volkswagen, who made their trade mark "Caravette" a generic name in the industry, are introducing at the 1970 London Motor Show two completely new motor caravan conversions on both the Volkswagen Micro Bus and Kombi. They are the Devon Sunlander and Devon Moonraker.

The Devon Sunlander is presented with all the comprehensive facilities usual in a Devon Motor Caravan, plus seats for five people in the body of the vehicle, two of which are reversible and fitted with comfortable armrests. The Sunlander offers the combination of two single beds, or one double bed, plus in both cases a child's double bed. The Devon Moonraker provides some extra equipment and in the place of one of the reversible seats is a swing-out cooker unit, which has been so successful in previous Devon models. In addition to other special Devon features, the Moonraker is fitted with an electric air extractor fan, the only one available on any Volkswagen motor caravan. Sleeping arrangements in the Moonraker allow an adult double bed plus a child's double or two adult singles, or one adult double...'

Having used the trading name of Devon Conversions for a time, the company name was finally changed to match in June 1971. Following a periodic reassessment of what was on offer, in 1972 Volkswagen (GB) Limited appointed Devon as their sole official converter, a move which not only led to a record market share of some 55 per cent of the total British market that year, but also to the publication of brochures and other marketing material interlinking Devon's products with those of Volkswagen, as already outlined earlier in this chapter.

Just as Westfalia was hit by the fuel crisis generated turbulence of 1973 and 1974, so too was Devon. In Britain, the government applied what can only be described as an excessive level of taxation on all Campers, leading to an inevitable market drop of some 50 per cent. Devon fought back as best they could, diversifying initially with the production of mini and midi-buses and later adding vehicles for the handicapped and an ambulance to the product portfolio. The programme of issuing new Camper conversions, however, continued, albeit perhaps not quite at the same level as was the case previously. The introduction of modern working methods led to suggestions by some of a general downgrading

Get the go-when-you-feel-like-it feeling

with a Devon Motor Caravan

in terms of quality, while the 1978 Sundowner was the first Devon conversion to be offered on the less prestigious Delivery Van.

Extracts from a company profile prepared for the press in 1979 indicate how much it had been forced to change in order to stay in business during those difficult years:

'Devon Conversions are one of the leading motor caravan manufacturers in Britain. They have been building motor caravans for more than 22 years and bus conversions since 1973. They not only have a

▲ This is the Sunlander on the cover of another go-ahead professional-looking brochure. *(RC)*

▼ When Volkswagen granted official converter status to a company they were likely to amalgamate their marketing with that of the supplier, in this instance Devon. This image was released under the heading of the 'VW Caravette', the word 'Devon' being singular by its absence. *(RC)*

substantial share of the UK market, they export an increasing number of motor caravans to France, Holland and Belgium. Until this year, they were exclusively involved in building conversions on the Volkswagen range of vehicles. But they have now expanded into converting the vehicles of other manufacturers including Mercedes-Benz and Ford.

Their factory at Sidmouth is the largest employer of labour in the town. They also have an expanding facility at the Vulcan Works in Exeter where the larger vehicles are converted. They have their own design department and over the years they have developed a self sufficiency in their production facilities. They mould and assemble their own patent elevating roofs, and make their own fittings and furnishings to rigorous quality standards.

'Part of the Devon-based travel, freight, fuel distribution, boat-building and motor trade Renwick Group, Devon employ their own marketing team of UK-based regional managers...'

In 1980, the Renwick Group was bought by a South African company, who decided to sell on the Devon division two years later, which led to a management and staff co-operative saving the business in 1985.

Devon's market share began to increase once more and expansion was back on the agenda.

Considering Devon's other interests, changes of ownership and commitment to manufacturers other than Volkswagen, the number of conversions and changes to the packages made for the third generation Transporter is quite surprising. In the beginning – which for Devon, like most other converters, was 1980 – the company saw no reason to introduce new designs under different brand names and instead merely tweaked the existing Moonraker and Sundowner conversions to suit the new model. By 1982 the Moonraker more or less carried the Volkswagen flag and as a result Devon introduced an even more luxurious offering, which was branded as the Sunrise. A great deal of emphasis was devoted to roof options, with increased maximum height availability being considered as significant. Devon offered both the 'amazing new Aerospace roof' and the Hi-Top, the former being described as 'remarkably roomy', and as 'rising easily on four gas struts'. 'What's more', the copywriter confirmed, 'you can open and shut it without getting out of the vehicle. ... And when closed for travelling, the Aerospace roof's aerodynamic design conserves fuel.' Text for the Hi-Top was equally effusive: 'With a towering 6' 4" of standing room throughout, a roof vent with fly-

◀ With the exception of the elevating roof, this brochure might easily have been promoting the VW Micro Bus. In 1976, when this cover was launched, the Devon range consisted of the Eurovette, the Devonette and the Continental, the last-mentioned being produced by Westfalia and sold by Devon through the Volkswagen dealerships. *(RC)*

▼ The air-cooled third generation Transporter in Devon Moonraker guise. No doubt clever and much admired in its day, the notion of a recipe, ingredients and a relaxing bottle has little visual appeal today. *(RC)*

In May 1985, the tranquil rural scene of cows ambling along to be milked formed not only the centrepiece of Devon's cover, but also extended to similar themes throughout the eight-page brochure. *(RC)*

From left to right on the cover of this 1986 Devon brochure are the folding, elevating roof on a Moonraker ('Flexibility, comfort and ease of use'); the 'Space Top' firmly clamped down on a Caravette ('Ferrying children to school, mobile site office, holiday home on wheels'); and a Moonraker Hi-Top and Eurovette Hi-Top ('The ultimate in design, comfort and quality'). *(RC)*

screen, 2 built-in radio speakers, interior mirror, luxury lining and lots more extra storage space, our Hi-Top is topping'.

By 1986 four models were on offer. In addition to the Moonraker and the Sunrise, both the Caravette and Eurovette names were resurrected. The former featured what Devon described as the 'new "Space Top" solid sided/insulated elevating roof or "Double Top" folding roof', while the latter, as previously, became the new flagship model, providing 'the ultimate in design, comfort and quality'.

In the hands of its current owners, in 1989 the company relocated to County Durham and set about establishing close ties with Toyota, of which they are now an approved converter. Volkswagen T4 models, which were found to be less suitable for conversion to Camper status than their predecessors, were restricted to the Moonraker and a new name, the Aurora.

DORMOBILE

To many people the name Dormobile occupies a similar position in colloquial dictionaries to both the biro and the hoover. Most of them know that these are not the correct names for a ballpoint pen, a vacuum cleaner or a Camper van, but they continue to use them regardless.

More than any other operation discussed thus far, Martin Walter Ltd of Folkestone – the company behind the Dormobile brand – was far from dependent on Volkswagen. Nevertheless, the Kent-based operation, with origins dating back to 1773, was careful to secure official endorsement for its Camper right from its launch at the Earl's Court Motor Show in October 1961. The Dormobile brand name itself – based at least loosely on the French *dormir*, meaning 'to sleep' – had been used regularly from 1952 onwards, but applied to makes as diverse as Bedford, Standard and Austin-Morris; and

Volkswagen undoubtedly saw the benefits of working with such a well-established firm.

Martin Walter Ltd's brochure carefully highlighted the official status of their conversion, stressing the 'joint' involvement in the product of VW Motors Ltd and the Camper company. Confidence glowed in their text, both in the heading – 'Famous the world over Volkswagen and the Dormobile Caravan' – and in the opening paragraphs:

The new Volkswagen Dormobile Caravan is the latest and most lavishly equipped of the famous Dormobile conversions by Martin Walter. The many novel and ingenious features introduced in the new Volkswagen are the outcome of practical experience.

The many new and extremely attractive features of this exciting caravan include new "Dormatic"

▼ With facilities and storage to the rear of the vehicle, patented innovative dormatic seating and a superior elevating roof, the success of the Volkswagen Dormobile 4-berth Caravan was virtually assured at its debut. It did have one major drawback, however. Although not too apparent in the photographs all the fittings were made of metal leading to problems with condensation. *(RC)*

THE VOLKSWAGEN DORMOBILE 4-BERTH CARAVAN
PRICE £915 COMPLETE (U.K.) *(No Purchase Tax)* Dual Colours Extra

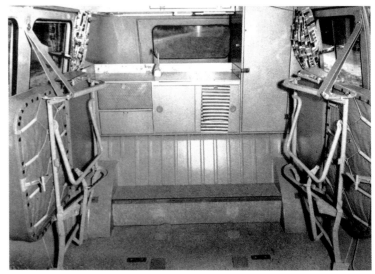

▲ ▶ One delightful image dating from 1965 of children enjoying the benefits of camping with a Dormobile is accompanied by another readily illustrating the amount of available space within the elevating roof area for two adults. Note the open and closed curtains in the roof area in the two pictures. (RC)

seating, a larger roof than ever (with a greatly increased window area), an improved interior layout for easier access and movement, fluorescent lighting which effectively illuminates the whole of the caravan from a point high in the roof, and many detail improvements to specification and fittings, including all-metal cabinets, to make this Volkswagen the finest motorised caravan ever.'

Working on an already well-established design, the layout remained more or less the same throughout the remaining years of first-generation Transporter production. Fortunately, more conventional wooden fitments replaced the condensation-prone metal cabinets of the earliest models! A best-selling highlight, though, had to be the undeniably ingenious 'Dormatic' seating, which came with the built-in advantage of several different layouts. Early brochures depict the 'Dormatic' seats 'arranged for sleeping', set up in their 'chair positions around the table', in 'bench position', and 'folded against the body sides leaving the floor absolutely clear for carrying goods or bulky objects'.

From 1963 it was also possible to order the Dormobile in two-berth guise, the elevating roof being deleted from the package.

The arrival of the second-generation Transporter in the summer of 1967 led Martin Walter Ltd to rethink their Volkswagen Dormobile layout, and, once again, the design determined upon included a truly radical improvement:

'In the country. On the Sand. Or just in the sun – Simply settle down where you please and discover Dormobile life in the new Volkswagen. You'll be feeling hungry after the drive down – so raise the front passenger seat for the best-designed caravan cooker ever! It's a big twin-burner and grill with metal worktop, shelf space and enough room around it to cook a real three-course meal in comfort...'

The D4/6, to give the new model its official designation, was based on the Kombi and thus in external appearance was invariably painted a single colour. The cooker position demanded that the 'famous Dormobile roof' had to be positioned closer to the cab, and in its general design the new model was more in keeping with the layouts offered by other manufacturers.

In 1970 Martin Walter Ltd added a further model to the range. Designated the D4/8, it was a multi-

◀ Used by Dormobile in their own literature and by Volkswagen when they wished to depict the Campers produced by each of their official converters, this vehicle is really only recognisable as a Dormobile by its elevating roof. (RC)

purpose vehicle – 'the new 8 seater that sleeps 1, 2, 3, 4 or even a family of 5' – aimed at the luxury rather than the economy end of the market. Highlights included forward-facing seating for eight people, a fitted but removable gold-coloured carpet 'to give that extra touch of luxury', and, for the first time in the history of the Dormobile, a refrigerator, a feature that quickly filtered down to the D4/6. As usual, Martin Walter aimed to place the spotlight on one attribute above all others:

'The outstanding feature of the new body design is the fully upholstered seating fitted in the body of the vehicle which allows for a low level double bed, 48" x 73" or a single bed, 32" wide with the outer seats left at bedside and gives exceptional locker accommodation in the steel framed and panelled seat boxes.'

Such was the Dormobile's reputation that not only could it be specified in left-hand-drive form, as it was exported to many nations across the world, but it also came to be manufactured under licence in countries such as Australia. Nevertheless, despite its heritage and size, Dormobile Ltd – by now part of the Charringtons Group – began to experience financial difficulties as the 1970s drew to a close, with the result that the third-generation Transporter never became the subject of a Dormobile conversion. The company struggled on, producing Campers based on vehicles other than Volkswagens, but finally ceased trading in 1984.

However, in the closing years of the 20th century the Dormobile name was revived when a group of ex-employees banded together to form a company supplying parts for earlier models, including roof canvases, skylights and even badges.

▲ Gone where the days when Dormobile Campers carried an identifying badge on the driver's door frame, but in the era of the D4/6 customers could opt for a delicate coach-line (1984) to be added to the vehicle's sides, while also specifying a roof rack (1613). *(RC)*

Campers in profusion and the copywriter's craft

Having concentrated on official and well-known names, in countries ranging from Germany to Australia, let us now turn our attention to the promotional literature generated by these and, more importantly, many smaller Camper companies over the years, which was often quirky, amusing or even downright bizarre.

Undoubtedly, a useful insight into the industry is provided by the varying quality of the copy found in the brochures produced in the latter years of the 1950s and the first half of the 1960s. Equally, it's important to see how from the 1970s onwards the story of a particular model or innovation was addressed once marketing budgets had become an essential requirement of all but a one-man band operating from a small unit in a backyard,

Archive imagery accompanied the story told by most of the firms included, and it is necessary to recognise that the almost blurred and sometimes doctored photographs of many represented the best endeavours of small companies and their printers, who lacked the resources not only of a giant organisation like Volkswagen, but even of well-established rival converters.

Camping in the days of the first-generation Transporter

Volkswagen's copywriters sold the story that follows in a 1961 brochure entitled 'The Volkswagen Camper', a publication printed in Germany but directed at the American market:

'Carefree vacations in a VW Camper – no need to make reservations, pack cases, tip porters. Rain can't spoil your trip – follow the sun and set up house wherever you like. The great outdoors is yours for the taking, and when you're ready for a bit of indoor comfort, just go back to your own living room, bedroom, kitchen, bar (no closing time) and bathroom (no waiting!). The elegant, space-saving fittings are the result of long experience and practical planning. A VW Camper means fresh air and fun for the family whether you're planning a weekend trip, a couple of weeks vacation or a long expedition. Welcome Volkswagen features for penny-wise travellers: low fuel consumption, good performance, ruggedness. Pictures can't tell the whole story, so if you'd like to see for yourself just ask a VW dealer for a demonstration. For the vacation of your life choose a VW Camper'.

European Cars Ltd of South Kensington, London – an operation that made its debut in the early months of 1958 and produced its final models during the course of 1964 – sold the story of its 'Slumberwagen' thus in literature produced in the latter part of 1959:

'With much ingenuity full use is made of the available space both when travelling or "in camp". Attention is drawn to locker space under seats, cupboards, small curtained hanging recess, water container, basin and wash cabinet. Rep curtains on non-rusting runners completely close off the interior. Combined with the mobility of this self-propelled caravan is the facility offered for either a quick one night stop or a longer stay with comfort.'

Born out of recognition that neither the Volkswagen Westfalia partnership nor the home-built 'Westfakia' could totally satisfy the demand for Campers in the USA, California-based **E-Z Camper** (pronounced 'e-zee') not only created its own but was also successful in negotiating a package whereby availability was through the Volkswagen dealer network. A remarkable degree of professionalism ensured a bullet point list of the Camper's key selling points, which, together with a crisp and enticingly clear introduction, is here reproduced in full:

'At last! A station wagon with a built-in "campsite". Now you can go to see those miles and miles of back country, far away from the city noise, smog and confusion. Now you can know for the first time the fun of camping without the need for elaborate planning, without the inconvenience and drudgery that takes up so much of the "fun time" of camping. Wherever you decide to go, it will take you only minutes to set up camp and begin to enjoy the great and wonderful outdoors.
● Diamondized polyclad plywall interiors ● 50-lb capacity ice box in coppertone ● old copper finish forged iron hardware ● 5 safety glass windows, aluminium screened ● 2 burner gasoline stove ● easy to clean vinyl floor tile on top of tempered masonite ● 54" x 108" awning with side curtains making an enclosed room which attaches to vehicle only... ● Husky 6' 2" bed with 4" plyafoam mattress ● man sized wardrobe and plenty of storage space ● insulation behind polyclad panelling ● folding tables with genuine "nevamar" tops, trimmed in chrome ● converts from beautiful station wagon to gleaming kitchen to lovely panelled bedroom in just seconds ● 12 gallon Calif. Code approved water system with pump.'

▶ ▼ The Slumberwagen Motor Caravan with Calthorpe elevating roof in all its glory is depicted here with pictures taken from a brochure dating from 1960. An even greater treat waits overleaf! *(RC)*

▲ ◄ From the sublime to the vaguely ridiculous – two images of the Slumberwagen, one with its elevating roof down, the other with it up. Would anyone really have stood peering out of the small window in the Calthorpe roof? Undoubtedly not, but the archetypal suited gentleman could at least be seen to be able to stand up in this conversion! (RC)

Northern England-based Volkswagen distributors **Moortown Motors** dabbled in the Camper business in the late 1950s and early 1960s. Perhaps unusually for a firm offering Volkswagens for sale in their showrooms, their activities extended to conversions on both Ford and Standard models. Like Devon, who relied on a member of the official Volkswagen dealership network to guarantee distribution, the Moortown operation was formed out of a partnership, with cabinet makers Bamforth combining their craftsmanship with the car distributor's sales and marketing abilities. Conversions were initially to the Micro Bus, but by 1960 the Kombi had been added. Following a revamp for the 1961 season and use of the 'Autohome' name as a brand, Moortown's final thrust was to produce what they described as 'a more modestly priced motorised caravan based on the Volkswagen Micro-Bus and Kombi', which was given the name of the Moortown Campahome. A letter from Moortown's Managing Director addressed to the Automobile Association's technical library, written in the autumn of 1963, advised, however, that 'we are discontinuing the production of motorised caravans as from October 1963'. The 'limited number of vehicles at present in stock', Moortown added, 'it is anticipated will be sold in the course of the next 2–3 months'.

▲ ▼ The well equipped E-Z Camper bears a passing resemblance in its interior layout to that of Westfalia's products. Initially developed out of recognition that demand for Volkswagen Campers outstripped supply in America, the E-Z Camper was available through the official Volkswagen dealer network. *(RC)*

▲ Moortown Motors was a Yorkshire firm based in Leeds. Although like Devon their Autohome range was formed out of a partnership between skilled craftsmen and the VW Distributors, not only did their vehicles struggle to capture a respectable chunk of the market, but also it was very much an unequal relationship with the firm of Bamforth of East Heslerton being little more than paid employees. *(RC)*

The specification of the Moortown Autohome Mark 2A included the following:

'Spacious dinette for four; foam rubber cushions; dining table, sleeping berths for 2 adults and 2 children; 2 storage lockers beneath the dinette seats; pumped water supply; water storage containers; fold away washbasin; 2 burner calor gas cooker; fitted cutlery draw; "Easicool" food storage container; full length wardrobe; table and horizontal surfaces covered in Formica. All cabinets in polished Jap oak; two large cupboards – one with fitted crockery compartment; two smaller cupboards for household utensils; interior electric light; hinged roof ventilator – 1ft 2ins square; interior of roof insulated and covered in washable PVC; curtains to all windows; lino tiled floor.'

As for the Moortown 'Campahome', the specification wasn't made entirely clear in the opening paragraph of a brochure specific to this budget model:

'The 'Moortown Campahome" has been specifically designed to provide the camping/touring enthusiast with a modestly priced vehicle whilst retaining the same degree of craftsmanship, comfort and quality as supplied in more expensive motorised caravans.'

◀ ▲ ▶ **The finest legacy of the Autohome range has to be the remarkable snap-shot images of life with a Camper in the late 1950s and early 1960s. From the lady cooking in her best attire, and business suit and pearl earring accessories for afternoon tea around the table, to the highly polished shoes of the gentleman kettle boiler and the collar and tie of the washer-up, the imagery is worth its weight in gold. The ingenious use of the cab for two children for many is further improved by the bored expressions of the two youngsters demonstrating the Camper's assets.** *(RC)*

INSIDE STORY

➡ of the finest motor - caravan value in the world !

▲ Although the name Service is singular by its absence, the image is of the cover of a brochure produced by the Garage in 1961. The brochure opens to reveal (as Service indicate) 'the finest motor-caravan value in the world!

▼ Undoubtedly the most unusual Camper conversion of all time – the Caraversions HiTop

'If you're handy to Colchester', wrote Essex-based **Service Garages Ltd**, a company possibly better known for its bespoke conversions on the Transporter – with mobile shops, refrigerated vans, and even the somewhat dubiously named 'Serv-ice' ice-cream van, springing to mind – 'it will be worth your while seeing the "Service Motor-Caravan"…for yourself.' However, the nub of the message came in the last sentence, where the phrase 'enquire from any Volkswagen Dealer or Distributor, and they will send you further details', clearly indicated tacit official approval for yet another Camper van manufacturer.

A basic form of press release written in the summer of 1961 not only set the scene for the purchase of a 'Motor-Caravan', but also summarised the specification:

'Even the most ardent caravanner will have to admit that there's a lot to be said for a 4-wheeled holiday home which can toil away for the rest of the year on such mundane jobs as shopping, getting you to and from the office and generally serving you well, giving at the same time a standard of comfort above that of the ordinary motor car.

'Bright ideas transform the Volkswagen Micro-Bus *'Such a vehicle is the Service Motor-Caravan. Developed by The Service Garages (South Eastern Limited)…this astonishingly successful holiday-home come-run-about vehicle is a conversion based on the Volkswagen Micro-Bus. Fitted out in polished wood and Formica surfaces the Service Motor-Caravan provides a wealth of cupboard space, a double bed with foam latex mattresses and sleeping accommodation for two children. A modern cooking unit with two burners; wardrobe, wash basin, 7 gallon water container; are part of the standard equipment, all of which either store or fold away quickly and easily and turn the vehicle into a functional every-day form of transport capable of passenger carrying up to 8 adults.'*

The Service Garages continued to produce their VW Camper until 1966, at which point they appear to have conceded defeat to the popularity of companies such as Devon and Dormobile.

No section dedicated to Camper conversions dating from the days of the first-generation Transporter could be considered complete without the inclusion of what has to be one of the oddest models of all time. Needless to say, very few HiTops by London-based **Caraversions** were either ordered or built and even fewer if any survive today. Unquestionably ugly, totally lacking in aesthetic appeal, the Kombi-based HiTop – which made its debut in 1962 – nevertheless had one advantage over some of its rivals:

'HiTop headroom allows US to furnish with standard height fittings and allows YOU to move around in comfort…HiTop headroom allows US to provide liberal bed and cupboard space and allows YOU to live and sleep in comfort.'

The near contemporaneous debut of the High Roofed Delivery Van, a vehicle with an overall height of 90in, should have been sufficient to suggest to Caraversions that their vehicle was top heavy and most definitely cumbersome in urban car parks, as its overall height stood at an amazing 98in.

A pinnacle of popularity: the second generation Transporter

Turning to the literature produced by Volkswagen initially, a delightful chunk of DDB prose adorns the third page of a picture-dominated brochure dating from 1969, enticingly entitled 'Camp down wherever you reach sundown'. Would-be purchasers must have been captivated by the message the agency sold so cleverly:

'This year, over 15-million will get into some kind of car and set out to discover the wonder, the relaxation and the sheer joy of the great outdoors. They'll stuff themselves and their gear into sedans and conventional station wagons. They'll haul boxes behind them. Some will hitch on a house. Some will convert their pick-up trucks into campers. And some, of course, will buy a rucksack for each member of the family and thumb their way to the nearest mountain. But there is a rapidly growing group who will be able to take off and go just about
anywhere they like
whenever they like
with the least fuss
the least planning
at the least cost
and get the most relaxation and fun out of it all.
Those are the people who own a Volkswagen Campmobile.'

Today the US Company **Sportsmobile** produces motorhomes and RVs based on vehicles from American manufacturers such as Chevrolet, Dodge and Ford, plus imported Mercedes vans. However, when the Indiana operation created its first Camper in 1961 it was to Volkswagen that they turned. In the spirit of both Westfalia and the emerging American dealer network-organised Campmobiles, the nature of the conversion was such that it could be removed within a matter of minutes, thus taking full advantage of the multifaceted intentions behind the Transporter's design. Well built and thought out, authorised Volkswagen dealers could fit a kit within five hours, but DIY versions were also readily available. The principles developed in the era of the first-generation Transporter were continued throughout production of the second-generation Transporter too, and, for that matter, for many more years thereafter.

Under the heading 'luxurious standard equipment', Sportsmobile listed what was included in a conversion made to either a Delivery Van or Kombi, although a kitted-out Microbus was also an option. As far as Sportsmobile were concerned this was an era when vinyl reigned supreme, with seats, mattresses and much more being covered in 'handsome' Naugahyde vinyl:

'Rear seat, Naugahyde w/inside pad; bed mattress, Naugahyde; front seat, Naugahyde w/storage base; table, free standing, recessed storage; ice box, w/pump, water container, sink, storage; utility cabinet, w/work table (attach to ice box), wardrobe, Naugahyde or solid cabinet; storage cabinet, w/ shelves, sliding doors; floor panels, cushioned vinyl; arm rest compartment, rear; ash tray; arm rest compartment, front; tire bracket (split seat vehicle); tire cover (split seat vehicle); curtains, all windows w/retaining cords; wall lamp, and two ceiling lights; 110v hook up, inside fused outlet; ceiling panels, vinyl clad; insulation, ceiling; ceiling compartment, w/padded front; wall, door, cab panels; curtain cornice, padded; windows, louvered, screened [3 panel van, 2 Kombi]'

Possibly of even more interest was Sportsmobile's optional elevating roof, a full-length pop-top affair designated the 'Penthouse':

'The Sportsmobile Penthouse will sleep two upstairs in privacy on a comfortable mattress. Spring counterbalanced crossarms float the top up or down in seconds. It's a wonderful option, ask the kids. Bedroom extends to 6' 2" to accommodate two adults. It's a little snug – but sleepable.'

Such was the ingenuity of the design of the Penthouse that for a period in the early 1970s Volkswagen of America offered it as on option on their own Camper based on the Westfalia.

In the latter years of second-generation Transporter production Sportsmobile were offering at least four variations on their Volkswagen-based 'pleasure wagons'. Sportsmobile 'V' included a removable seat in place of the icebox console standard with 'model IV', while 'model VI' included an ice box located in the back of the passenger seat and a full-height, permanently mounted 'closet and storage cabinet'. Undoubtedly, the quirkiest offering was the Sportsmobile Clubcar, which to all extents and purposes contained vinyl-covered fireside chairs, carpets that any '70s household would have been proud of, and an abundance of dubious decor that nearly 30 years later would raise many an eyebrow:

'Clubcar – Soft, quiet, luxurious comfort…everywhere you go! Clubcar's rear seat is comfort designed. Steel frame with springs, 3" firm foam topped with 2.5" soft stratafiber with glove soft fabric backed vinyl means "super comfort". Soft, fiber filled, bolsters add to your lounging pleasure. Back cushion locks in two

▲ Although unfortunately depopulated, this image of the Sportsmobile illustrates the Camper's Penthouse roof to perfection. (RC)

Past the days of the second-generation Transporter, Sportsmobile offered conversions on both the T3 and T4, although increasingly the mainstream element of their business, the RV, took precedence.

California-based **Sundial** was another business that was created out of Volkswagen of America's inability to prise more Westfalia Campers out of the German firm to satisfy the insatiable demands of customers. Initially at least, the interior of a Sundial closely mimicked that of a Westfalia, even to the extent of utilising parts from the latter to make copies. Although both Kombis and Micro Buses were used as a basis for Sundial conversions, the more readily available Delivery Van was used as the base model. As such, Sundial conversions, although relatively rare nowadays, are recognisable by their characteristic windows – louvred in the days of the first-generation Transporter and of 'large safety glass sliding…with screens for van conversion' in the period when the company worked with the second-generation model.

Although some insist that the quality of a Sundial wasn't comparable with that of a Westfalia, the company took great pride in their endeavours to continually upgrade their products:

'Sundial is always concerned about building the best. We believe that our customers value fine workmanship and post-sales service. With a policy of constant improvement of our products, we cannot guarantee that the specifications of conversions and accessories will necessarily be identical to those shown in…[the] brochure.'

In the early years of second-generation Transporter production, Sundial offered two variations on a theme, both being available in a variety of finishes. For example, woodwork could be specified in light, medium, or dark hues, while '20 different vinyl upholstery patterns' were 'offered in three price ranges' to suit the customer's budget. Eight choices of curtain designed to 'match or contrast' were on offer, while four options in table and cabinet-top patterns were available. Despite the tag 'De luxe' being applied to one, in reality each of the two conversions was designed with different demands and requirements taken into account:

positions – upright or lounge. Headrest swings down, for couch effect, when desired.

'Sportsmobile's deluxe recliner seat is a co-pilot's delight. Driver seat includes special matching covers with soft padding. Skylight with shag trim, and roof vent, are popular Clubcar options. Quality, thick shag, carpet enriches and brightens the Clubcar interior throughout. Soft, upholstered black trim panels highlight the interior.'

▶ The Sportsmobile was a well appointed and designed Camper made better still by the fact that the children could be banished to the upper deck! (RC)

'The King Size Bed Model features: full width seat and bed; table hinged to wall; six separate storage areas; water pump and portable plastic sink near door for easy access from outside; drinking glass rack on ice cabinet; excellent wardrobe accessibility; antique copper hardware.

'The De luxe Model features: extra large counter top with built-in stainless steel sink; large cupboard with three drawers; nine separate storage areas; handy medicine cabinet with large mirror; clip on

*table for outside use; exterior wheel mount provided
for split seat type; hand polished brass hardware.'*

Key, though, to the advantages of a Sundial model
over the offerings from other manufacturers had to be
the company's assurance regarding availability:

*'You can own a Sundial converted Volkswagen fitted
with your choice of accessories for less than the cost
of most new station wagons. Decide on a floor plan
and select the accessories you want…Your Sundial
Camper can be ready for the road in a few days.'*

Sadly, the fuel crisis of the mid-'70s – intrinsically
linked as it was to a downturn in the Camper
business and the economy in general – led to
Sundial's demise.

The **Viking**, launched by Motorhomes of
Berkhamsted in 1970, was at first little different
from other conversions offered by a variety of
manufacturers, despite the lavish claims made in the
company's literature:

*'Viking. So much more than a Volkswagen. Viking is
an entirely new concept in motor caravan design. Its
versatile use of space, ingenious design and superb
quality sets it apart from all other Volkswagens.
Viking is ahead of the field – in every field.'*

Even the Viking's guarantee was interesting in its
extravagance:

*'Volkswagen (GB) Limited guarantee the engine,
transmission and other mechanical components
within the terms of their normal warranty. The
Viking conversion is guaranteed unconditionally
by Viking Motorhomes for a period of twelve months
from the date of purchase.'*

It is possible that statements such as this aroused
Volkswagen in Britain to take what they deemed
appropriate action, but it is also probable that their
exclusive contract with Devon and, by default,
Westfalia precipitated a move destined to shake
many a manufacturer and stir Motorhomes into a
frenzied whirl of denial. A press release entitled 'VW
Warning on Unauthorised Motor Caravans' slated
manufacturers who cut through the Volkswagen's
roof, suggesting such conversions were unsafe, as
the vehicles lacked sufficient strengthening both
in the roof section and in the vital underfloor area,
and the Viking was cited as a prime example of
such malpractice. Volkswagen's ultimate weapon,
the retraction of their warranty, was duly employed.
Motorhomes hit back with a vitriolic release of
their own, demanding that Volkswagen carry out a

▲ ◀ Despite observations that the
quality of Sundial Campers wasn't
comparable to those despatched to the
United States by Westfalia, reference to
these brochure images would seem to
indicate otherwise. The picture at the
top shows the interior of the De luxe
model, while the close up interior shot
illustrates some of the basics of the
King Size Bed model. *(RC)*

full technical appraisal and accusing the company of deliberately attempting to discredit the Viking because it was better than the products of the firm VW were endorsing. As Motorhomes continued to produce their Viking model and customers were not difficult to find, the skirmish appeared to have been won by the underdog.

However, despite the publicity surrounding this foray, if it hadn't been for an innovation dating from 1974, at a point when the company had renamed itself Motorhomes International and relocated to Stanbridge in Hertfordshire, perhaps the Viking name wouldn't be as well known as it is today, many years after its demise.

The Spacemaker concept – essentially a new style of elevating roof, branded as the Viking and Pioneer Spacemaker – was launched in the aggressive marketing style with which Motorhomes International were becoming increasingly associated, although perhaps, in this instance, the operation had a genuine reason to make their voice heard:

'A system so far advanced as to make all the others seem almost obsolete.
'As leaders in the field of leisure vehicle engineering we have a special responsibility to raise standards and research new systems. To develop ways of making the most from a little space; and then to make space where none exists.'

The mechanics of the Spacemaker, however, were described in a practical rather than an openly belligerent way:

'We wanted an elevating roof that was semi-automatic, simple and spacious. It had to be full-length to create extra space above the cab for sleeping or storage. This called for an improved lifting mechanism…So we used gas-filled arms, pressurised to provide exactly the lifting power we needed for this giant roof. Now, lifting a Spacemaker roof is rather like opening the tailgate of an estate car.
'A problem with most elevating roofs is the limited space between bunks. Access is difficult unless the bunks are tapered. To overcome this the Spacemaker roof is side-hinged; so as it opens it overhangs the side of the van. The side-hinged feature also ensures positive location when the roof is lowered. We then developed an "overhang" feature along the opposite side. We've created space for both bunks to be moved outwards over the sides of the van – leaving more room to move about inside.
'Spacemaker is the most technically advanced elevating roof available anywhere …'

The Spacemaker concept, an arrangement that was also available as an aftermarket extra that could be fitted to conversions produced by other manufacturers, ensured that Motorhomes International remained at the forefront throughout the remaining production years of the second-generation Transporter. It also guaranteed that Motorhomes International were ready to launch a similar product, suitably updated and rebranded as the Xplorer, when the third-generation Transporter made its debut. However, the storm clouds were gathering for Motorhomes International and the double attack of particularly stiff competition and a downturn in sales forced the company to cease trading in the mid-1980s. Extracts from a brochure designed to promote the new Xplorer and its Spacemaker roof hark back to the controversy of earlier years, but also go some way towards explaining how the company had not exactly endeared itself to its competitors, and may well have encouraged a concerted effort amongst them to push Motorhomes International over the edge:

'To create the necessary standing space we are allowed to cut away the roof panel between the ribs and all three VW approved converters, Devon, Danbury and Motorhomes International have done this…'

Of Devon conversions, Motorhome International were delighted to put the following in print:

'The Devon has two small beds to the front and rear of the roof opening…They are suitable only for two small children. A double bed is possible by sliding the back bed forward to make one big bed…Access to it is via a second "hole" in the roof…which is directly above the ground floor double bed. It is a matter of some inconvenience that one reaches the upper bed only by putting at risk the credentials of anyone occupying the bed below. And, of course, the upper bed now seals off the standing area, so at night one must crouch at all times.'

Danbury's product was dismissed in two short sentences:

'The Danbury has a double bed at the back end of the roof system. When fully extended to its maximum length of 72" it seals off all but 14" of the original roof opening.'

After outlining the Spacemaker arrangement, the summary was blunt in the extreme.

'…NO INTRUSION of the normal standing area. Four adults in the Spacemaker, two in the Devon and Danbury. One hundred percent more space. And that is the measure by which Spacemaker leads in design know-how.'

This is the Isabella awning. The most fabulous side tent ever made by man.
Chosen for the Viking because of its quality and style.
It has room enough for three berths and is guaranteed for five years.
It's free standing, of course.

From the early and relatively anonymous days of Campers with the Viking name as illustrated in the picture top left, Motorhomes, later Motorhomes International, bade to carve a name for themselves with the introduction of the innovative Spacemaker roof. The line up of newly completed third generation conversions branded the Xplorer might attest to the company's success but by the mid 1980s it had ceased to trade – a victim of a general downturn in business and conceivably its own aggressive marketing. *(RC)*

Pictured in the lee of York Minster and with St William's College as a backdrop, the York with its moulded fibre glass roof was a conversion carried out on customers' Transporters new or old. (RC)

Impossible as it is to include every manufacturer in this section, it is worth a moment's diversion to look at at least one of the less well-known operations on the periphery of the bigger picture. Few will have heard of the **York Motor Caravan Company**, based in the heart of the historic city of York, but snippets from a press pack provided by the firm in 1976 are of more than passing interest. York's work appears to have been concentrated solely around the conversion of vehicles already owned by potential customers. In addition to the straightforward fitting of an interior to either a Kombi or Micro Bus, York offered both High Top and Elevating Roof conversions. The depiction of an early model second-generation High Top Transporter on the front cover of their 1976 brochure is indicative of the operation's status:

'The stream-lined, moulded fibre glass roof with louvred side windows gives an overall headroom of 5' 10" within the caravan, and incorporates extensive storage lockers over the driving cabin at the rear.'

The High Top wasn't simply an adapted version of the High Roof Delivery Van, for the roof could be purchased as nothing more than a moulding, or fitted to include side windows, front and rear lockers and a headlining. As for the Elevating Roof conversion:

'This incorporates our unique easy to operate raising mechanism (patent pending) to the fibre glass roof unit which gives a comfortable headroom. The size of the aperture avoids cutting through roof cross members – thus ensuring that the strength of the structure is unimpaired.'

In their press pack, York proudly included a lengthy review of their conversions, an article full of compliments but devoid of any reference to its origin! Of greatest interest to the wider community of the by now relatively hard-pressed firms offering Campers must have been the opening remarks by the anonymous 'reviewer':

'When the York Motor Caravan Company was formed 15 years ago, production concentrated on Rootes chassis. Now public preference demands that nearly all the one-a-week turnout utilises customer's Volkswagen chassis, though Commer van conversions and coach-builts will be made on request.'

Increasing sophistication in the era of the third generation Transporter

Volkswagen of America undoubtedly had the ideal Camper story knitted together, as has been seen earlier in this chapter. A further extract from another brochure of 1982 vintage serves to illustrate the liquid smooth text that few if any could emulate:

'The comforts of home and the ride of a car. If you're off to see America, it's the only way to go. With the cost of a vacation home even more prohibitive than the cost of getting to it, here's a way to save on them both. Now, we're not suggesting that a Vanagon can substitute for luxury accommodations, but it is an attractive alternative. And the Camper is ideal for overnights or weekend trips. You can also use your Vanagon Camper on the weekdays for commuting or shopping. As regular daily transportation it will seat four with so much comfort – amid luxurious, contemporary furnishings – it may be the ultimate in van-pool vehicles...' – Vanagon and Vanagon Camper 1982, printed in the USA.

Despite the degree of sophistication readily evident in a new, much-improved range of vehicles from Westfalia, in general the era of the T3 can be distinguished by increasing diversity and ingenuity on the part of independent companies, most of which were far from reliant on Volkswagen to make their living.

Typical of these was, and remains, the already alluded to firm of **Auto-Sleepers**. Based close to the delightful Cotswold village of Broadway in Worcestershire, the business came into being in 1961 when the Trevelyan family built their own Camper based on a Morris J2 van. This took both parents and their two young sons to the South of France for a holiday. A second Camper, this time based on an Austin, benefited from a series of refinements developed in the light of their earlier holiday experience. This second vehicle soon attracted the attention of dealers Henlys of Bristol, who promptly placed an order for five more such Campers. The family went into partnership with local builder Bob Hallin, and from these humble origins Auto-Sleepers was born. However, it was more than 20 years before the company dabbled with a Camper based on a Volkswagen, by which time not only had the first-generation Transporter been eclipsed by the second but the third-generation model had been updated to include modern water-cooled engines.

Well-built conversions using the finest materials had been a recognisable feature of the company virtually from its inception, although whether its slogan 'The Hallmark of Quality' led Volkswagen to award conversion design approval with almost immediate

The increasingly sophisticated nature of Camper conversions during the course of the third generation Transporter's eleven year production cycle is epitomised by the content of the pictures designed to promote the Auto-Sleeper Hi-Top. *(RC)*

effect when Auto-Sleepers produced its first VW Camper will inevitably be a matter for debate.

The tone of the brochure produced to promote the Auto-Sleepers Hi-Top must have been music to the ears of Volkswagen, whose own products, although not necessarily the cheapest, always exuded finesse.

'The new Volkswagen Auto-Sleeper is extremely attractive and is almost "car-like" to drive. The beautifully styled high-top roof has been designed with aerodynamics in mind with the resultant benefit in fuel consumption.

The Volkswagen Auto-Sleeper is extremely well equipped and the high level of specification includes carpeting throughout, a swivelling passenger seat enabling maximum utilisation of the interior space, and even a chemical toilet in a specially designed locker. The external appearance of the Volkswagen Auto-Sleeper is eye-catching, as not only is there an attractive paint scheme with contrasting coachlines, but the wheel trims, roof rack and ladder are fitted as standard. Auto-Sleepers and Volkswagen have produced the ideal combination: a perfectly planned, fitted and equipped interior powered by precision engineering ensuring economy and reliability.'

CI Autohomes, a division of Caravans International, was another manufacturer that produced its first Volkswagen-based camper in the early days of the third-generation Transporter. Although trouble lay ahead, this was not foreseen when the Dorset-based company devised a brand new story in the evolution of the Camper:

'Following their appointment as official converters of the popular Volkswagen Kombi, CI Autohomes are proud to announce their first ever model on a Volkswagen – the CI Kamper – which has been specifically designed for the Volkswagen Kombi. The entirely new high rise roof – double skinned and fully insulated – provides headroom of 7' 5" over the complete standing area, plus quiet, warm and spacious surroundings for the occupants of the upper double bed located at the level of the roof. The Kamper roof is easily elevated with the assistance of gas filled struts and incorporates a wind-up rooflight with built in flyscreen. For even greater ventilation or to facilitate spectating at sporting events one of the roof side panels can also be folded away without affecting the stability of the roof…'

Caravans International spiralled into receivership at the end of 1982, but fortunately the Autohome division was rescued, re-emerging as Autohomes (UK) with renewed vitality. Shortly after this the company developed further models, while remaining one of Volkswagen's approved converters. Essentially Autohomes – whose strap-line was 'Leaders by design' – produced three models of varying names over the years. From the early days of the Kamper, which was revamped and subsequently known as the Kamper II, each conversion bore a remarkable resemblance in interior layout design, but differed in terms of the type of roof fitted:

'Now the Kamper II takes the original concept of a true dual-purpose vehicle equipped for either summer or winter use, a further great step forward with a vast number of improvements including superb new interior decor, new lighter furniture, improved curtain location, thicker upper bed mattress, more comprehensive kitchen facilities, increased storage space, detail improvements to the elevating roof and a much simplified method of converting the rear seat to a double bed.'

If Autohomes (UK)'s products demonstrated both quality and individuality, so too did 'the all new Autocruiser', an infrequently seen conversion

▲ 'Still the only Volkswagen Caravan with a rigid, fully insulated elevating roof', proclaimed CI Autohomes shortly after their debut as official Volkswagen conversion specialists. *(RC)*

▼ Autohomes (UK), the successor company to CI Autohomes developed the range of Campers offered. Here from left to right we have the Karisma, the Kamper, and the Kameo. The Karisma was the best equipped of the three conversions. *(RC)*

Unassuming from the outside save the by now commonplace high-top look, the interior of Diamond RV's Autocruiser was distinctive, especially as the conversion came complete with a shower unit. *(RC)*

from the little-known firm of **Diamond RV**: 'The first radical rethink of a VW Design for 15 years. That is what is being said about the Autocruiser. We think you will like it.' Their high-top conversion was most unusual in that the layout included a shower and toilet compartment and completely separated the area set aside for cooking, washing up and food storage from the living or sleeping area:

'A most intriguing design with space for living. A large lounge/dinette area separated completely from the galley which offers fridge, large sink, hob with hot plate and grill, good work surfaces, roof storage pod and an abundance of cupboard space. Even a toilet and shower compartment with hot and cold water is provided. Two single beds are ingeniously provided leaving full access to toilet and galley, even when the beds are in use. The high quality carpet and soft interior lining together with a choice of three interior trim materials add up to give a feeling of true quality and luxury. A complete motorhome in a parking meter sized vehicle.'

Luxury and individuality also extended to firms other than Westfalia in Germany, two of the most notable being Dehler and Tischer, both of which survive today, although only the latter is still involved in the Camper business. **Dehler,** originally yacht builders, diversified into the Camper business in the 1980s, when they offered the luxuriously upmarket Profi. Apart from its fixed but aerodynamic high roof, the exterior of a Profi could be readily identified through the inclusion of a multitude of customised fibreglass panels ranging from bumper and lower side-skirts to elegant waistline additions, all of which were finished in a contrasting shade to the vehicle's main body colour. The Profi also sported alloy wheels, both a cab and main body sunroof, and a largely concealed rack built into the roof towards the rear. Interior quality and a level of sumptuousness difficult to adequately describe in words alone matched its exterior opulence. Reference to a built-in TV in the roof space, and the inclusion of a compartment for showering, hint at the vehicle's attributes, as does mention of meticulously padded upholstery, carefully moulded fittings which even extended to the dashboard, and the inclusion of polished wood trim in the style of upmarket executive cars. In summary, the Profi was aimed at wealthy customers yearning for the fun of an outdoor holiday or weekend without having to suffer the traditional indignities of the average period campsite.

Alloy wheels and an abundance of carefully crafted fibreglass panels suggests that the interior of Germany's Dehler Profi conversion might well be luxurious... (RC)

Based on an idea originating from the USA, **Tischer** started to produce demountable Campers in the 1970s, during the second-generation Transporter era. However, it was during the lifetime of its successor that business grew considerably, and the demountable has since been offered on all subsequent generations of Volkswagen Pick-ups or chassis cabs. An English-language version of Tischer's brochure not only shows that the company's biggest success lay in the field of double cab models, but also gives us the brand name for the conversion: *Das Huckepack-System*, which is translated into English as 'Pick-a-Back'. Overall Tischer were eager to emphasise to potential customers that the demountable was another viable option in the search for an ideal Camper, *Die Alternative* in the German original becoming 'The Alternative' in the English version:

The cabin is quickly removable from the base vehicle so both may be used independently. Note the optional cab/cabin door access…Now you can use the pick-up for excursions or as your everyday vehicle when at home (the pick-up sides are easily replaced and we also offer a polyester hardtop)…It only takes a few minutes to remove the cabin – much easier than

... which indeed it was. (RC)

packing everything away every time…The double cab version provides comfortable travelling for 4–5 people even without the cabin fitted…The kitchen area is fully equipped and invites you to cook your favourite dinner…The beautifully appointed bathroom with full size shower…Interior panelling is in hi-class plywood with synthetic surfaces, practical, hardwearing and attractive…Full insulation, double glazing and central heating ensure your comfort regardless of weather.'

▼ The ingenious piggy back Camper arrangement made its debut in the era of the second generation Transporter. Although both models illustrated are based on the single cab Pick-up the double cab version allowed more people to travel in the van when not enjoying the home-from-home comforts of what was essentially a mini caravan. (RC)

Touching on the T4 and even the T5

Sadly, without turning this volume into a book about Volkswagen-based Campers it is not practical to do more than skim the surface of conversions based on the fourth-generation Transporter. Thus restricted, two firms have been selected to fly the flag for vehicles built between 1990 and 2003. The name of one, Karmann, might be considered synonymous with that of Volkswagen, but not because of its Camper conversions; the other, Holdsworth, was another British manufacturer that had benefited from official approval for its conversions from Volkswagen Commercial Vehicles VAG (United Kingdom) Ltd, but, as previously mentioned, by the mid-1990s had hit hard times. Receivership followed, and although the company was relaunched as Cockburn Holdsworth its grip on the marketplace was no longer secure.

Karmann coachbuilt Campers in second-generation guise are sometimes seen at the many gatherings of enthusiasts held each year. Numbers pale into insignificance compared to those conversions based on the third generation model and if truth be told, more vehicles of that kind of age are evident than those of fourth generation lineage. This is looking, of course, at matters from a British perspective, as for many years Karmann did not offer a right-hand-drive version of any of their models. For this, a would-be purchaser would have to turn to Jurgens in South Africa, whose Auto Villa, first conceived in 1973, bears an uncanny resemblance to the Karmann models, except that the conversion extends over the cab area. This similarity in design was not just coincidence, for while a member of the

Karmann family was on holiday in South Africa he came across examples of the Auto Villa. Quickly appreciating that there was nothing even remotely similar available in Europe, let alone Germany, he negotiated a deal whereby his company could build its own version under licence.

Launched in 1974, the Karmann Mobil featured an aluminium-clad body on an aluminium frame. With a walk-through cab that led into a private bathroom area fully equipped with shower, sink and toilet, and provided in addition with an electric fridge, plentiful storage cupboards, a two-burner hob and stainless steel sink, there was little to match such a specification at the time. Living accommodation was at the rear of the van, with a U-shaped seating arrangement, plentiful windows and a table that when laid down contributed to the formation of a double bed.

The advent of the third-generation Transporter saw few changes in the general layout of the conversion other than the addition of a Jurgens-style additional sleeping area over the cab. Marketed as the Karmann Gipsy, the model sold well, and in later years it was supplemented by the Karmann Cheetah, which, although far from a budget model, lacked some of the equipment of the more expensive Gipsy, such as a chemical toilet.

The advent of the fourth-generation Transporter in 1990 provided Karmann with the benefits of a longer wheelbase on which to work and resulted in the first dramatic design change in nearly 20 years. Now both the kitchen and the bathroom were to be found at the rear of the vehicle in the case of the Gipsy, although the Cheetah retained the essentials of the older style of layout.

With a total length of 5,970mm, a width of 2,170mm and a height of 2,780mm, the T4 Karmann motorhomes were far from compact. Karmann offered conversions not only on the Transporter but also on the LT, as well as models manufactured by Mercedes and Ford. From humble origins in the field of Campers, if not in product price, Karmann had become a leading motorhome manufacturer. Nevertheless, towards the end of the run of the fourth-generation Transporter the company decided to concentrate on its core business and put its motor-caravan division up for sale. Ownership duly passed into the hands of Eura Mobil, a firm already noted for both technical advances and build quality. Transferring production to its own site and adding new buildings to accommodate additional production lines, the change was completed in time to welcome the arrival of the fifth generation of Transporters. The new company's Colorado range, which comprised not only four over-cab versions but also a similar number of lower profile models, was launched to great acclaim at the 2004 Düsseldorf Caravan show.

Although by no means the oldest of the firms in

▼ With the advent of the chassis cab and long-wheel base options – made possible by the front mounted engine of the fourth generation Transporter – converters could offer much larger vehicles than previously. This is Karmann's Cheetah model – a fully fledged motorhome with numerous storage areas, gadgets and gizmos. *(RC)*

Britain offering Camper conversions on the Volkswagen Transporter, **Richard Holdsworth Conversions** – who made their debut around the time that the second-generation Transporter was launched – soon established an enviable reputation. By 1972 the company had outgrown its original premises in Ashford, Middlesex, and had relocated to Reading, where its new factory could accommodate the assembly of 50 Campers at a time, resulting in an increase in production from 150 units to an astonishing 300 per day.

From the start, Transporter conversions played only a relatively small part in the company's activities. However, the quality of both the design and work carried out, along with the use of handcrafted furniture and delightful weave fabrics, virtually guaranteed success for Holdsworth. Many examples of both their Villa and Variety models, based on the third-generation Transporter, have not only survived the test of time but also admirably demonstrate the robust and practical nature of the materials used. Following Holdsworth's victories at both the Camping and Caravan Show and the National Motor Caravan Fair in 1984, the company felt justified in presenting potential purchasers with their assurance of quality in their brochures:

'Quality. In the world of motor caravans, Richard Holdsworth has an unrivalled name for quality. Richard Holdsworth craftsmen work only in solid timber. Furniture units have rounded edges and worktops have expensive roll edges. Rich weaves in woollen-based fabrics grace deep comfortable seats and beds. Full-length brass piano hinges are used extensively and carpet type trim gives excellent insulation even in "out of season" touring.'

The tragedy of Holdsworth's demise in the 1990s was compounded by its successor company's absorption into Autocruise CH within a very short space of time. The T4-based Caprice produced by Cockburn Holdsworth was a vehicle of elegance in the style of its predecessors. A brief extract from the sales brochure for the model is perhaps most interesting for its list of extras at additional cost; for this demonstrates that, despite the write-up, other manufacturers had gained significant ground in the specification of the products they offered:

'The Caprice offers the attention to details you would expect from Cockburn Holdsworth … Flexible but never capricious, the Caprice is the two-in-one the best of both worlds.

'Optional extras ● Arm rest to cab seats ● blown air heating ● second battery ● water level indicators ●RM4213 Electrolux refrigerator with mains hook-up and 220v socket ● Thetford Porta Potti ● cassette flyscreens on all opening windows ● quality china-ware ● cab swivels ● low line elevating roof.'

▲ ▼ Holdsworth had debuted at the start of the second generation production run and had enjoyed great success until the 1990s, with many third generation models (as above) remaining sought after even today. The fourth generation Transporter, seen below at a time when Holdsworth had been bought by Cockburn, failed to capture Richard Holdsworth's imagination. *(RC)*

◀ Despite the vehicle's unusual appearance this image is available for journalists to download from Volkswagen's website – confirmation that the Transporter in Camper guise is a recognised symbol of the hippy movement.

▶ The extreme Camper – a rat-look Delivery Van with grass flattening suspension and little more than a duvet in home-from-home comforts. *(RC)*

Concluding the Camper story

While the casual observer might think that the ultimate goal of any potential owner of an older Volkswagen Camper is to acquire the best original vehicle with the most pristine interior imaginable, this is not necessarily the case. If the desire is concours prizes and little else, then such an assumption could be well founded, but this is not why the cult of the Camper has spiralled to astronomic proportions over the last decade and more.

For many an enthusiast a major part of the fun of owning a Volkswagen Camper is in the creation of a personalised home-from-home living space. To the amazement of the ultra-conservative traditionalist, many a first or second generation Transporter not only

▼ Taken in 2007, this official image replicates the outdoor lifestyle enjoyed by elements of the community in the late 1960s and 1970s.

looks spot on, but also feels right, despite being laden with the trappings of 21st-century living. Equally, the rescue of a fine old interior from a past-its-sell-by-date vehicle to install in another carefully restored shell might engender cries of 'fake' if entered in a concours competition, but the owner and many others will undoubtedly delight in his or her retro creation. Some enthusiasts have even been known to fit-out their vans with units carefully engineered to look like the work of craftsmen from decades ago, again to the accolade of many. Another option for those who don't want to indulge in modern-day external styling might be to turn to the current Transporter from the Brazilian factory, a modified incarnation of the much-loved second generation Transporter now fitted with a 1.4 water-cooled engine. It can be bought either fully converted to Camper status, most likely under the reincarnated Danbury brand-name, or an individualised interior could be created for it either at home or through the auspices of a local craftsman.

Some people will buy a 20- to 25-year-old Camper – and here we are realistically thinking of the third generation Transporter in water-cooled guise, the earlier air-cooled models already proving something of a collectors' item – and if necessary will be satisfied to patch and repair the interior to ensure its ongoing serviceability. With such a vehicle, depreciation can be more or less overlooked, as there is a distinct possibility that ever firmer prices for the older vehicles will succeed in driving a growing number towards more recent vehicles, in turn increasing the demand for these. Apart from the well-known conversions of the likes of Devon and Danbury, not to mention Westfalia, As we have seen, Autohomes produced a series of conversions based on the third generation

model, with names ranging from the simplistic Kamper to Kameo and Karisma, Auto-Sleepers offered the Hi-Top (later renamed the Trident), Diamond RV produced the singularly unusual Autocruiser, while Holdsworth presented models ranging from the High Flyer and Villa to later top-of-the-range model the Vision. Tischer's demountables are also reasonably easy to acquire, and so on.

Others, who look to the performance and reliability of a modern vehicle, but who possibly are unable to afford the asking price of any of the latest models, will opt for the newest available at a sum the household budget can absorb. For the next few years at least conversions on the T4, including those of Volkswagen's approved UK manufacturers referred to above, the inevitable Westfalia California and its attendant limited edition specials – such as the California Event, California Generation, California Exclusive and the run-out California Freestyle – plus Karmann's Gipsy and Cheetah, fit this bill perfectly. Some owners will undoubtedly be Volkswagen enthusiasts, as an ever-increasing presence at enthusiasts' meetings attests; others might well have chosen a conversion based on the product of another manufacturer, with scant regard to the significance of the letters V over W.

Finally, there are those who simply buy a new Camper to use for the purpose for which it was built. Realistically only a small percentage of such purchasers will have an ingrained loyalty to the Volkswagen marquee, and less still will decide that an in-house manufactured California is the only option. With an enviable array of conversions to select from – Auto-Sleepers' Trooper, Trident, Topaz and Sandhurst; Bilbo's Celex, Elegans, Komba, Lezan and Nexa; Devon's Sundowner; IH Motor Campers' J1000; Karmann's Colorado; Murvi's Mallard; and Torbay's Maverick, to name but some of the best-known examples – perhaps it's not surprising that

out of the 13,817 T5 Transporters sold in Britain in 2006, only 142 were Californias.

Whichever generation is chosen and whatever model is selected, it is thanks to the Camper, official or unofficial, that the Transporter is the cult vehicle it has become. Campers fit with the lifestyle sought by so many in today's pressurised world – a back-to-basics, outdoor, carefree existence mingled with the genuine camaraderie shared amongst like-minded folk. Can this be achieved with a Pick-up, or a Micro Bus De Luxe? Assuredly not, despite their attraction as individual Volkswagen Transporter models, for it's the addition of the 'nest' dimension that makes the Volkswagen Camper special. Despite the knowledge that until 2004 Volkswagen hadn't ever manufactured a Camper, no volume dedicated to 60 years and five generations of Transporter would be complete without them.

▲ Music, camera, action – another starring role for the Volkswagen Camper. (RC)

▼ An old Camper and modern youth – the vehicle's popularity has never been greater as Volkswagen intend to convey in this image snapped in 2006.

Final thoughts – 60 years and many more

For 60 diamond-encrusted years, and through five generations, Volkswagen's Transporter – in both workhorse and people-carrying modes – has been both the enduring market leader and the undoubted envy of other manufacturers.

Unquestionably, the fifth generation Transporter has proved itself not only a worthy successor to its four predecessors but also an ideal representative of the genre both on the arrival of the ten millionth model, which rolled off the production line in 2004, and now on the occasion of the 60th anniversary of the original version's launch in 1949.

The legend of the Transporter will endure, and no doubt ten years hence a sixth generation model will hold the mantle during any celebrations to mark yet another glittering achievement. Whether Heinz Nordhoff envisaged such a dynasty when he stood before the world's automotive press in 1949 is hardly worth asking. It had become his life's aim to propel Volkswagen to the pinnacle of European automotive achievement. That he achieved this goal in part through the success of the Transporter ensures that he would have been the first to congratulate the current holder of his position as Director General, Professor Dr Martin Winterkorn, on the occasion of the vehicle's diamond jubilee.

However, it is to the memory of Heinz Nordhoff and such worthy successors as Rudolf Leiding and Carl Hahn, who strove to take the Transporter concept even further forward in order that its supremacy was not only maintained but advanced, that this book must be dedicated.

Congratulations Volkswagen on your overwhelming achievement, and here's to another 60 glorious years!

◀ 55-years after its launch - give or take a month or two - Volkswagen celebrated the arrival of the 10,000,000th Transporter. This picture was taken on 22nd September 2004.

Index